WINDOWS® 7 SP1

QuickSteps™

About the Author

Marty Matthews' experience with computers extends from some of the early mainframe computers to the most recent personal computers. He has been a programmer, systems analyst, computer service company vice president, and software company president. He has firsthand knowledge of how to program and use a computer, as well as how to use what a computer can do.

Marty also has a knack for explaining how to use computers in such a way that makes it easy to understand. For 28 years Marty and his wife Carole have authored, co-authored, or been responsible for the production of over 100 computing-related books, including ones on desktop publishing, web publishing, Microsoft Office, and Microsoft operating systems—from MS-DOS through Windows 7 SP1. Recent books published by McGraw-Hill include *Windows 7 QuickSteps, Windows 7 for Seniors QuickSteps*, and *Computing for Seniors QuickSteps*.

Marty and Carole live on an island in Puget Sound, in Washington state.

About the Technical Editor

John Cronan has more than 30 years of computer experience and has been writing and editing computer-related books for 18 years. His recent books include *eBay QuickSteps Second Edition, Dynamic Web Programming: A Beginner's Guide, Microsoft Office Excel 2010 QuickSteps*, and *Microsoft Office Access 2010 QuickSteps*. John and Faye (and cat Little Buddy) reside in Everett, WA.

WINDOWS® 7 SP1
QuickSteps™

MARTY MATTHEWS

New York Chicago San Francisco
Lisbon London Madrid Mexico City
Milan New Delhi San Juan
Seoul Singapore Sydney Toronto

The McGraw·Hill Companies

Cataloging-in-Publication Data is on file with the Library of Congress

McGraw-Hill books are available at special quantity discounts to use as premiums and sales promotions, or for use in corporate training programs. To contact a representative, please e-mail us at bulksales@mcgraw-hill.com

Trademarks: McGraw-Hill, the McGraw-Hill Publishing logo, QuickSteps™, and related trade dress are trademarks or registered trademarks of The McGraw-Hill Companies and/or its affiliates in the United States and other countries and may not be used without written permission. All other trademarks are the property of their respective owners. The McGraw-Hill Companies is not associated with any product or vendor mentioned in this book.

Information has been obtained by McGraw-Hill from sources believed to be reliable. However, because of the possibility of human or mechanical error by our sources, McGraw-Hill, or others, McGraw-Hill does not guarantee the accuracy, adequacy, or completeness of any information and is not responsible for any errors or omissions or the results obtained from the use of such information.

WINDOWS® 7 SP1 QUICKSTEPS™

1234567890   QDB QDB   10987654321

ISBN   978-0-07-177247-1
MHID   0-07-177247-2

SPONSORING EDITOR / Roger Stewart

EDITORIAL SUPERVISOR / Jody McKenzie

PROJECT MANAGER / Vasundhara Sawhney, Cenveo Publisher Services

ACQUISITIONS COORDINATOR / Joya Anthony

TECHNICAL EDITOR / John Cronan

COPY EDITOR / Lisa McCoy

PROOFREADER / Paul Tyler

INDEXER / Valerie Perry

PRODUCTION SUPERVISOR / Jean Bodeaux

COMPOSITION / Cenveo Publisher Services

ILLUSTRATION / Cenveo Publisher Services

ART DIRECTOR, COVER / Jeff Weeks

COVER DESIGNER / Pattie Lee

SERIES CREATORS / Marty and Carole Matthews

SERIES DESIGN / Bailey Cunningham

To Carole and Michael
with my love and appreciation
for sharing your lives with me

Contents at a Glance

1
2
3
4
5
6
7
8
9
10

Contents

5

6

10

Acknowledgments

This book is a team effort of truly talented people who I have worked with for many years and in the process we have become good friends. This team includes: **John Cronan**, technical editor; **Lisa McCoy**, copy editor; **Paul Tyler**, proofreader, **Valerie Perry**, indexer; **Joya Anthony**, acquisitions coordinator; **Vasundhara Sawhney**, project manager; **Jody McKenzie**, project supervisor; and **Roger Stewart**, editorial director. A lot of effort and a part of themselves have gone into this book. It wouldn't be the book it is without all of them. Thanks, John, Lisa, Paul, Valerie, Joya, Vas, Jody, and Roger!

Introduction

QuickSteps books are recipe books for computer users. They answer the question "How do I..." by providing a quick set of steps to accomplish the most common tasks with a particular operating system or application.

The sets of steps are the central focus of the book. QuickSteps sidebars show how to quickly perform many small functions or tasks that support the primary functions. Notes, Tips, and Cautions augment the steps, and are presented in a separate column so as not to interrupt the flow of the steps. The introductions are minimal, and other narrative is kept brief. Numerous full-color illustrations and figures, many with callouts, support the steps.

QuickSteps books are organized by function and the tasks needed to perform that function. Each function is a chapter. Each task, or "How To," contains the steps needed for accomplishing the function, along with the relevant Notes, Tips, Cautions, and screenshots. You can easily find the tasks you want to perform through:

- The table of contents, which lists the functional areas (chapters) and tasks in the order they are presented

- A How To list of tasks on the opening page of each chapter

- The index, which provides an alphabetical list of the terms that are used to describe the functions and tasks

- Color-coded tabs for each chapter or functional area, with an index to the tabs in the Contents at a Glance (just before the table of contents)

Conventions Used in This Book

Windows 7 QuickSteps uses several conventions designed to make the book easier for you to follow. Among these are:

- A 🌐 or a ✐ in the table of contents or the How To list in each chapter references a QuickSteps or QuickFacts sidebar in a chapter.

- **Bold type** is used for words on the screen that you are to do something with, like "…click the **File** menu, and click **Save As**."

- *Italic type* is used for a word or phrase that is being defined or otherwise deserves special emphasis.

- <u>Underlined type</u> is used for text that you are to type from the keyboard.

- SMALL CAPITAL LETTERS are used for keys on the keyboard, such as ENTER and SHIFT.

- When you are expected to enter a command, you are told to press the key(s). If you are to enter text or numbers, you are told to type them.

How to...

- *Log On to Windows*
- *Use the Mouse*
- *Using the Mouse*
- *Use the Screen*
- *Using the Notification Area*
- *Open the Start Menu*
- *Use the Start Menu*
- *Starting a Program*
- *Use a Window*
- *Changing the Windows Explorer Layout*
- *Use a Menu*
- *Use a Dialog Box*
- *Navigate the Windows Desktop*
- *End Your Windows Session*
- *Having Fun with Windows*
- *Get Help*
- *Play FreeCell*

Chapter 1

Stepping into Windows 7 SP1

Windows 7 SP1 as an *operating system* performs *the* central role in managing what a computer does and how it is done. An operating system provides the interface between you and the computer hardware: It lets you store a file, print a document, connect to the Internet, or transfer information over a local area network (LAN) without knowing anything about how the hardware works.

This chapter explains how to start and/or log on to Windows 7 SP1; how to use its screens, windows, menus, and dialog boxes; and how to shut it down. You will also learn how to get help and discover some ways to have fun with Windows.

"SP1" stands for "Service Pack 1," which is the first major upgrade to Windows 7. Many believe that only with the

NOTE

If you don't already have Windows 7 SP1 on your computer and haven't been notified by Windows Update of the SP1 availability, you can install it manually by clicking **Start**, clicking **All Programs**, and clicking **Windows Update**.

NOTE

The desktop on your screen may be different from the one shown in Figure 1-1. Each manufacturer has its own default desktop, and if you upgrade to Windows 7 SP1, you will see still a different one.

NOTE

If you are logging on to a domain (see Chapter 9), you will be asked to press **CTRL+ALT+DEL** at the same time. Do so, then enter your user name and password, and press **ENTER** or click **OK**.

SP1 upgrade does the operating system become fully mature. SP1 adds many fixes and security updates plus a number of changes in the areas of communications, audio, printing, document restoration, and authentication. In addition, Windows 7 SP1 comes with a new version of Internet Explorer (IE 9) and a new version of Windows Live Essentials, which includes Windows Live Mail. This book will discuss Windows 7 in its SP1 incarnation.

Start Windows

To start Windows, you need to turn on the computer. Sometimes, that is all you need to do. If, when you turn on the computer, you see a screen similar to Figure 1-1, you have started Windows. In some cases, in addition to turning on the computer, you need to log on.

Log On to Windows

If, when you start Windows, you see a Log On screen on which you can click one of several users, click your name or that of the default user and, if requested, enter your password. Windows will log you on to the system. If someone else, such as a system administrator, installed Windows 7 SP1 on your computer, he or she should have given you a user name and password, if one is needed. If you purchased a computer with Windows 7 SP1 installed on it or you upgraded to Windows 7 SP1, a default user is shown on the logon page. As you will see in Chapter 8, you can change and add users if you wish.

Use the Mouse

A *mouse* is any pointing device—including trackballs, pointing sticks, and graphic tablets—with two or more buttons. This book assumes you are using

The Recycle Bin icon opens
a folder of deleted files

The desktop is used for windows,
dialog boxes, and icons

The mouse pointer shows where
the mouse is pointing

Desktop icon for a program
you can run, or a file or
folder you can open

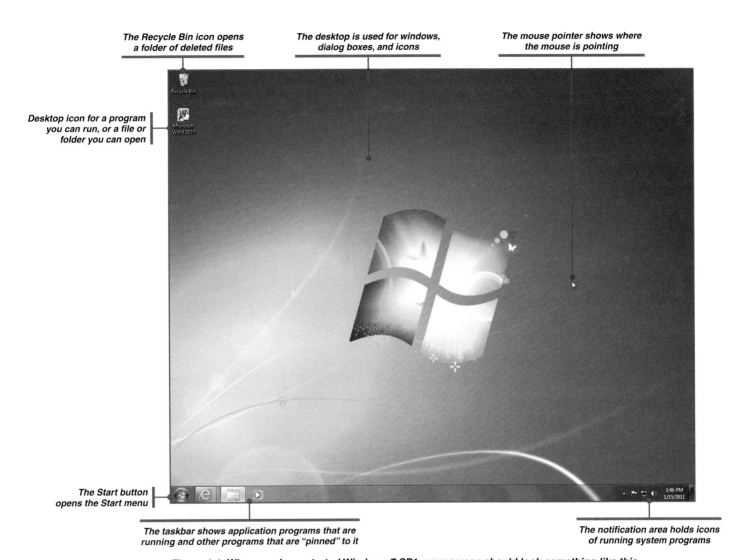

The Start button
opens the Start menu

The taskbar shows application programs that are
running and other programs that are "pinned" to it

The notification area holds icons
of running system programs

Figure 1-1: When you have started Windows 7 SP1, your screen should look something like this.

1

USING THE MOUSE

HIGHLIGHT AN OBJECT ON THE SCREEN

Highlight an *object* (a button, an icon, a border, etc.) on the screen by pointing to it. *Point* at an object on the screen by moving the mouse until the tip of the pointer is on top of the object.

SELECT AN OBJECT ON THE SCREEN

Select an object on the screen by clicking it. *Click* means to point at an object you want to select and quickly press and release the left mouse button.

OPEN AN OBJECT OR START A PROGRAM

Open an object or start a program by double-clicking it. *Double-click* means to point at an object you want to select and press and release the mouse button twice in rapid succession.

OPEN A CONTEXT MENU FOR AN OBJECT

Open a context menu, which allows you to do things specific to an object, by right-clicking it. *Right-click* means to point at an object you want to select and quickly press and release the right mouse button.

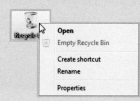

MOVE AN OBJECT ON THE SCREEN

Move an object on the screen by dragging it. *Drag* means to point at an object you want to move, and then press and hold the mouse button while moving the mouse. You will drag the object as you move the mouse. When the object is where you want it, release the mouse button.

a two-button mouse. Moving the mouse moves the pointer on the screen. You *select* an object on the screen by moving the pointer so that it is on top of the object and then pressing the left button on the mouse.

You can control the mouse with either your left or right hand; therefore, the buttons may be switched. (See Chapter 2 to switch the buttons.) This book assumes you are using your right hand to control the mouse and that the left mouse button is "the mouse button." The right button is always called the "right mouse button." If you switch the buttons, you must change your interpretation of these phrases.

Use the Screen

The Windows 7 SP1 screen can hold windows and other objects. In its simplest form, shown in Figure 1-1, you see a background scene, a bar at the bottom with a button on the left and the time and date on the right, and some icons in the upper-left area.

The parts of a screen are:

- The **desktop**, which takes up most of the screen.
- The **Start button** in the lower-left corner, which opens the Start menu.
- The **taskbar** across the bottom, which identifies programs that either are running or "pinned" to it.
- The **notification area** in the lower-right area, which holds icons of running system programs.
- The **Show Desktop** button, at the rightmost area of the taskbar, minimizes all open windows so you can see the desktop.
- **Desktop icons**, which can be in any number and anywhere on the desktop, are in the upper-left corner of Figure 1-1. Desktop icons are used to start programs or open files or folders.
- The **mouse pointer**, which can be anywhere on the screen.

QUICKSTEPS

USING THE NOTIFICATION AREA

The *notification area* on the right of the taskbar contains the icons of special programs and system features, as well as the time and date.

SHOW HIDDEN ICONS

- Click the up arrow to see the icons of hidden programs, and then click any you wish to open.

OPEN A SYSTEM FEATURE

- Click one of the icons in the middle to open a system feature.

SET THE TIME AND DATE

- Click the time and date area to see a calendar and an analog clock, and then click **Change Date And Time Settings** (see related Note).

SHOW THE DESKTOP

- On the far right of the taskbar is an unmarked rectangular area, which, if you click it, will minimize all open windows and dialog boxes and display the desktop. Clicking it again restores all open windows and dialog boxes. Simply moving the mouse over (also known as *to mouse over*) this button temporarily clears from the screen all open windows and dialog boxes until you move the mouse away.

NOTE

If you are connected to the Internet, you should never need to set your time and date, even when changing to or from daylight saving time, because Windows automatically synchronizes your computer's time with a local time server.

USE THE DESKTOP

The *desktop* is the entire screen, except for the bar at the bottom. Windows, dialog boxes, and icons, such as the Recycle Bin, are displayed on the desktop. You can store *shortcuts*, which are icons for your favorite programs, on the desktop (see Chapter 2). You can drag windows, dialog boxes, files, and icons around the desktop. Double-click an icon on the desktop to open it.

USE THE START BUTTON

The *Start button*, located on the left of the taskbar, opens the Start menu when clicked. This provides you with primary access to the programs, utilities, and settings that are available in Windows.

USE THE TASKBAR

The *taskbar* at the bottom of the screen contains the active *tasks*, which are icons and titles of the programs that are running on the computer or folders that are open. The taskbar also holds the Start button on the left and the notification area and Show Desktop button on the right. Click a program on the taskbar to open it.

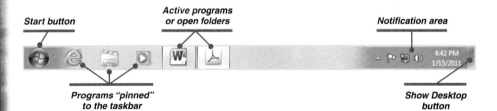

USE A DESKTOP ICON

A *desktop icon* represents a program or folder that can be started or opened and moved about the screen. The Recycle Bin is a desktop icon for a folder that contains all of the files that have been deleted since the Recycle Bin was last emptied. Double-click a desktop icon to open or start what it refers to.

NOTE

Your taskbar may have more or fewer objects than those shown in the previous illustration.

NOTE

The icons you have in the notification area will depend on the programs and processes you have running and the system features you have available. The icons shown here include system messages, which access the Action Center ; Network, which accesses the Network And Sharing Center ; and Speakers, which allows you to control the sound from your computer . In a laptop or notebook computer, you probably have two additional icons: Power and Wireless .

NOTE

The two steps describing how to open the Start menu can be replaced with the two words "click **Start**." You can also open the Start menu by pressing the Windows flag key on your keyboard, if you have that key, or by pressing both the **CTRL** and **ESC** keys together (**CTRL+ESC**). In the rest of this book, you will see the phrase "click **Start**." This means open the Start menu using any technique you wish.

USE THE MOUSE POINTER

The *mouse pointer,* or simply the *pointer* or *mouse,* shows where the mouse is pointing. Move the mouse to move the pointer.

Open the Start Menu

To open the Start menu:

1. Point at the **Start** button by moving the pointer so that it is over the Start button. You will see that the button changes color. When this happens, the button is said to be *highlighted.*

2. Press and release the left mouse button (given that your mouse buttons have not been switched) while the pointer is on the Start button. The Start menu will open, as you can see in Figure 1-2.

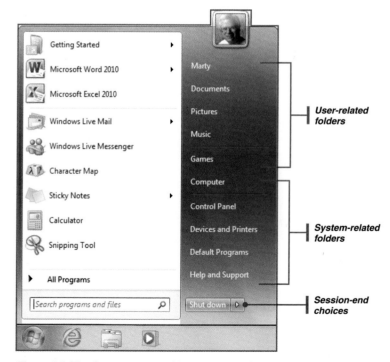

Figure 1-2: *The Start menu provides access to the programs, utilities, and settings in Windows.*

NOTE

Depending on the edition of Windows 7 SP1 you have (Starter, Home Basic, Home Premium, Professional, Enterprise, or Ultimate), your Start menu may be slightly different from the one shown here for Windows 7 SP1 Ultimate edition.

NOTE

If you are looking for Internet-accessing programs on the Start menu, you'll see how to add them in Chapter 4.

Use the Start Menu

The Start menu contains icons for programs and folders, as well as access to control functions and other menus, as shown in Figure 1-2. The most important menu item is All Programs, which opens a menu within the Start menu of all your programs. The buttons in the lower-right corner—Shut Down and session-ending choices—are important control functions discussed later in this chapter. The text box in the lower-left corner allows you to enter criteria and search the files and folders on the computer or the Internet for those that contain a match. All other options on the menu open folders, start programs, or both. The lower icons on the left (six of them in Figure 1-2) change to reflect the programs you have used most recently (which are probably different from those shown here). In Figure 1-2 these are the programs that Windows 7 SP1 initially displays by default. The upper icons on the left (three in Figure 1-2) are semi-permanently "pinned" to the Start menu, which is something you can control, as you will see in Chapter 2.

The remaining icons in the Start menu fall into two categories: user-related folders and system-related folders, programs, and options.

OPEN USER-RELATED FOLDERS

The top five options on the right in Figure 1-2 (including the user's name at the top) are used to access folders related to the user who is logged on. These options start the Windows Explorer program and display the folder identified. Clicking the user's name opens a folder containing the user's libraries (with four subsidiary folders), as well as other features, as shown next. Windows Explorer will be discussed later in this chapter and again in Chapter 3.

OPEN SYSTEM-RELATED FOLDERS

The remaining five icons in the bottom-right area of the Start menu (see Figure 1-2) help you manage your computer and its resources or get help. The function of each is as follows:

- **Computer** starts the Windows Explorer program and displays disk storage devices on the computer. From this point you can open any disk, folder, and file that is available to you on your computer and the network to which you are connected.

2 3 4 5 6 7 8 9 10

STARTING A PROGRAM

The method for starting a program depends on where the program icon is located. Here are the alternatives:

ON THE DESKTOP

- Double-click the program icon, or "shortcut," on the desktop.

ON THE START MENU

- Click the program icon on the Start menu.

A PINNED ICON ON THE TASKBAR

- Click the program icon on the taskbar.

IN THE NOTIFICATION AREA

- Click the program icon in the notification area.

ON THE ALL PROGRAMS MENU

1. Click **Start**.
2. Click **All Programs**.
3. Click the relevant folder or folders.
4. Click the program icon, as shown in Figure 1-3.

FROM THE RUN COMMAND

1. Click **Start** and click **All Programs**.
2. Click **Accessories** and then click **Run**.
3. Type the path and program name, and press **ENTER** or click **OK**.

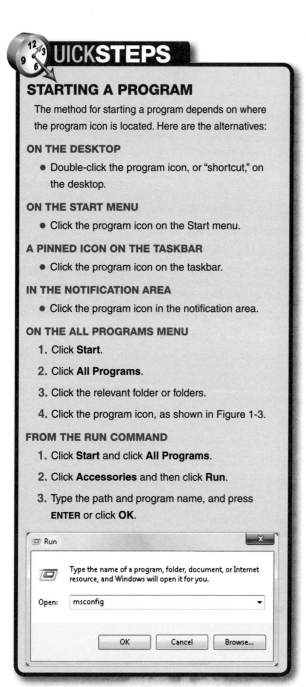

- **Control Panel** provides access to many of the settings that govern how Windows and the computer operate. This allows you to customize much of Windows and to locate and solve problems. Control Panel is discussed primarily in Chapter 2.

- **Devices And Printers** allows you to check the status of and change the settings on the hardware devices and printers in or connected to your computer.

- **Default Programs** allows you to associate a program with a file type and automatically start that program when you double-click the related type of file.

- **Help And Support** opens a window from which you can search for information on how to use Windows 7 SP1. It includes a tutorial and a troubleshooting guide. Help is discussed in more detail later in this chapter.

Your computer's manufacturer may have added an icon that connects you to the manufacturer's Internet Help center.

Figure 1-3: All Programs on the Start menu may lead you through several folders before you find the program you want.

TIP

In Chapter 3 you will see how to start programs with Windows Explorer.

Use a Window

When you start a program or open a folder, the program or folder appears in a "window" on your screen, as shown with the Windows Explorer window in Figure 1-4.

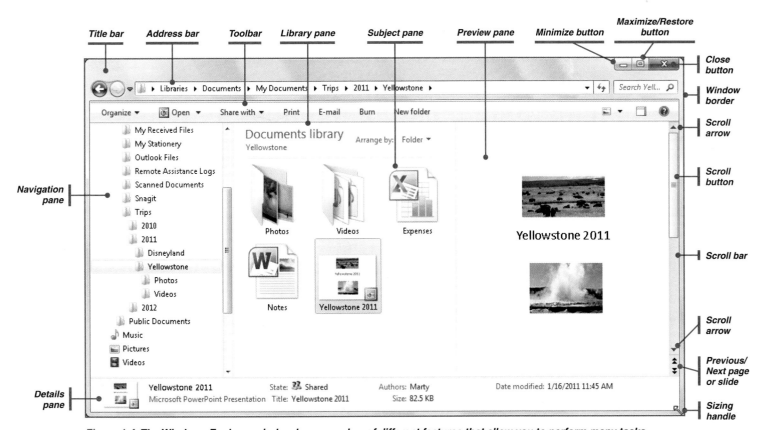

Figure 1-4: *The Windows Explorer window has a number of different features that allow you to perform many tasks.*

TIP

When you move the pointer to a program on the Start menu, the program takes on a colored background and becomes selected, as shown earlier in Figure 1-3. If you don't immediately click the item, a little message box, or *screen tip,* will appear. It gives you information about the program you selected.

The window in Figure 1-4 has a number of features that are referred to in the remainder of this book. Not all windows have all of the features shown in the figure, and some windows have features unique to them.

- The **title bar** is used to drag the window around the screen, and may contain the name of the program or folder in the window (the Windows Explorer window in Windows 7 SP1 does not contain a name in the title bar).

- The **address bar** displays the complete address of what is being displayed in the subject pane. In Figure 1-4, this is the Yellowstone folder, in the 2011, Trips, My Documents, and Documents parent folders in Libraries.

- The **toolbar** contains tools related to the contents of the window. Click a tool to use it. The toolbar is always displayed.

- The **library pane**, which only appears while you are in the library, displays the current library and the open folder, and allows you to arrange the content.

- The **subject pane** displays the principal subject of the window, such as files, folders, programs, documents, or images. The subject pane is always displayed.

- The **preview pane** displays the object selected in the subject pane. For example, in Figure 1-4, the navigation pane points to a particular folder whose files of screenshots are shown in the subject pane, where one particular file is selected and displayed in the preview pane. By default, the preview pane is turned off.

- The **Minimize button** decreases the size of the window so that you see it only as a task on the taskbar.

- The **Maximize/Restore button** increases the size of the window so that it fills the screen. When the screen is maximized, this button becomes the **Restore button**, which, when clicked, returns the screen to its previous size.

- The **Close button** shuts down and closes the program, folder, or file in the window.

- The **window border** separates the window from the desktop, and can be used to size the window horizontally or vertically by dragging the horizontal or vertical border, respectively.

- **Scroll arrows**, when clicked, move the window contents in small increments in the direction of the arrow.

- The **scroll button** can be dragged in either direction to move the contents accordingly.

- The **scroll bar** allows you to move the contents of the pane within the window so that you can see information that is not displayed. Clicking the scroll bar itself moves the

TIP

Double-clicking a window's title bar toggles between maximizing and restoring a window to its previous size. This may be easier than clicking the Maximize and Restore buttons.

QUICKSTEPS

CHANGING THE WINDOWS EXPLORER LAYOUT

The window shown in Figure 1-4 has all of its panes turned on. By default, the preview pane is not visible. You can turn these panes on and turn other panes off.

TURN ON PANES

Click **Organize** on the toolbar, click **Layout**, and click **Preview Pane** (see Figure 1-5).

TURN OFF PANES

Click **Organize** on the toolbar; click **Layout**; and click **Details Pane**, **Library Pane**, or **Navigation Pane**.

TURN ON CLASSIC MENUS

If you miss the menus that were in Windows Explorer in earlier versions of Windows, you can turn them on:

- Permanently by clicking **Organize** on the toolbar, clicking **Layout**, and clicking **Menu Bar**.
- Temporarily by pressing **ALT**.

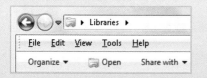

contents in larger increments. The scroll bar only appears when there is more content than what can be displayed.

- The **previous** and **next buttons** on a scroll bar display the page or slide that comes before or after the current one. These buttons only appear when there are multiple pages to be displayed.

- The **sizing handle** in each corner of the window allows it to be sized diagonally (shown in Figure 1-4 with the related mouse pointer), increasing or decreasing the window's height and width when you drag a handle.

- The **details pane** displays detailed information about the object that is selected in the subject pane. The details pane is turned on by default.

- The **navigation pane** provides links to the most commonly used folders related to the user who is logged on, as well as an optional hierarchical list of disks and folders on the computer. The navigation pane is turned on by default.

Use a Menu

A *menu* provides a way of selecting an action, such as turning on the preview pane, as shown in Figure 1-5. To use a menu in an open window:

1. Click the menu name on the menu bar.
2. Move the pointer to the option you want.
3. Click the option you want.

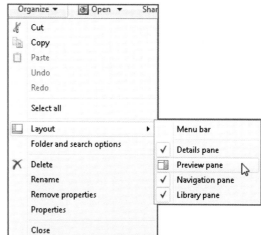

Figure 1-5: By default, menus are not available in Windows Explorer, but you can turn them on if you wish.

NOTE

To turn the library pane on or off, you have to be in a library. Otherwise, the option is not available.

NOTE

The line between windows and dialog boxes is becoming fuzzier. The purpose of a window is to display information, while the purpose of a dialog box is to gather information. Most windows have a title bar with the Minimize, Maximize/Restore, and Close buttons. The title bars of program windows also have a control menu icon on the left of the title bar and the program name in the middle of the title bar. All windows also have a border and sizing handles, both of which can be used to change the size of the window. Some dialog boxes can now be sized, and many windows do not have menus or a system menu icon, but generally dialog boxes do not have a control menu icon, a menu bar, or Minimize and Maximize buttons.

Use a Dialog Box

Dialog boxes gather information. A *dialog box* uses a common set of controls to accomplish its purpose. Figures 1-6 and 1-7 show two frequently used dialog boxes with many of the controls often seen.

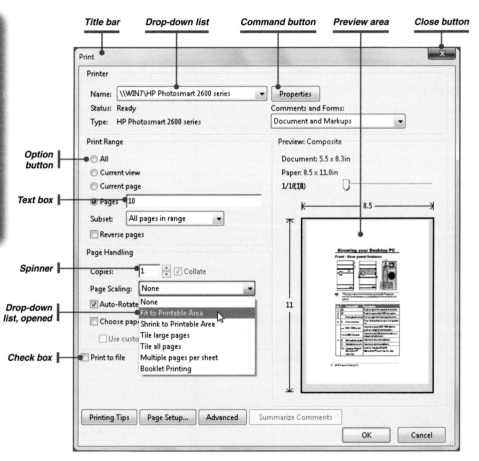

Figure 1-6: **This dialog box demonstrates some of the standard controls you'll find in dialog boxes.**

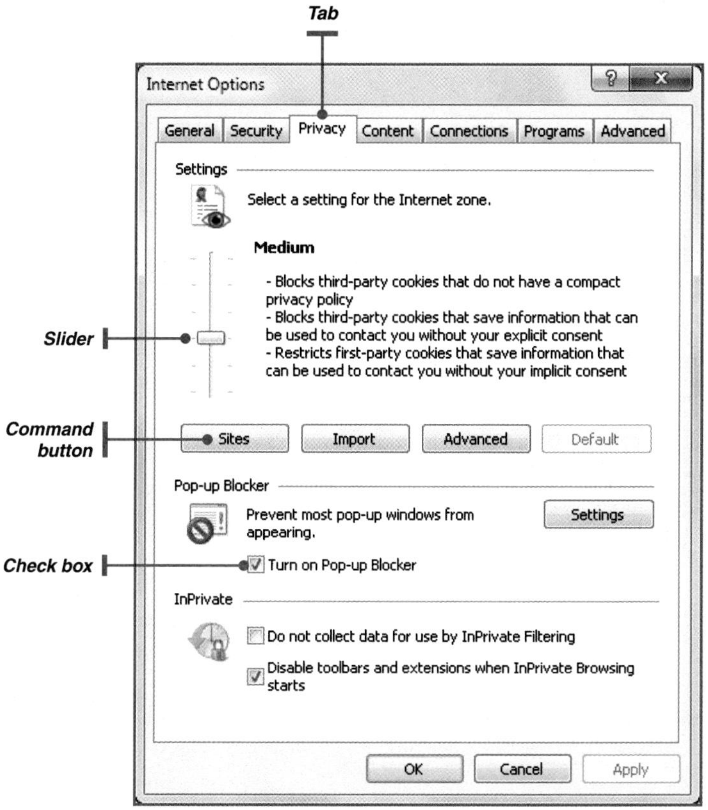

Tab

Slider

Command button

Check box

Figure 1-7: **Dialog boxes come in many different sizes and with different controls.**

The common controls in dialog boxes are used in the following ways:

- The **title bar** contains the name of the dialog box and is used to drag the box around the desktop.
- **Tabs** let you select from among several pages in a dialog box.
- A **drop-down list box** displays a list from which you can choose one item that will be displayed when the list is closed.
- A **list box** (not shown) lets you select one or more items from a list; it may include a scroll bar.
- **Option buttons**, also called radio buttons, let you select one among mutually exclusive options.
- **Check boxes** let you turn features on or off.
- A **preview area** shows you the effect of the changes you make.
- A **text box** lets you enter and edit text.
- **Command buttons** perform functions such as closing the dialog box and accepting any changes (the OK button), closing the dialog box and ignoring the changes (the Cancel button), or opening another dialog box (the Properties button).
- A **spinner** lets you select from a sequential series of numbers.
- A **slider** lets you select from several values.

You will have many opportunities to use dialog boxes. For the most part, you can try dialog boxes and see what happens; if you don't like the outcome, you can come back and reverse the setting.

NOTE

While all the references in the "Navigate the Windows Desktop" section say "windows," they at times also refer to dialog boxes. There can be some differences in behavior between dialog boxes and windows. For example, Aero Peek works the same for both, but when using Aero Shake, shaking a dialog box closes all open windows, but shaking a window doesn't close dialog boxes.

Navigate the Windows Desktop

When multiple windows are open, and possibly a dialog box or two, navigating among them and displaying the one(s) you want could be difficult. Figure 1-8, for example, shows such a situation. Earlier versions of Windows tried to address this, but Windows 7 added a number of features to handle it elegantly, including:

- **Aero Peek** to see what's hidden on the screen
- **Aero Shake** to minimize other open windows

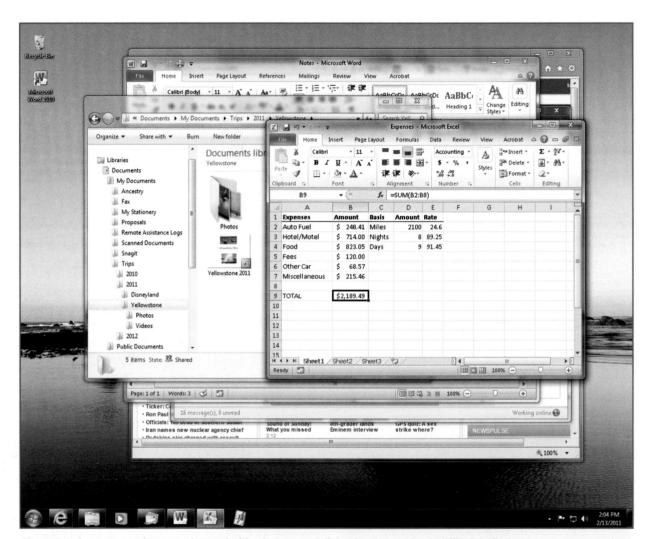

Figure 1-8: A screen can become cluttered with windows and dialog boxes, making it difficult to find what you want.

- **Aero Snaps** to resize and position windows
- **Jump lists** to see recent files and program options
- **Taskbar previews** to see what is open in a program

AERO PEEK

Aero Peek allows you to see what's hidden on the desktop behind all the open windows. You can do this on a temporary (or "peek") basis or a more long-lasting one.

- **Temporarily peek** at the desktop:

  Move the mouse pointer to ("mouse over") the **Show Desktop** area on the far right of the taskbar. All the open windows will become transparent ("glass") frames, as you can see in Figure 1-9, and you can then see what was hidden on the desktop, such as the email messages and folder in Figure 1-9.

- **Return** to the original desktop after a temporary peek:

  Move the mouse pointer away from the Show Desktop area. All the open windows will reappear, as shown in Figure 1-8.

- **Hide** all open windows so you can see and work on the desktop:

  Click the **Show Desktop** area on the far right of the taskbar. All the open windows will be hidden, and you can move the mouse around the entire desktop.

- **Unhide** all open windows and return to the original desktop:

  Click the **Show Desktop** area on the far right of the taskbar. All the open windows will be returned to their original position.

AERO SHAKE

Aero Shake allows you to minimize all open windows except for the one you are "shaking." To "shake" a window:

Point to the title bar of the window you want to remain open. Press and hold the mouse button while moving the mouse rapidly to the left and then to the right, as if you were shaking it.

–Or–

Figure 1-9: **With Aero Peek, all open windows become transparent.**

Select the window you want to keep displayed. Press and hold the Windows Flag key while pressing **HOME**.

To return the minimized windows to their original size and position, repeat the same steps.

AERO SNAPS

Aero Snaps "snaps" a window to various parts of the screen, a function similar to the Maximize/Restore button (which can still be used) on the title bar of a selected, floating (not already maximized) window, with some useful additions.

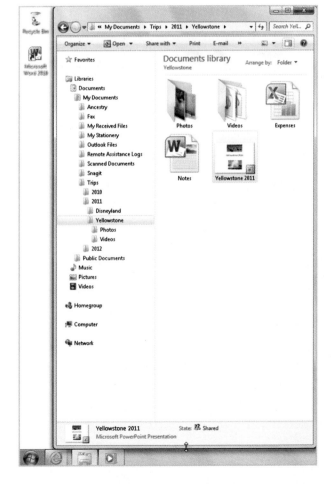

- **Maximize** a floating window:

  Point within the title bar or the window, not on its edge, and drag it to the top of the screen. The window will be maximized to fill the screen.

  –Or–

  Press and hold the Windows Flag key while pressing **UP ARROW**.

- **Restore** a maximized window (independent of how it was maximized):

  Double-click the title bar.

  –Or–

  Select the window you want to be maximized. Press and hold the Windows Flag key while pressing **DOWN ARROW**.

- **Vertically maximize** a floating window while not spreading it out horizontally (as shown):

  Point to the top or bottom edge of a window, and drag it to the corresponding edge of the screen. The window will be vertically maximized.

  –Or–

  Select the window you want to be maximized. Press and hold the Windows Flag key while pressing **SHIFT+UP ARROW**.

- **Left-align** a floating window and have it occupy 50 percent of the screen:

  Point to the title bar of a window, and drag it to the left edge of the screen. When the mouse pointer (not the window's edge) reaches the edge of the screen, the window will fill the left 50 percent of the screen.

  –Or–

  Select the window you want to be aligned. Press and hold the Windows Flag key while pressing **LEFT ARROW**.

- **Right-align** a floating window and have it occupy 50 percent of the screen:

  Point at the title bar of a window, and drag it to the right edge of the screen. When the mouse pointer reaches the edge of the screen, the window will fill the right 50 percent of the screen.

  –Or–

  Select the window you want to be aligned. Press and hold the Windows Flag key while pressing **RIGHT ARROW**.

- **Restore** a window that is filling 50 percent of the screen:

  Double-click the title bar twice.

  –Or–

  Select the window you want to be restored. Press and hold the Windows Flag key while pressing the key opposite to the one used to enlarge it.

  –Or–

  Point at the title bar of a window, and drag it down and away from the window edge it was aligned to.

JUMP LISTS

Jump lists are a context or pop-up menu for application icons on the taskbar or the Start menu. When you right-click a program icon on either the Start menu or taskbar, or click the right arrow to the right of a program on the Start menu, a menu will appear containing a list of recent files or web pages, as well as options to close the application, pin or unpin it from the Start menu or taskbar, and open the application with a blank file or web page.

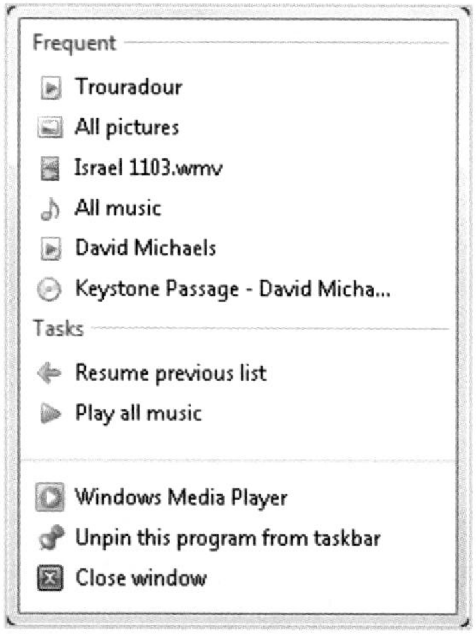

Frequent
Trouradour
All pictures
Israel 1103.wmv
All music
David Michaels
Keystone Passage - David Micha...
Tasks
Resume previous list
Play all music
Windows Media Player
Unpin this program from taskbar
Close window

TIP

Look at the icons on the taskbar in Figure 1-10. It is obvious by its bright highlight that the Windows Explorer icon is selected and the one displaying the thumbnails. You can also tell that the Internet Explorer and Windows Media Player icons, by their lack of any highlight and border, do not have open windows.

TASKBAR PREVIEWS

Taskbar previews are a miniature image, or thumbnail, of an open window attached to a taskbar icon. When you mouse over an icon on the taskbar, a thumbnail of the open window or windows related to that icon will temporarily appear, as shown next. If you then move the mouse to the thumbnail, a temporary full-sized image will appear (see Figure 1-10). When you move the mouse off the thumbnail or the icon, the corresponding image will disappear. Open a window by clicking its thumbnail. Close a window by clicking the **Close** button on the thumbnail.

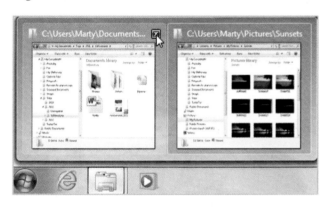

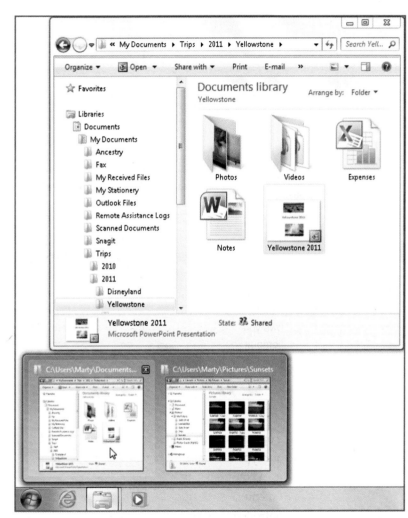

Figure 1-10: *The natural instinct is to move the mouse from the thumbnail to the temporary larger window to open it, but that causes both images to disappear. You must click the thumbnail.*

End Your Windows Session

You can end your Windows session in several ways, depending on what you want to do. All of these can be found on the Start menu.

1. Click **Start**. Note in the lower-right area of the Start menu that there is a button marked Shut Down and a right-pointing arrow that opens a menu of options that are in addition to Shut Down.

NOTE

In the previous illustration of the lower-right area of the Start menu there is an exclamation mark in a shield on the Shut Down button. This tells you that when you shut down, updates will be installed and then the computer will be shut down.

NOTE

The function of the Shut Down button can be changed to any of the other session-end options (see Chapter 5).

TIP

There are two distinct schools of thought on whether you should use Sleep or Shut Down when you leave the computer for any length of time. There are two primary considerations: security and power usage. Older computers used less power running in Sleep mode than the power consumed during shutting down and starting up. New computers have reduced the power consumed during these events, so it is now a toss-up. From a security standpoint, there is no security like having your computer completely turned off. A computer is also fairly secure in Sleep mode, but it is theoretically possible for a hacker to awaken it. The choice becomes a matter of preference. I turn my computers off; my wife leaves hers on.

2. Click either **Shut Down** or the right arrow, and click the option you want.

The meanings of the various options are:

- **Shut Down** closes all active programs and network connections and logs off all users so that no information is lost, and then turns off the computer (if it is done automatically) or tells you when it is safe for you to turn it off. When you start up the computer, you must reload your programs and data and reestablish your network connection (done by Windows) to get back to where you were when you shut down.

- **Switch User** leaves all active programs, network connections, and your user account active but hidden while you let another person use the computer.

- **Log Off** closes all active programs, network connections, and your user account but leaves Windows 7 SP1 and the computer running so another person can log on.

- **Lock** leaves all active programs, network connections, and your user account active but displays the Welcome screen, where you must click your user icon and potentially enter a password, if you have established one, to resume using the computer.

- **Restart** closes all active programs and network connections and logs off all users so that no information is lost. Windows is then shut down and restarted. This is usually done when there is a problem that restarting Windows will fix or to complete setting up some programs.

- **Sleep** leaves all active programs, network connections, and your user account active and in memory, but also saves the state of everything on disk. Your computer is then put into a low-power state that allows you to quickly resume working exactly where you were when you left. In a desktop computer, it is left running in this low-power state for as long as you wish. In a mobile computer (laptops, notebooks, netbooks, and tablet PCs), after three hours or if the battery is low, your session is again saved to disk and the computer is turned off.

RESUME FROM SLEEP

There are several ways to resume operation after a computer has been put into Sleep mode, which depend on your type of computer, how it was put to sleep, and how long it has been sleeping. A computer can be put into Sleep mode either by your action on the Start menu or as the result of the computer not being used for a time, which is controlled in the Power Options (see Chapter 5). The ways to resume include:

- Press any key on your keyboard. This works with most desktop computers and mobile computers that have only been asleep a short time.

UICKSTEPS

HAVING FUN WITH WINDOWS

Windows 7 SP1 has a number of games besides FreeCell. The following sections explain how to play three more.

PLAY HEARTS

Hearts is a card game that can be played by as many as four people on the network.

1. Click **Start**, click **Games**, and double-click **Hearts**. The game board will appear. By default, you will have three simulated opponents.

2. Click three cards you want to give away, and click the arrow to give your cards to the person in the direction of the arrow.

The objective is to have the lowest score by *not* taking tricks with hearts or the queen of spades in them *unless* you can take all such tricks. You take a trick by playing the highest card in the suit led for that trick. You begin the game by passing three cards from your hand to another player. You want to pass your highest hearts and spades. The person with the two of clubs leads. You must follow suit if you can. If you can't, you may throw away your high hearts or spades or any other card. Whoever takes a trick plays the first card for the next trick. Play continues until all cards have been played. At the end of a game, one point is assessed for each heart in the tricks you took plus 13 points for the queen of spades. If you get all the hearts

Continued . . .

- Quickly press the power button on your computer. This works with most recent computers of all types. Holding down the computer's power button will, in most cases, either fully turn off the computer or cause it to restart (shut fully down and then restart).

- Open the top. This works with most mobile computers.

Get Help

Windows 7 SP1 Help provides both built-in documentation and online assistance that you can use to learn how to work with Windows 7 SP1. For example, to use Help to start a program:

1. Click **Start** and click **Help And Support**. The Windows Help And Support window, like the one shown in Figure 1-11, opens.

Figure 1-11: The Windows 7 SP1 Help And Support window provides you with several options for getting help.

QUICKSTEPS

HAVING FUN WITH WINDOWS

(Continued)

plus the queen of spades, you get zero points and all other players get 26 points.

PLAY MINESWEEPER

Minesweeper is a game of chance in which you try to accumulate points by not encountering mines.

1. Click **Start**, click **Games**, and double-click **Minesweeper**. The first time you play, you are asked to click the level of difficulty you want to use. The game board will then appear.

2. The object is to find the mines hidden in the squares without clicking one. Click a square. You will see one or more squares showing numbers or blanks or a mine. The number tells you how many mines are contained in the eight surrounding squares. Mark the suspected mines with the right mouse button. Clicking a mine ends the game.

3. After a game has ended, to restart the game, click **Restart This Game**; to start a new game, click **Play Again**; or click **Exit**. To continue a game, click the **Game** menu, and click **Save**.

PLAY SOLITAIRE

Solitaire is a game of chance and strategy. The object of the game is to end up with the deck of cards arranged sequentially in suits from ace to king.

1. Click **Start**, click **Games**, and double-click **Solitaire**. The game board is displayed.

Continued . . .

2. In the Search Help text box, type start a program. A number of options related to starting a program will be displayed.

3. Click the **Close** button to close the Help And Support window.

Play FreeCell

There are a number of games you can play in Windows 7 SP1. Probably the most addictive of them all is a solitaire-like card game called FreeCell. To start playing:

1. Click **Start**, click **Games** on the right, and double-click **FreeCell**. The game board will be displayed, and a new hand will be dealt.

   The objective is to get the complete set of cards in each of the four suits in order from ace to king in the home cells in the upper-right area. You can temporarily place up to four cards in the free cells in the upper-left area. You can also temporarily place a card on the next highest card of the opposite color in the stacks at the bottom.

2. To move a card, click it and then click where you want it to go. If it is not a legal move, you will be told that. If you get an empty column at the bottom, you can build your own sequence in it.

   The secret is to think several moves in the future and never fill up the free cells without having a way to empty them. The game is lost if you have no moves left and haven't moved all the cards to the home cells. Figure 1-12 shows a game that was played for a few minutes and is all but won. The eight of diamonds is the only card left to move. When all your cards are in order, they will be moved to the home cells automatically and you will be told you won.

3. When you are done playing, click **Close** and, if you did not finish it, decide if you want to save the game by clicking **Save**.

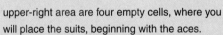

HAVING FUN WITH WINDOWS *(Continued)*

2. You will see a row of seven stacks of cards; all are face-down except the top card. You move the cards between the stacks to create columns of alternating suits, exposing the hidden cards so you can eventually move them to the empty cells. In the upper-left area of the board is another turned-down stack of cards, which you can click and move to a proper place on one of the seven stacks. In the upper-right area are four empty cells, where you will place the suits, beginning with the aces.

3. Start a new game by clicking **Game** and clicking **New Game**.

TIP

FreeCell has two neat features. You can undo your moves (on the Game menu click **Undo** or press **CTRL+Z**) and get a hint (on the Game menu, click **Hint** or press **CTRL+H**). Also, if you wait a minute without making a move, a hint will automatically appear.

*Figure 1-12: **Many people spend a lot of time playing FreeCell.***

Chapter 2

Customizing Windows 7 SP1

Windows 7 SP1 has many features that can be customized. You can keep the default setup or you can change the display, Start menu, taskbar, and sounds. You can also rearrange the desktop and enable accessibility options.

Change the Look of Windows 7 SP1

An important aspect of Windows that leads to your enjoyment and efficient use of it is how it looks. Windows 7 SP1 provides significant flexibility in this area. You can change how the screen looks, including the desktop, the Start menu, and the taskbar.

Use the Personalization Window

Much of what you see on the screen is controlled by the Personalization window. Open it to make many of the changes in this chapter. (Several of the

In Windows 7 SP1, when you first attempt to change various aspects of the program, you'll see a User Account Control (UAC) dialog box appear and ask you if you want to allow a program to make changes to your computer. This prevents a hacker from changing your system over the Internet or malicious software from harming your computer. When you see these dialog boxes and if you are an administrator and, in fact, want to continue, click **Yes**. If you are not logged on as an administrator, you will need to enter a password. If you don't want to do whatever is being requested, click **No**. To simplify the instructions in this book, I have left out the UAC dialog box and its associated steps. If you see one while following the instructions here, just process it as you want and continue with the instructions. UAC is discussed in depth in Chapter 8.

features controlled in the Personalization window, such as sounds and the mouse pointer, are discussed on their own later in this chapter.)

1. With Windows 7 SP1 running and displayed on your computer, right-click a blank area of the desktop. The desktop *context menu* is displayed.

2. Click **Personalize**. The Personalization window opens, as shown in Figure 2-1.

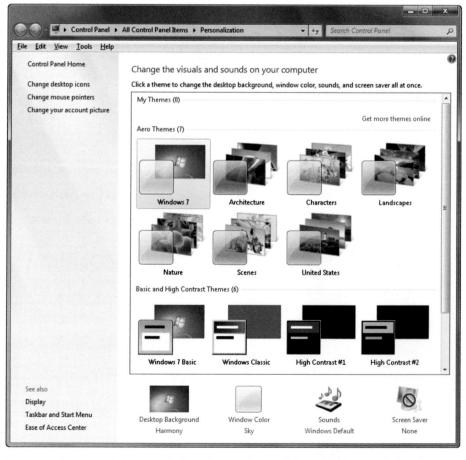

Figure 2-1: The Personalization window lets you change the appearance of Windows 7 SP1.

CHANGE THE DESKTOP THEMES AND COLORS

You can use any picture, color, or pattern you want for your desktop background. Windows 7 SP1 comes with a number of alternatives. From the Personalization window:

1. Drag the scroll bar on the right and review the themes that are available with Windows 7 SP1 (or click **Get More Themes Online** to view Microsoft's online library). Click the theme you want to use. With each theme you can select a desktop background and a window color, as well as the sounds used and a screen server.

2. Click **Desktop Background**. Click the **Picture Location** down arrow, and select a source of pictures (see Figure 2-2), or click **Browse** and navigate to a location on your computer where you have a picture you want to use (Chapter 3 explains how to navigate on your computer). Click **OK**, and click the picture or pictures desired.

3. Click **Save Changes** to close the Desktop Background window.

4. At the top of the themes list, click **Save Theme** to save any changes to a current theme or to save a new theme.

5. In the Save Theme As dialog box, name the theme, and click **Save**.

CHANGE THE RESOLUTION AND TEXT SIZE

Depending on your computer and monitor, you can display Windows 7 SP1 with various resolutions and text sizes. You can select the text and object size in the Display window and then go on to adjust the resolution. From the Personalization window:

1. Click **Display**. The Display window will appear, as shown in Figure 2-3.

2. Click the text and object size you want to use, and click **Apply**.

3. Click **Adjust Resolution**. If you have more than one display device, click **Identify**. The display's number appears on each screen. In the Display drop-down list, click the display whose resolution you want to change.

Figure 2-2: Selecting a background picture causes it to be displayed instantly as your background.

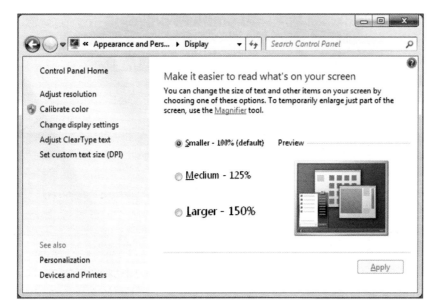

Figure 2-3: *Increasing the text and object size lets you see less of what's on the screen, but what you see is larger and possibly easier to read.*

4. Click the **Resolution** drop-down arrow. Drag the slider up or down to adjust the resolution. (You can try this and if you don't like it, come back and change it.)

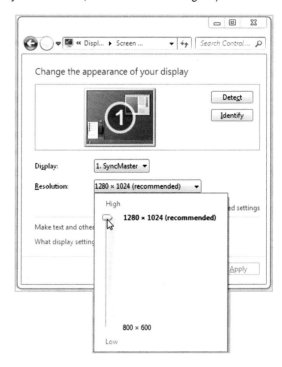

NOTE

The Advanced Settings link at the right of the Screen Resolution window will provide access to settings that are specific to your display hardware.

5. Click **Apply** to save the settings, and then click the **Back** arrow in the upper-left area until you are back to the Personalization window.

ALTER THE APPEARANCE OF OBJECTS

You can alter the appearance of windows, icons, and dialog boxes, changing their shapes and colors, as well as the font used in those objects. From the Personalization window:

1. Click **Window Color** at the bottom of the window. The Window Color And Appearance window will open.

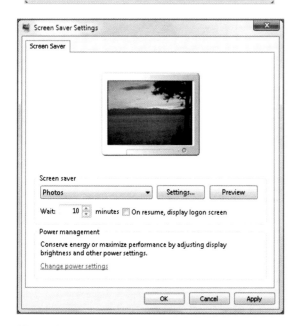

Figure 2-4: *You can use your own photos with the Photos screen saver option.*

2. Click a different color scheme, if desired; turn off transparency if you don't like looking through window borders; or change the color intensity.

3. Click **Advanced Appearance Settings** to open the old style (circa Windows XP) Window Color And Appearance dialog box, shown here. Select an object whose color and/or font you want to change, and make those changes. All settings made here will provide a Windows Classic look or style.

4. When you are ready, click **OK** to close the Window Color And Appearance dialog box. Then click **Save Changes** to return to the Personalization window.

PICK A NEW SCREEN SAVER

When the computer is left on but not in use, the unchanging image on the screen can be burned into the face of a cathode-ray tube (CRT) monitor. The newer, thin, flat-screen liquid crystal display (LCD) monitors are not as affected by this, but plasma displays can be. To prevent this damage, you can choose to use a *screen saver,* which constantly changes the image on the screen when the computer is not in use. Windows 7 SP1 provides a number of alternative screen savers you can use. From the Personalization window:

1. Click **Screen Saver** in the lower-right corner. The Screen Saver Settings dialog box appears.

2. Click the **Screen Saver** down arrow, and review the options in the drop-down list.

3. Click a screen saver option to see it previewed in the dialog box (see Figure 2-4).

4. Click **Preview** to see the screen saver on your full screen. Press **ESC** to return to the dialog box.

5. Click the up or down arrow on the **Wait** spinner to set the inactivity time to wait before enabling the screen saver.

6. When you have the screen saver you want, click **Settings**, if it is enabled, to see what settings are available for your screen saver. With the Photos option, you can select the folder, such as Pictures, from which to display photos.

7. When you are ready, click **OK** to close the dialog box.

Figure 2-5: *Your sounds can be associated with various events.*

SELECT THE SOUNDS WINDOWS 7 SP1 PLAYS

You can select the sounds that are played when various events occur, such as a critical stop or Windows shutdown, in the Sound dialog box. From the Personalization window:

1. Click **Sounds**. The Sound dialog box will appear, displaying the Sounds tab, as shown in Figure 2-5.

2. Click the **Sound Scheme** down arrow, and select one of the options.

3. Double-click a **Program Events** option to hear its current sound played.

4. Click the **Sounds** down arrow to select a different sound for the event. Click **Test** to hear the sound.

5. When you have made all the changes you want to the association of sounds and events, click **Save As** to save your changes as a new scheme. Type a name for the new scheme, and click **OK**.

6. When you are ready, click **OK** to close the Sound dialog box.

USE A DIFFERENT MOUSE POINTER

If it is difficult for you to see the mouse pointer, you can change how it looks and behaves in the Mouse Properties dialog box. From the Personalization window:

1. Click **Change Mouse Pointers**. The Mouse Properties dialog box will appear with the Pointers tab displayed, as shown in Figure 2-6.

2. Click the **Scheme** down arrow, and choose the scheme you want to use.

3. If you want to customize a particular mouse pointer, select that pointer, click **Browse**, locate and select the pointer you want to use, and click **Open**.

4. Click **OK** to close the Mouse Properties dialog box.

Add Windows Program Icons

When you first install and start up Windows 7 SP1, you will only have a couple of icons on the desktop, including the Recycle Bin, which is the only one Windows has by default. Some computer manufacturers may include additional icons. The purpose of having program icons on the desktop, called *shortcuts*, is to be able to easily start the programs by double-clicking their icons. To add

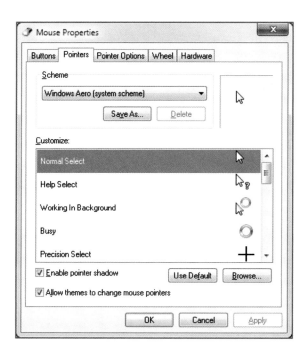

Figure 2-6: *The mouse pointer should be easily seen and instantly informative for you.*

Windows program icons, such as Windows Explorer and Control Panel, to the desktop and customize them:

1. Right-click a blank area of the desktop, and click **Personalize** to open the Personalization window.

2. Click **Change Desktop Icons** on the left to open the Desktop Icon Settings dialog box, shown in Figure 2-7.

3. In the Desktop Icons area, click one to five icons that you want to have on the desktop. For example, you might want icons for Computer and Control Panel. The others you might use less often, and they can be accessed quickly from the Start menu.

4. To customize a Windows program icon, click the icon and click **Change Icon**. A dialog box will appear displaying alternate icons.

5. Select the alternative you want, and click **OK**.

6. When you are satisfied with the Windows program icons you have selected and/or changed, click **OK**.

7. Click the **Close** button to close the Personalization window.

Figure 2-7: *Add the icons to the desktop for the programs you use most often.*

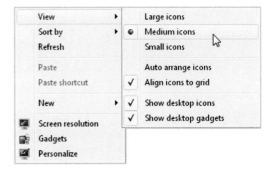

View	▶		Large icons
Sort by	▶	●	Medium icons
Refresh			Small icons
Paste			Auto arrange icons
Paste shortcut		✓	Align icons to grid
New	▶	✓	Show desktop icons
		✓	Show desktop gadgets
🖥 Screen resolution			
🖳 Gadgets			
🖥 Personalize			

Change Desktop Icons

When you have the icons that you want on the desktop, you can change the size of the icons, their order, and their alignment through the desktop context menu.

Right-click a blank area of the desktop to open the context menu, and click **View** to open the View submenu.

RESIZE ICONS

Windows 7 SP1 gives you the choice of three different sizes of icons. The size you choose is a function of both the resolution you are using on your display and your personal preference. By default (the way Windows is set up when you first install and/or start it), your icons will be medium size. From the View submenu:

Click each of the sizes to see which is best for you.

Large   **Medium**   **Small**

ALIGN ICONS

You can drag desktop icons where you want them; by default, Windows 7 SP1 will align your icons to an invisible grid. If you don't like that, from the View submenu:

Click **Align Icons To Grid** to clear the check mark and allow any arrangement on the desktop that you want.

If you should move your icons around and then change your mind, reopen the **View** submenu, and:

Click **Align Icons To Grid** to reselect it. Your icons will jump to the invisible grid and be aligned.

ARRANGE ICONS

By default, there is no particular order to the icons on the desktop, and you can drag them into the order that suits you. However, you can have Windows arrange and sort the icons in several ways. From the **View** submenu:

Click **Auto Arrange Icons**. By default, the icons will be placed in a column alphabetically by name, except that the system icons (Computer, Recycle Bin, Internet Explorer, user's files, Control Panel, and Network) will be at the top.

QUICKSTEPS

ADDING OTHER PROGRAM ICONS TO THE DESKTOP

The method for adding other program icons, or shortcuts, to the desktop depends on where the icons are.

ADD ICONS FROM THE START MENU

Click **Start** to open the menu, and drag the icon from the menu to the desktop.

ADD ICONS FROM THE PROGRAMS MENU

1. Click **Start** and click **All Programs**.

2. Locate and point to the icon, hold down the right mouse button, and drag the icon to the desktop. (This is called *right-drag*.)

3. Click **Copy Here**.

ADD ICONS FROM OTHER MENUS

1. Click **Start**, click **All Programs**, and open additional folders as needed.

2. Point to the icon, and right-drag the icon to the desktop.

3. Click **Copy Here**.

ADD ICONS NOT ON A MENU

1. Click **Start** and click **Computer**.

2. In the Computer window, open the drive and folder(s) needed to locate the program (most programs are stored in their own folder within the Program Files folder on the C: drive).

3. Drag the program icon to the desktop.

NOTE

Changing the size of icons only affects the icons on the left of the Start menu. The purpose of smaller icons is to list more programs.

If you want to change the order in which Windows 7 SP1 arranges desktop icons:

1. Right-click a blank area of the desktop to open the context menu, and click **Sort By** to open that submenu.

2. Click one of the options to have the icons sorted in that manner.

RENAME DESKTOP ICONS

When you add program icons to the desktop, they may have the word "Shortcut" in their names, or they may have names that are not meaningful to you. To rename desktop icons:

1. Right-click an icon name you want to change, and click **Rename**.

2. Type the new name that you want to use, and press **ENTER**.

Change the Start Menu

The Start menu has several areas you can customize, including the size of the icons, the number of programs on it, the programs to use for the Internet and for email, and how the Start menu operates.

CHANGE WHAT IS DISPLAYED ON THE START MENU

Windows 7 SP1 gives you considerable flexibility as to what is displayed on the Start menu and how those items work.

1. Right-click **Start** and click **Properties** to open the Taskbar And Start Menu Properties dialog box.

2. With the Start Menu tab selected, click **Customize**. The Customize Start Menu dialog box will appear (see Figure 2-8).

3. Scroll through the list of links, icons, and submenus. Select the ones you want included on the Start menu and indicate how they should operate. Toward the end of the list there is an option that lets you change the size of the icons on the Start menu.

4. Use the **Number Of Recent Programs To Display** spinner to select the number displayed in the lower-left corner of the Start menu.

5. Use the **Number Of Recent Items To Display In Jump Lists** spinner to select the number displayed in jump lists (see Chapter 5).

6. To return to the original default settings, click **Use Default Settings**.

7. When you have made the changes you want, click **OK** twice.

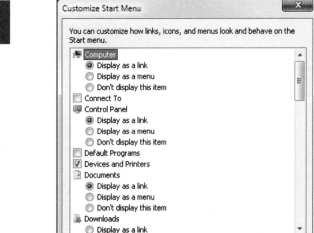

Figure 2-8: *You can customize what is displayed on the Start menu and how those items work.*

ADD PROGRAMS TO THE START MENU

You can add programs to the upper-left corner of the Start menu, where they will remain unless you remove them.

1. Click **Start**, click **All Programs**, and open the appropriate folders to display the program you want on the Start menu.

2. Right-click the program and click **Pin To Start Menu**. The program will appear on the Start menu. For example, if you want to add Internet Explorer, click **Start**, click **All Programs**, right-click **Internet Explorer**, and click **Pin To Start Menu**.

3. Click outside the Start menu to close it.

Figure 2-9 shows a changed Start menu, which you can compare with Figure 1-2 in Chapter 1.

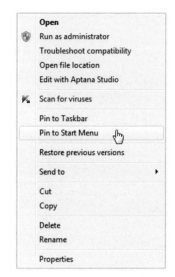

Change the Taskbar

The taskbar at the bottom of the Windows 7 SP1 screen has four standard areas: the Start button on the left, the task list in the middle, and the notification area and the Show Desktop button on the right. In addition, there is an optional "pin-to" area next

Figure 2-9: *A Start menu with changes described in this chapter.*

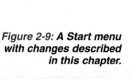

TIP

To remove a program from the Start menu, click **Start**, right-click the program, and if it is one you added in the upper-left corner of the menu (semipermanent area), click **Unpin From Start Menu**. If the program you want to remove is in the lower-left corner (recently used program area), click **Remove From This List**. Then click outside the Start menu to close it.

The picture that is displayed on the Start menu comes from your user account, as described in Chapter 8. To change this picture, right-click the desktop, click **Personalize**, click **Change Your Account Picture** on the left, click one of the pictures shown, click **Change Picture**, and click **Close** to close the Personalization window; or click **Browse for More Pictures**, navigate to the drive and folder with the picture you want (see Chapter 3), click that picture, and click **Open**. Click **Close** to close the User Accounts dialog box.

You can turn on a second optional area on the taskbar next to the notification area that lets you open the Tablet PC Input Panel to enter text on the screen without a keyboard. Instead, you write with a mouse or stylus, or click a keyboard layout on the screen. See the "Changing Taskbar Properties" QuickSteps to see how to turn this on.

to the Start button. You can change the taskbar by moving and sizing it and by changing its properties.

Start button   Programs currently running   Notification area and clock

Programs pinned to the taskbar   Show Desktop button

MOVE AND SIZE THE TASKBAR

You can move the taskbar to any of the four sides of the screen. Do this by dragging any empty area of the taskbar to another edge. For example, Figure 2-10 shows the taskbar moved to the right edge of the screen.

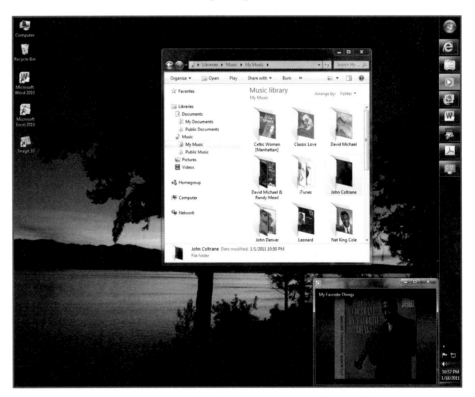

Figure 2-10: *A taskbar can be moved to any of the four sides of the screen.*

QUICKSTEPS

CHANGING TASKBAR PROPERTIES

A number of taskbar features can be changed through the Taskbar And Start Menu Properties dialog box (see Figure 2-11).

OPEN TASKBAR PROPERTIES

Right-click an open area of the taskbar, and click **Properties**. The Taskbar And Start Menu Properties dialog box appears with the Taskbar tab selected. (Click **Apply** to test a change without closing the dialog box.)

UNLOCK THE TASKBAR

By default, the taskbar is locked. To move or resize the taskbar, it must be unlocked.

Click **Lock The Taskbar** to remove the check mark and unlock the taskbar.

HIDE THE TASKBAR

Hiding the taskbar means that it is not displayed unless you move the mouse to the edge of the screen containing the taskbar. By default, it is displayed.

Click **Auto-Hide The Taskbar** to select the check box and hide the taskbar.

USE SMALL ICONS

If you want to conserve desktop space and you have good eyesight, you can make the icons smaller, the size they were in previous versions of Windows.

Click **Use Small Icons** to select the check box and make the icons smaller.

CUSTOMIZE TASKBAR BUTTONS

There are three choices for customizing taskbar buttons:

- Always combine similar items and hide the labels, such as program names.

Continued . . .

Figure 2-11: *You will use the taskbar often, so it should look and behave the way you want.*

You can size the taskbar by dragging the inner edge (top edge when the taskbar is on the bottom) in or out. Here is a taskbar at double its normal size.

In either case, you must first unlock the taskbar. See the "Changing Taskbar Properties" QuickSteps to do this.

Permanently Pin Icons to the Taskbar

Windows 7 SP1 provides the ability to permanently "pin," or attach, frequently used program icons to the taskbar next to the Start button. Once there the icons are always visible (unless you hide the taskbar), and the related program can be started by a single click. By default Windows 7 SP1 has three icons pinned to the taskbar: Internet Explorer, Windows Explorer, and Media Player. You can pin additional icons, you can remove those that are currently pinned, and you can rearrange the current icons.

PIN AN ICON TO THE TASKBAR

After you have used Windows 7 SP1 for a while you may find that you use a program more often than others and would like to have it more immediately available. This is what pinning to the taskbar is for. You can do that by either:

Locating the program icon in Windows Explorer, any part of the Start menu, or on the desktop; right-clicking it; and clicking **Pin To Taskbar**.

–Or–

Starting the program in any of the ways described in Chapter 1. When it has started, right-click its icon on the taskbar, and click **Pin This Program To Taskbar**.

REMOVE AN ICON PINNED TO THE TASKBAR

To remove a program icon pinned to the taskbar:

Right-click the icon and click **Unpin This Program From Taskbar**.

REARRANGE ICONS PINNED TO THE TASKBAR

The icons that are pinned to the taskbar can be moved around and placed in any order.

Drag icons pinned to the taskbar to where you want them.

Change How Windows 7 SP1 Operates

How Windows 7 SP1 operates is probably more important to you than how it looks. For that reason, Windows 7 SP1 has a number of facilities that allow you to customize its operation.

QUICKSTEPS

CHANGING THE NOTIFICATION AREA

The notification area on the right of the taskbar can also be changed through the Taskbar And Start Menu Properties dialog box (see the "Changing Taskbar Properties" QuickSteps for instructions on displaying the dialog box). The notification area, which can get crowded at times, contains program icons put there by Windows and other programs. You can control which icons are displayed along with their notifications, which icons are hidden but their notifications are displayed, or which icons are not there at all. To change the notification area:

Click **Customize** under Notification Area. The Notification Area Icons window will appear, as shown in Figure 2-12.

CUSTOMIZE NOTIFICATION ICONS

To customize the behavior of icons in the notification area:

Click the drop-down list opposite the icon you want to change, and select the behavior you want.

DISPLAY SYSTEM ICONS

Up to five system icons—Action Center, Network, Volume, Power (on mobile computers), and Clock—are shown in the notification area by default. You can turn them off if you wish.

1. Click **Turn System Icons On Or Off**.

2. Click the drop-down list opposite an icon name, and click **Off** to not display it.

3. When you have made the changes you want, click **OK**.

CLOSE TASKBAR PROPERTIES

After you've made any of these changes to the notification area, click **OK** to enable them and close the Notification Area Icons window. Click **OK** again to close the Taskbar And Start Menu Properties dialog box.

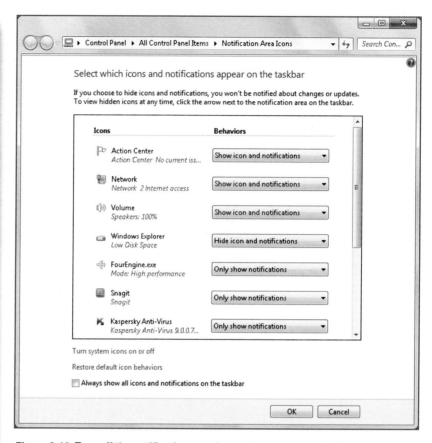

Figure 2-12: *Turn off the notification area icons that are not useful to you.*

Set and Use the Date and Time

The time and date in the lower-right corner of the screen may seem simple enough, but significant capability lies behind these basic numbers.

1. Move the mouse until your cursor is on the time in the notification area. The current day and date will appear.

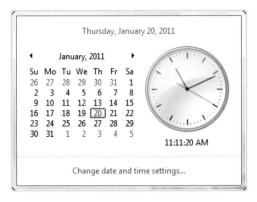

2. Click the time. The full calendar and clock appear, as you can see on the left.

3. Click **Change Date And Time Settings**. The Date And Time dialog box will appear, as shown in Figure 2-13.

4. With the Date And Time tab selected, click **Change Date And Time**. The Date And Time Settings dialog box appears.

5. Use the arrows on the calendar to change the month. Or, click the month to display the year, use the arrows to change the year, click the month, and then click a day.

6. Double-click an element of time (hour, minute, second, A.M./P.M.), and use the spinner to change the selected time element. Click **OK** to close the Date And Time Settings dialog box.

7. Click **Change Time Zone**, click the **Time Zone** down arrow, and click your time zone.

8. Click **Automatically Adjust Clock For Daylight Saving Time** if it isn't already selected and you want Windows 7 SP1 to do that. Click **OK** to close the Time Zone Settings dialog box.

9. Click the **Additional Clocks** tab to add one or two clocks with different time zones. Click the first **Show This Clock** checkbox, open the drop-down list box, and click a time zone. Enter a display name, and repeat for a second additional clock, if desired. (The additional times will appear when you point to the time in the notification area.) Click **OK** when done.

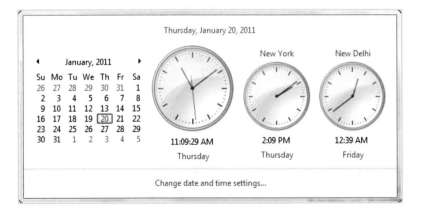

Figure 2-13: Setting the date and time is normally automated using an Internet time server.

10. Click the **Internet Time** tab and see how your computer's time is currently being synchronized. If you want to change that, click **Change Settings**.

The blue and yellow shield on the Change Date And Time button tells you that the function being selected requires administrator permission. You must be an administrator or have a password for an administrator, to change the date and time.

11. Click **Synchronize With An Internet Time Server** if it isn't already selected, open the drop-down list, click a time server, and click **Update Now.** Once turned on, Windows will check the time every seven days. Click **OK** to close the Internet Time Settings dialog box.

12. Click **OK** to close the Date And Time dialog box.

Change Ease-of-Access Settings

Ease-of-access settings provide alternatives to the normal way the mouse and keyboard are used, as well as some settings that make the screen more readable and sounds more understandable.

1. Right-click a blank area of the screen, click **Personalize**, and click **Ease Of Access Center** in the lower-left area. The Ease Of Access Center window will open, as shown in Figure 2-14.

   –Or–

   Press and hold the **Windows Flag** key while pressing **U**.

2. Select the options you want to use in the common tools area at the top (see Table 2-1 for a description). You can also turn the options on or off using the keyboard shortcuts shown.

3. Click any of the blue text links in the lower part of the window to review, and possibly change, the ease-of-access settings that apply to various areas of the computer. Within links there are a number of assistive tools, shown in Table 2-2, that can be turned on, either in these links or with the keyboard shortcuts shown.

4. When you have set up the accessibility options you want, click **Close**.

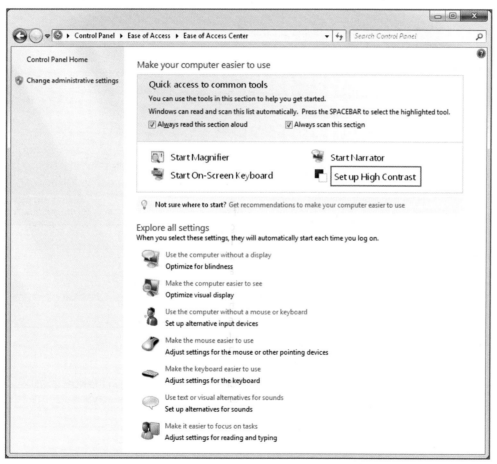

Figure 2-14: Ease-of-access settings let you work with Windows 7 SP1 and your programs in ways that facilitate use with various physical limitations.

TIP

You can also turn on the most common ease-of-access options from the Windows 7 SP1 logon screen by clicking the **Ease Of Access** icon in the lower-left corner of the screen.

NOTE

By default, and if you have speakers and a sound card, Windows 7 SP1 will scan and read aloud the four options in the Quick Access section.

NOTE

Many Control Panel components are also available from other locations. For example, the Date And Time component opens the same dialog box that appears when you click the time in the taskbar and click **Change Date/Time**.

OPTION	DESCRIPTION	KEYBOARD SHORTCUT
Magnifier	Enlarges a part of the screen around the mouse.	
On Screen Keyboard	Displays an image of a keyboard on the screen that you can click to select the appropriate keys.	
Narrator	Reads aloud selected text on the screen.	
High Contrast	Uses high-contrast colors and special fonts to make the screen easy to use.	Press left **SHIFT**+left **ALT**+and **PRINT SCREEN** all together.

Table 2-1: *Ease-of-Access Reading Tools*

OPTION	DESCRIPTION	KEYBOARD SHORTCUT
Mouse Keys	Uses the numeric keypad to move the mouse around the screen.	Press left **ALT**+left **SHIFT**+and **NUM LOCK**.
Sticky Keys	Simulates pressing a pair of keys, such as CTRL+A, by pressing one key at a time. The keys **SHIFT**, **CTRL**, and **ALT** "stick" down until a second key is pressed. This is interpreted as two keys pressed together.	Press either left or right **SHIFT** key five times in succession.
Filter Keys	Enables you to press a key twice in rapid succession and have it interpreted as a single keystroke; also slows down the rate at which the key is repeated if it is held down.	Hold down the right **SHIFT** key for eight seconds.
Toggle Keys	Hear a tone when **CAPS LOCK**, **NUM LOCK**, or **SCROLL LOCK** is turned on.	Hold down the **NUM LOCK** key for five seconds.

Table 2-2: *Ease-of-Access Typing Tools*

QUICKSTEPS

USING THE CONTROL PANEL

The Control Panel is a facility for customizing many of the functions available in Windows. The individual components of the Control Panel are discussed throughout this book (several in this chapter); this section is an introduction to the Control Panel itself.

OPEN THE CONTROL PANEL

Click **Start** and click **Control Panel** on the right. The Control Panel is displayed. By default, it will be as shown in Figure 2-15. (Mobile computers will show additional hardware devices unique to them.)

SWITCH THE CONTROL PANEL VIEW

The Control Panel has three views: the default Category view, shown in Figure 2-15, which groups Control Panel functions; and Large and Small Icons views (Figure 2-16 shows Small Icons view), which shows all the Control Panel components in one window.

When in Category view, click the **View By** down arrow on the right, and click either **Large Icons** or **Small Icons**.

When in Large or Small Icons view, click the **View By** down arrow on the right, and click **Category** to switch back to that view.

OPEN A CONTROL PANEL CATEGORY

Category view groups components into categories that must be opened to see the individual components, although some subcategories are listed.

Click a category to open a window for it, where you can either select a task you want to do or open a Control Panel component represented by an icon.

Continued . . .

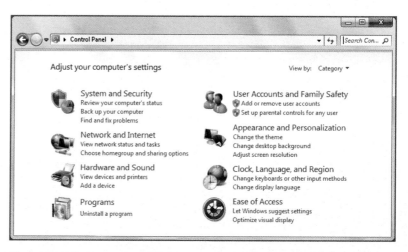

Figure 2-15: *Category view provides a hierarchy of windows that leads you to the settings you want to change.*

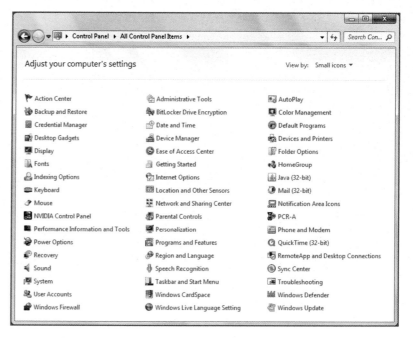

Figure 2-16: *The Control Panel's Small and Large Icons views show all of the components in the Control Panel.*

UICKSTEPS

USING THE CONTROL PANEL
(Continued)

OPEN A CONTROL PANEL COMPONENT

When Category view's secondary windows are opened in the previous step, the icons for individual Control Panel component icons are displayed. In either Large or Small Icons view, these component icons are directly displayed. To open a component:

Click the component's icon.

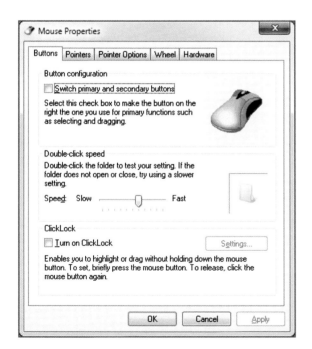

Figure 2-17: *The mouse is the primary way you operate in Windows 7 SP1.*

Customize the Mouse

The mouse lets you interact with the screen and point at, select, and drag objects. You also can start and stop programs and close Windows using the mouse. While you can use Windows without a mouse, it is more difficult, making it important that the mouse operates in the most comfortable way possible. Change the way the mouse works through the Control Panel Mouse component.

1. Click **Start** and click **Control Panel**.

2. In Category view, click **Hardware And Sound**, and under Devices And Printers, click **Mouse**.

   –Or–

   In Large or Small Icons view, click **Mouse**.

   Either way, the Mouse Properties dialog box will appear, as you can see in Figure 2-17.

3. If you want to use the mouse with your left hand, click **Switch Primary And Secondary Buttons**.

4. Double-click the folder in the middle-right area of the Buttons tab. If the folder opens, your double-click speed is okay. If not, drag the **Speed** slider until the folder opens when you double-click it.

5. Select the options you want to use on the **Buttons**, **Pointer Options**, **Wheel**, and **Hardware** tabs.

6. Click the **Pointers** tab. If you want to change the way the pointer looks, select a different scheme (see "Use a Different Mouse Pointer," earlier in the chapter).

7. When you have set up the mouse the way you want, click **OK**.

Customize the Keyboard

Windows requires a keyboard for manual communications (speech recognition can replace the keyboard in many instances). You can change the length of the

NOTE

If you have purchased a mouse separately from your computer and have installed its software, your tabs may be different and its features may not be as described here.

delay before a key that is held down is repeated and the rate at which the key is repeated.

1. Click **Start** and click **Control Panel**.

2. In Category view, click **Large** or **Small Icons** view, and then click **Keyboard**. The Keyboard Properties dialog box appears.

3. Click in the text box in the middle of the dialog box, and press a character key to see how long you wait before the key is repeated and how fast the repeated character appears.

4. Drag the **Repeat Delay** slider in the direction desired, and then test the repetition again.

5. Drag the **Repeat Rate** slider in the direction desired, and then test the repetition again.

6. Drag the **Cursor Blink Rate** slider in the direction desired, and observe the blink rate.

7. When you have set up the keyboard the way you want, click **OK**.

Change Sounds

Windows 7 SP1 uses sounds to alert and entertain you. Through the Control Panel's Sound component, you can select the sound scheme you want (see Figure 2-18).

1. Click **Start** and click **Control Panel**.

2. In Category view, click **Hardware And Sound**, and then click **Sound**.

   –Or–

   In Large or Small Icons view, click **Sound**.

   In either case, the Sound dialog box appears.

3. Click **Speakers**, click **Configure** in the lower-left corner, select your configuration in the Audio Channels list, and click **Test** to test your setup. When you are ready, click **Next**.

4. If you select a configuration that has more speakers than you actually have, for example if you have a subwoofer and a pair of speakers, you must select the 5.1 Surround configuration. Then click the speakers that aren't present—the Center and Side Pair in the Center in the example, and click **Next**. Click the speakers that are full-range speakers, and click **Next**. When you are done, click **Finish**.

5. Double-click **Speakers**, click the **Levels** tab, and drag the slider(s) in the direction desired to set the volume. Click **OK** to close the Speakers Properties dialog box.

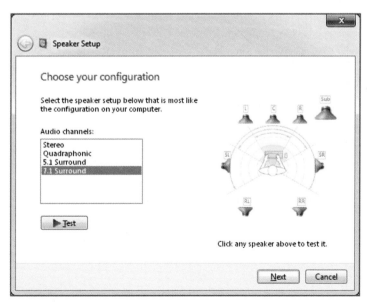

Figure 2-18: Windows 7 SP1 can handle up to seven-speaker surround sound.

CAUTION

Changing the format used for dates and times might affect other Windows programs, such as Excel.

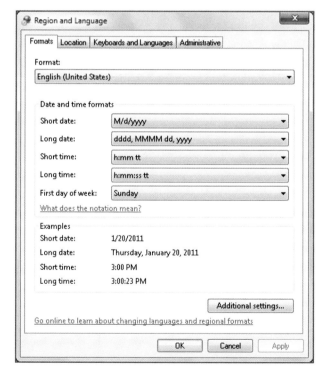

Figure 2-19: Regional and language options allow Windows 7 SP1 to be used almost anywhere in the world.

6. Click the **Sounds** tab, and select a different sound scheme to change it, if desired (see "Select the Sounds Windows 7 SP1 Plays" earlier in the chapter).

7. When you have set up the sounds the way you want, click **OK**.

Change Regional Settings

Windows 7 SP1 lets you determine how numbers, dates, currency, and time are displayed and used, as well as the languages that will be used. Choosing a primary language and locale sets all the other settings. You can customize these options through the Regional And Language options component in the Control Panel.

1. Click **Start** and click **Control Panel**.

2. In Category view, click **Clock, Language, And Region,** and then click **Region And Language**.

   –Or–

   In Large or Small Icons view, click **Region And Language**.

   In either case, the Region And Language dialog box will appear, as you can see in Figure 2-19.

3. In the Formats tab, click the **Format** drop-down list, and select the primary language and region in which the computer will be used. This changes the standards and formats that will be used by default.

4. Customize the date and time formats by clicking the down arrow associated with each setting and selecting the option that you want.

5. Click **Additional Settings** and then go to the individual tabs for numbers, currency, time, and date; and set how you want these items displayed. Click **OK** when you are done.

6. Review the **Location**, **Keyboards And Languages**, and **Administrative** tabs, and make any desired changes.

7. When you have set up the regional settings the way you want, click **OK**.

Manage Gadgets

The Gadgets feature displays a clock and other gadgets—initially on the right side of the screen, but they can be moved. To manage gadgets:

1. Click **Start** and click **Control Panel**.

2. In Category view, click **Appearance And Personalization**, and then click **Desktop Gadgets**.

   –Or–

   In Large or Small Icons view, click **Desktop Gadgets**.

In either case, the Gadgets window will open, as shown on the left.

3. Double-click the gadgets that you want displayed.

4. If you want to see more gadgets, click **Get More Gadgets Online**. Internet Explorer will open and display the gadgets that are available. Under the gadget that you want, click **Get Now**. On the Windows Live page that appears, review the gadget and, if you want it, click the **Download** button and then click **Save**, click **Run**, and click **Install**. Close Internet Explorer. The new gadget appears on your desktop.

5. When you are ready, click **Close** to close the Gadgets window. Gadgets for headlines, weather, and central processing unit (CPU) usage are shown here on a desktop.

Chapter 3
Storing Information

The information on your computer—documents, email, photographs, music, and programs—is stored in *files*. So that your files are organized and more easily found, they are kept in *folders,* and folders can be placed in other folders for further organization. For example, a folder labeled "Trips," which is contained in the My Documents folder, contains separate folders for each of the years 2010, 2011, and 2012. The 2011 folder contains folders for Yellowstone and Disneyland. The Yellowstone folder contains folders of photos and videos, as well as files for notes, expenses, and a presentation. Such a set of files and folders is shown in the My Documents folder in Figure 3-1.

In this chapter you'll see how to create, use, and manage files and folders like these. The term "objects" is used to refer to any mix of files, folders, and disk drives.

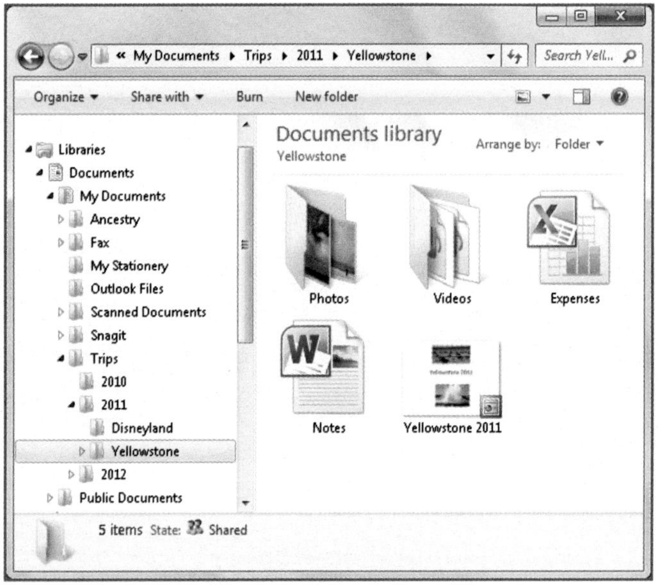

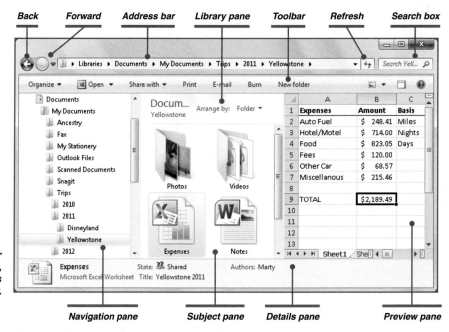

Figure 3-1: Windows stores files in folders, which can be within other folders.

Use the Windows File System

The tool that Windows 7 SP1 provides to locate and work with files and folders is *Windows Explorer* (often called "Explorer," not to be confused with Internet Explorer discussed in Chapter 4). Windows Explorer has a number of components and features, most of which are shown in Figure 3-2 and described in Table 3-1. Much of this chapter is spent exploring these items and how they are used.

When you open Windows Explorer, you can choose what you want it to initially display from among the choices on the right of the Start menu. These choices give you access to (from top to bottom):

- Your personal folder, which contains your documents, pictures, music, and games

- Your documents

Figure 3-2: Windows Explorer provides the means to access files, folders, disks, and memory devices on your computer.

NOTE

Depending on the permissions you have and whether you are connected to a network, you may have Network on your Start menu.

AREA	FUNCTION
Back and Forward buttons	Displays an object previously shown
Address bar	Displays the location of what is being shown in the subject pane
Toolbar	Contains tools to work with objects in the subject pane
Refresh	Updates what is displayed in the address bar
Search box	Provides for the entry of text you want to search for
Preview pane	Displays the contents of the object selected in the subject pane
Details pane	Provides information about the object selected in the subject pane
Subject pane	Displays the objects stored at the address shown in the address bar
Navigation pane	Facilitates moving around among the objects you have available
Library pane	Displays a header for the subject pane when a library is opened

Table 3-1: Windows Explorer Components

Figure 3-3: Windows 7 SP1 starts with a number of standard folders that are a part of the personal folder.

- Your pictures
- Your music
- Your games
- The computer on which you are working

Open Windows Explorer

To open Windows Explorer:

1. Start your computer, if it's not running, and log on to Windows if necessary.

2. Click **Start**. The Start menu will open, and you'll see the Windows Explorer choices on the upper-right corner of the menu.

3. Click your personal folder. Explorer will open and display in the subject pane the files and folders that either come standard with Windows 7 SP1 or that have been placed there by you or somebody else, as shown in Figure 3-3. You can:

   Click an object in the subject pane to *select* it and get information about it in the details pane, preview it in the preview pane, or use the toolbar tools with that object.

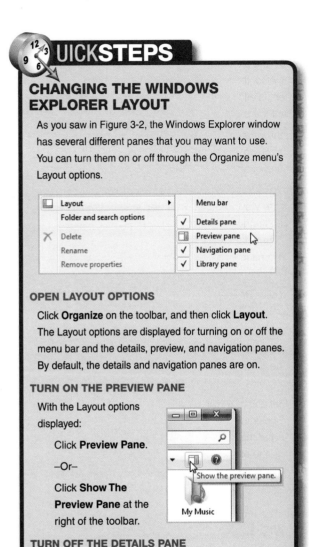

QUICKSTEPS

CHANGING THE WINDOWS EXPLORER LAYOUT

As you saw in Figure 3-2, the Windows Explorer window has several different panes that you may want to use. You can turn them on or off through the Organize menu's Layout options.

Layout	▶	Menu bar
Folder and search options		✓ Details pane
✗ Delete		▣ Preview pane
Rename		✓ Navigation pane
Remove properties		✓ Library pane

OPEN LAYOUT OPTIONS

Click **Organize** on the toolbar, and then click **Layout**. The Layout options are displayed for turning on or off the menu bar and the details, preview, and navigation panes. By default, the details and navigation panes are on.

TURN ON THE PREVIEW PANE

With the Layout options displayed:

Click **Preview Pane**.

–Or–

Click **Show The Preview Pane** at the right of the toolbar.

TURN OFF THE DETAILS PANE

With the Layout options displayed:

Click **Details Pane**.

–Or–

Double-click an object in the subject pane to *open* it so that you can see and work with its contents.

Customize Windows Explorer

You can customize how Windows Explorer looks and which features are available with the toolbar.

1. If Windows Explorer is not already open, click **Start** and click your personal folder.

2. Click **Pictures** in the navigation pane, and then double-click **Sample Pictures** in the subject pane. Windows 7 SP1's sample pictures should open, as you can see in Figure 3-4.

3. Click one of the pictures. The toolbar changes to something like this:

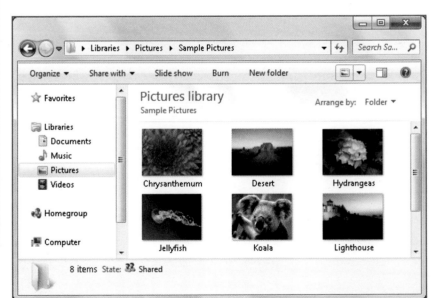

Figure 3-4: Windows Explorer's toolbar changes to provide commands for what is selected in the subject pane.

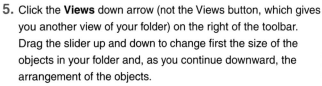

These toolbar options are specific to a picture. Selecting other types of files would have generated different options. Also, the second option, "Preview," in the menu shown here might be "Open" after installing Windows Live Essentials, as suggested in Chapter 4 for email and shown in Figure 3-5.

4. Click **Organize** to open the Organize menu. Here you can perform operations on the object you have selected using menu options such as Cut, Copy, Paste, Delete, and Rename, and perform folder-related operations with menu options such as Layout, Folder And Search Options, and Close.

5. Click the **Views** down arrow (not the Views button, which gives you another view of your folder) on the right of the toolbar. Drag the slider up and down to change first the size of the objects in your folder and, as you continue downward, the arrangement of the objects.

6. Click the **Views** down arrow, and click **Details**, which is shown in Figure 3-5.

7. Click **Name** at the top of the left column in the subject pane. The contents of the subject pane will be sorted alphanumerically by name. Click **Name** again, and the contents will be sorted by name in the opposite direction.

8. Click one of the other column headings, and then click the same column heading again to see the contents sorted that way, first in one direction, and then in the other.

9. Click the **Close** button in the upper-right corner of the Explorer window to close it.

Use Windows Explorer Menus

The Windows 7 SP1 Explorer does not display the menu bar by default, although earlier versions of Windows Explorer did. Most of the menu commands are available on the toolbar, but, if you prefer, you can turn on and use the menus.

1. Click **Start**, click **Pictures**, and then click **Sample Pictures** to open the Windows Explorer window and display the sample pictures.

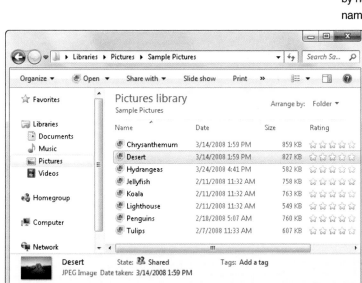

Figure 3-5: Folder Details view gives you further information about the objects in a folder.

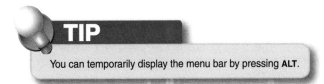

TIP

You can temporarily display the menu bar by pressing **ALT**.

2. Click **Organize**, click **Layout**, and click **Menu Bar**. The Windows Explorer menu bar will appear between the address bar and the toolbar.

3. Click the **File**, **Edit**, and **View** menus; and review the available options. The toolbar's Organize and View menus in Windows 7 SP1 Explorer, along with the features of the column heading, replace many of the options in the first three menus on the menu bar. The Help menu is equivalent to the Help icon on the toolbar.

4. Click the **Tools** menu. The first three options are discussed in Chapter 9. Click **Folder Options** (also available from the Organize menu). The Folder Options dialog box will appear with the General tab displayed, as shown in Figure 3-6. This allows you to:

- Open a new window for each folder you open.

- Use a single click in place of a double click to open a window.

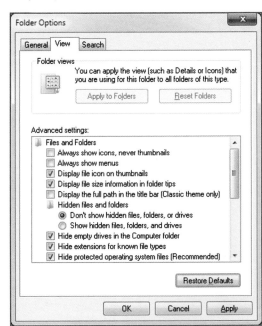

- If you choose single click, you can also determine whether to permanently underline an icon title, as in an Internet browser, or underline an icon only when you point at it.

- Display more or fewer folders in the navigation pane.

Figure 3-6: Folder options allow you to determine how folders look and behave.

5. Click the **View** tab, which is shown in Figure 3-7. This gives you a number of options that determine what is displayed for the current folder and allow you to apply these changes to all folders. The default settings generally work for most people.

Figure 3-7: There are a number of options in the way that Explorer can display folder and file information.

6. When you are ready, click **OK** to close the Folder Options dialog box. (The Search tab will be discussed under "Search for Files and Folders" later in this chapter.)

7. If you want to turn off the menu bar, click **Organize**, click **Layout**, and click **Menu Bar**.

8. Click **Close** to close the Explorer window.

Locate and Use Files and Folders

The purpose of a file system, of course, is to locate and use the files and folders on your computer, and possibly on other computers connected to yours (accessing other computers is called *networking* and is discussed in Chapters 9 and 10). Within your computer, there is a storage hierarchy that starts with storage devices, such as disk drives, which are divided into areas called folders, each of which may be divided again into subareas called subfolders. Each of these contains files, which can be documents, pictures, music, and other data. Figure 3-1 showed folders containing subfolders and eventually containing files with information in them. Figure 3-8 shows a computer containing disk drives, which in turn contain folders. Windows Explorer contains a number of tools for locating, opening, and using disk drives, folders, and files.

Identify Storage Devices

Files and folders are stored on various physical storage devices, including disk drives, CD and DVD drives, memory cards and sticks, and Universal Serial Bus (USB) flash memory. You will have some, but not necessarily all, of the following:

- Primary floppy disk, labeled "A:" (most computers no longer have a floppy drive)
- Primary hard disk, labeled "C:"
- CD or DVD drive, labeled "D:"
- Other storage devices, labeled "E:" and then "F:" and so on

Your primary hard disk is always labeled "C:." Other drives have flexible labeling. Often, the CD or DVD drive will be drive "D:," but if you have a second hard disk drive, it may be labeled "D," as you can see in Figure 3-8.

Figure 3-8: Your computer stores information in a hierarchy of disk drives and folders.

Select and Open Drives and Folders

When you open Windows Explorer and display the items in Computer, you see the disk drives and other storage devices on your computer, as well as several folders, including Program Files, Users, and Windows, as you saw in Figure 3-8. To work with these drives and folders, you must select them; to see and work with their contents, you must open them.

1. Click **Start** and click **Computer** to open Windows Explorer and display the local disk drives.

2. In the subject pane (right pane), click disk **(C:)**. Disk (C:) will be highlighted and its characteristics will be displayed in the details pane (bottom pane).

3. Double-click disk **(C:)** in any pane. Disk (C:) will open and its folders will be displayed in the subject pane.

4. Double-click **Users** to open that folder and display your folder along with a Public folder.

5. Double-click your personal folder (the folder with your name on it). The subject pane displays the files and folders in your folder. This will include Contacts, Desktop, My Documents, My Music, and others, as shown in Figure 3-9.

6. Keep double-clicking each folder to open it until you see the contents you are looking for.

Figure 3-9: Double-clicking a drive or folder will open it in the subject pane.

Navigate Folders and Disks

Opening Windows Explorer and navigating through several folders—beginning with your hard disk—to find a file you want is fine. However, if you want to quickly go to another folder or file, you won't want to have to start with your hard disk every single time. The Windows 7 SP1 Explorer gives you three ways to do this: through the Libraries folder in the navigation pane, by using the folder tree in the navigation pane, or by using the address bar.

NAVIGATE USING LIBRARIES

The Windows 7 SP1 suggested way to navigate is through the Libraries folder, which contains links to the folders within your personal folder (called a "library" in this case, as shown next). By clicking a library in the navigation pane and then double-clicking folders within the subject pane, you can move around the folders and files within your personal folder. For example, given the folder structure shown in Figure 3-1, here are the steps to open the hypothetical Yellowstone folder:

1. Click **Start** and click **Documents**, which opens the Documents library within your personal Libraries folder.

2. In the navigation pane, click the right-pointing triangle or arrow opposite the Documents library to open it.

3. Still in the navigation page, click the right-pointing arrow opposite My Documents to open it.

4. If you had such a set of folders, you would repeat step 3 to open the Trips and 2011 folders, and then click the **Yellowstone** folder to open it in the subject pane.

NAVIGATE USING FOLDERS

The portion of the navigation pane starting with Computer is a folder tree that contains all the disk drives, folders, and files on your computer in a tree, or hierarchical, structure. To open the same folder structure shown in Figure 3-1 through Computer:

1. Click **Start** and click **Computer**, which opens Computer in the navigation pane, as you saw in Figure 3-8.

2. In the navigation pane, click the right-pointing arrow opposite the (C:) disk drive to open it.

3. Still in the navigation page, click the right-pointing arrow opposite Users to open it.

4. Repeat step 3 to open your personal folder and then the My Documents, Trips, and 2011 folders.

5. Click the **Yellowstone** folder to open it in the subject pane.

   You can see that Libraries saves a couple of steps, but at the cost of possible confusion.

NAVIGATE USING THE ADDRESS BAR

Windows 7 SP1 gives you another way to quickly navigate through your drives and folders by clicking segments of a folder address in the address bar, as shown here:

TIP

It is easy to become confused by the various folders in the navigation pane. Both Favorites and Libraries are folders with *shortcuts,* or links to folders and files on your computer. (See "Create Shortcuts" later in this chapter.) The shortcuts in Libraries are links to the actual folders in the C:/Users/Personal Folder/My Documents path, as you can see in "Navigate Using Folders."

TIP

The folder tree is also useful for copying and moving files and folders, as you will see in the "Copying and Moving Files and Folders" QuickSteps in this chapter.

By clicking the down arrow on the far right of the address bar, you can see how this same address looked in previous versions of Windows and use the address bar as it was in the past.

C:\Users\Marty\Documents\Trips\2011\Yellowstone

With Windows 7 SP1, if you click any segment of the address, you will open that level in the subject pane. If you click the arrow to the right of the segment, it displays a drop-down list of subfolders that you can jump to. By successively clicking segments and their subordinate folders, you can easily move throughout the storage space on your computer and beyond to any network you are connected to.

QUICKSTEPS

RENAMING AND DELETING FILES AND FOLDERS

Sometimes, a file or folder needs to be renamed or deleted (whether it was created by you or by an application) because you may no longer need it or for any number of reasons.

RENAME A FILE OR FOLDER

With the file or folder in view but not selected, to rename it:

In the subject pane, slowly click the name twice (don't double-click), type the new name, and press **ENTER**.

–Or–

In either the navigation or subject pane, right-click the name, click **Rename**, type the new name, and press **ENTER**.

DELETE A FILE OR FOLDER TO THE RECYCLE BIN

With the file or folder in view in either the navigation or subject pane, to delete it:

Click the icon for the file or folder to select it, press **DELETE**, and click **Yes** to confirm the deletion.

–Or–

Right-click the icon, click **Delete**, and click **Yes** to confirm the deletion.

Continued . . .

Create New Folders

While you could store all your files within one of the ready-made folders in Windows 7 SP1—such as Documents, Music, or Pictures—you will probably want to make your files easier to find by creating several subfolders.

For example, to create the Trips folder discussed earlier:

1. Click **Start** and click **Documents**. Make sure nothing is selected.

2. Click **New Folder** on the toolbar. A new folder will appear with its name highlighted.

3. Type the name of the folder, such as Trips, and press **ENTER**. Double-click your new folder to open it (you will see it's empty).

As an alternative to clicking New Folder on the toolbar, right-click the open area in the subject pane of Windows Explorer. Click **New** and click **Folder**. Type a name for the folder, and press **ENTER**.

QUICKSTEPS

RENAMING AND DELETING FILES AND FOLDERS (Continued)

RECOVER A DELETED FILE OR FOLDER

To recover a file or folder that has been deleted:

Click the **Organize** menu, and click **Undo**. This only works if you perform the undo operation immediately after the deletion.

–Or–

Double-click the **Recycle Bin** on the desktop to display the Recycle Bin. Right-click the file or folder icon, and choose **Restore**.

PERMANENTLY DELETE A FILE OR FOLDER

If you're sure you want to permanently delete a file or folder:

Click the icon to select it, press and hold **SHIFT** while pressing **DELETE**, and click **Yes** to confirm the permanent deletion.

–Or–

Right-click the icon, press and hold **SHIFT** while clicking **Delete**, and click **Yes** to confirm the permanent deletion.

TIP

To select all objects in the subject pane, click **Organize** and click **Select All**; or click any object in the subject pane, and press **CTRL+A**.

Select Multiple Files and Folders

Often, you will want to do one or more operations—such as copy, move, or delete—on several files and/or folders at the same time. To select several files or folders from the subject pane of an Explorer window:

Move the mouse pointer to the upper-left area, just outside of the top and leftmost object. Then drag the mouse to the lower-right area, just outside of the bottom and rightmost object, creating a shading across the objects, as shown in Figure 3-10.

–Or–

Click the first object, and press and hold **CTRL** while clicking the remaining objects, if the objects are noncontiguous (not adjacent to each other). If the objects are contiguous, click the first object, press and hold **SHIFT**, and click the last object.

Figure 3-10: Drag across multiple objects to select all of them.

Figure 3-11: *The Recycle Bin holds deleted items so that you can recover them until you empty it.*

Use the Recycle Bin

If you do a normal delete operation in Explorer or the desktop, the deleted item or items will go into the Recycle Bin. Should you change your mind about the deletion, you can reclaim an item from the Recycle Bin, as explained in the "Renaming and Deleting Files and Folders" QuickSteps earlier in this chapter.

The Recycle Bin is a special folder that can contain both files and folders. You can open it and see its contents as you would any other folder by double-clicking its desktop icon. Figure 3-11 shows a Recycle Bin after deleting several files and folders. What makes the Recycle Bin special are the two special tasks in the toolbar:

- **Empty The Recycle Bin** permanently removes all of the contents of the Recycle Bin.

- **Restore All Items** returns all the contents to their original folders, in effect, "undeleting" all of the contents. If you select one item, this option changes to Restore This Item.

Obviously, there is a limit to how much the Recycle Bin can hold. You can limit the amount of space it takes so that it doesn't take over your hard disk. That and other settings are configured in the Recycle Bin's Properties dialog box.

1. Right-click the **Recycle Bin** on the desktop, and click **Properties**. The Recycle Bin Properties dialog box will appear, as you can see here.

2. If you have multiple hard disks, select the drive you want to set. In any case, make sure **Custom Size** is selected, select the size, and type the number of megabytes you want to use ("3082" megabytes is 3.082 gigabytes).

3. If you don't want to use the Recycle Bin, click **Don't Move Files To The Recycle Bin**. This is strongly discouraged since this means that files will be permanently deleted with no hope of recovery.

4. If you don't need to see the deletion confirmation message, click that check box to deselect it. Again, this is discouraged since the message tells you what is happening to the files in case it is not what you want.

5. When you are ready, click **OK** to close the dialog box.

Create Shortcuts

A shortcut is a link to a file or folder that allows you to quickly open the file or folder from places other than where it is stored. For example, you can start a program from the desktop even though the actual program file is stored in some other folder. To create a shortcut:

1. In Windows Explorer, locate the folder or file for which you want to create a shortcut.

2. If it is a program file (one identified as an "application," or with an .exe extension), drag it to a different folder, for example, from a folder to the desktop.

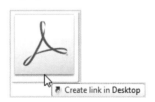

Create link in Desktop

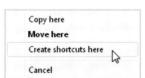

Copy here
Move here
Create shortcuts here
Cancel

3. If it is any other file or folder, hold down the right mouse button while dragging the file or folder to a different folder, release the right mouse button, and then click **Create Shortcuts Here**.

   –Or–

1. In Windows Explorer, open the folder in which you want to create a shortcut.

2. Right-click a blank area in the subject pane of the folder, click **New**, and click **Shortcut**.

New   ▸   Folder
                     Shortcut
Properties

QUICKSTEPS

COPYING AND MOVING FILES AND FOLDERS

Copying and moving files and folders are similar actions, and can be done with the mouse alone, with the mouse and a menu, and with the keyboard.

COPY WITH THE MOUSE

To copy with the mouse, hold down **CTRL** while dragging any file or folder from one folder to another on the same disk drive, or drag a file or folder from one disk drive to another.

MOVE NONPROGRAM FILES ON THE SAME DISK WITH THE MOUSE

Move nonprogram files from one folder to another on the same disk with the mouse by dragging the file or folder.

MOVE NONPROGRAM FILES TO ANOTHER DISK WITH THE MOUSE

Move nonprogram files to another disk by holding down **SHIFT** while dragging them.

MOVE PROGRAM FILES WITH THE MOUSE

Move program files to another folder or disk by holding down **SHIFT** while dragging them.

COPY AND MOVE WITH THE MOUSE AND A MENU

To copy and move with a mouse and a menu, hold down the right mouse button while dragging the file or folder. When you release the right mouse button, a context menu opens and allows you to choose whether to copy, move, or create a shortcut (see "Create Shortcuts" in this chapter).

Copy here
Move here
Create shortcuts here

Cancel

Continued . . .

3. In the dialog box that appears, click **Browse** and use the folder tree to locate and select the file or folder for which you want to make a shortcut.

4. Click **OK** and click **Next**. Type a name for the shortcut, and click **Finish**.

Search for Files and Folders

With large and, possibly several, hard disks, it is often difficult to find files and folders. Windows Explorer's Search feature addresses that problem.

1. Click **Start** and notice the blinking cursor in the Search Programs And Files text box at the bottom of the menu.

2. Type all or part of the folder name, filename, or keyword or phrase in a file in the Search box. As you type, Windows 7 SP1 will start locating files and folders that match your criteria and display them in the top of the Start menu.

   Initially, the search will be of all indexed files (by default, Windows 7 SP1 will index your files and folders automatically) and will show all results.

3. If you see the file or folder you are searching for, click it and it will be displayed in Windows Explorer (if a folder) or in the program that created it (if a file).

4. If you want to see more results, click **See More Results** at the bottom of the menu. Windows Explorer will

open. Review the list in the subject pane; if you see the file or folder you want, click it to open it.

5. If you still are not finding what you want, scroll the subject pane to the bottom and you'll see some additional options, as shown in Figure 3-12.

6. In the Search Again In options, you can choose several specific places to search, or click **Customize** to select one or more other places to search.

7. To filter the search results, click in the search text box in the upper-right corner of the Windows Explorer window. Two options will appear that let you filter the search results by the date it was modified and by the size of the file.

8. To change search options, click **Organize** in the toolbar, and click **Folder And Search Options**. The Folder Options dialog box will appear. Click the **Search** tab. Make any change to the settings that you want, and click **OK**.

9. If you want to save the search, click **Save Search** on the toolbar, select the folder in which you want to store the file, type the filename, and click **Save**. If you don't select another folder, saved searches are available in the Searches folder by default. Saved searches also appear under Favorites in the navigation pane.

10. When you are done, close Windows Explorer.

Create Files

Files are usually created by applications or by copying existing files; however, Windows has an additional file-creation capability that creates an empty file for a particular application.

1. Click **Start**, click **Documents**, and open the folder in which you want to create the new file.

2. Right-click a blank area of the subject pane in Windows Explorer, and choose **New**. A menu of all the file types that can be created by the registered applications on your computer will appear.

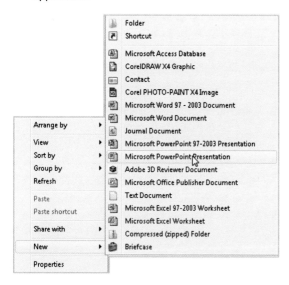

Figure 3-12: *You may need to refine your search criteria to get only the files you are looking for.*

3. Click the file type you want to create. If you want to work on the file, double-click it to open it in its application.

NOTE

You can let someone else use an encrypted file by giving him or her your logon user name and password. In addition, in many organizations, an administrator will have the ability to decrypt files so that information cannot be lost through encryption.

TIP

To remove encryption, follow the steps used to encrypt and deselect the relevant option.

Encrypt Files and Folders

Windows 7 SP1 Professional, Enterprise, and Ultimate editions, but not Windows 7 SP1 Starter, Home Basic, or Home Premium editions, have the ability to encrypt files and folders so that they cannot be read without the key to decrypt them. The key is attached to the person who performed the encryption. When she or he logs on to the computer, the files can be used as if they were not encrypted. If someone else logs on, the files cannot be accessed. Even if someone takes the disk to another computer, all that will be displayed is gibberish. To encrypt a file or folder:

1. Click **Start** and click **Computer**. In the navigation pane, open the drive and folders necessary to display the files or folders you want to encrypt in the subject pane.

2. Right-click the file or folder, and choose **Properties**. In the General tab, click **Advanced**. The Advanced Attributes dialog box appears, as shown.

3. Click **Encrypt Contents To Secure Data**.

4. Click **OK** twice.

   If you are encrypting a file, you will see an Encryption Warning dialog box stating that the file is not in an encrypted folder, as shown below, which means that when you edit the file, temporary or backup files might be created that are not encrypted. Options include whether to encrypt the file and its parent folder or just the file.

   If you are encrypting a folder, you will see a Confirm Attribute Changes dialog box that asks if the change applies to this folder only or applies to this folder and its subfolders and files.

5. Choose the option you want, and click **OK**. You may see a message from the Encrypting File System that you should back up your encryption key. Click the icon in the notification area to choose how you want to back up your key. The title under the file or folder icon turns a different color, normally green.

Change Other File and Folder Attributes

Encryption, described in the previous section, is one of five or six file or folder attributes. The others are shown in Table 3-2.

To set the additional attributes:

1. Click **Start** and click **Computer**. In the navigation pane, open the drive and folders necessary to display in the subject pane the files or folders whose attributes you want to set.

2. Right-click the file or folder, and choose **Properties**. In the General tab, you can click **Read-Only** and **Hidden**. Do that if you wish, and click **OK**.

3. If you want to set archiving or indexing, click **Advanced**. The Advanced Attributes dialog box appears.

4. Click the attribute you want to set, and click **OK** twice.

ATTRIBUTE	DESCRIPTION
Read-Only	The file or folder cannot be changed.
Hidden	The file or folder cannot be seen unless Show Hidden Files, Folders, And Drives is selected in the Folder Options View tab.
File Or Folder Is Ready For Archiving	This serves as a flag to backup programs that the file or folder is ready to be backed up.
Allow Files In This Folder Or This File To Have Contents Indexed	This allows the Windows Indexing Service to index the file or folder so that searching for the file can be done quickly. (See Chapter 6 for how to use the Indexing Service.)
Compress Contents To Save Disk Space	The file or folder is rewritten on the disk in compressed format. The file can still be read, but the reading will take a little longer while it is decompressed.

Table 3-2: Additional File and Folder Attributes

![QUICKSTEPS](clock icon)

ZIPPING FILES AND FOLDERS

Windows 7 SP1 has a way to compress files and folders called "zipping." *Zipped* files have the extension .zip and are compatible with programs like WinZip. Zipped files take up less room on a disk and are transmitted over the Internet faster.

CREATE A ZIPPED FOLDER

You can create a new zipped folder and drag files to it.

1. Click **Start** and click **Documents**.

2. Navigate to the folder that you want to contain the zipped folder.

3. Right-click in a blank area of the subject pane, click **New**, and click **Compressed (Zipped) Folder**. The zipped folder will appear.

4. Click the folder name, type a new name, press **ENTER**, and drag files and folders into it to compress them.

New Compressed (zipped) Folder

SEND FILES OR FOLDERS TO A ZIPPED FOLDER

1. In Windows Explorer, select the files and/or folders you want zipped.

2. Right-click the selected objects, click **Send To**, and click **Compressed (Zipped) Folder**. A new zipped folder will appear containing the original files and/or folders, now compressed.

EXTRACT ZIPPED FILES AND FOLDERS

To unzip a file or folder, simply drag it out of the zipped folder, or you can extract all of a zipped folder's contents.

1. Right-click a zipped folder, and click **Extract All**. The Extract Compressed (Zipped) Folders dialog box will appear.

Continued . . .

Back Up Files and Folders

Backing up copies important files and folders on your disk and writes them on another device, such as a recordable CD or DVD, a USB flash drive, or to another hard disk. To start the backup process:

1. Click **Start**, click **Control Panel**, click **System And Security**, and click **Backup And Restore**. If this is the first time you are doing a backup, you will be asked to set up Windows Backup.

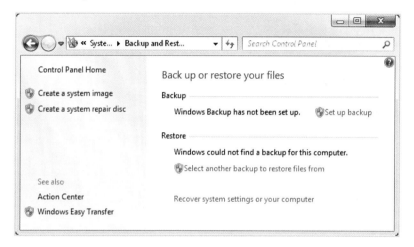

2. Click **Set Up Backup**. The Set Up Backup dialog box will appear, as shown in Figure 3-13.

3. Click a local backup destination drive, or click **Save On A Network**.

4. If you chose to save on a network, click **Browse**, select a network drive and folder where you want the backup, click **OK**, and enter your network user name and password. Click **OK**. The network drive will appear on the list of destination drives. Click it.

5. Click **Next**. Accept the recommended Let Windows Choose What To Backup, or click **Let Me Choose**, and then click **Next**.

6. If you chose the latter option, select the files and drives you want to back up, and click **Next**.

UICKSTEPS

ZIPPING FILES AND FOLDERS

(Continued)

2. Enter or browse to the location where you want the extracted files and folders, and click **Extract**.

3. Close Windows Explorer when you are done.

TIP

When you zip a group of files, right-click the file whose name you want to give to the zip folder, and then click **Send To**. The file's name will automatically be given to the zip folder.

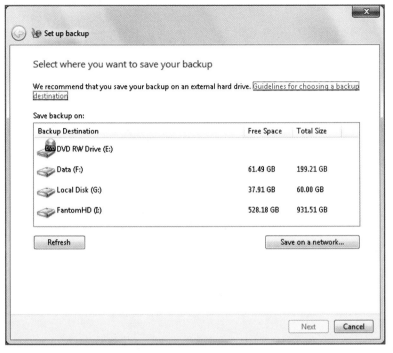

Figure 3-13: *If possible, back up to an external drive.*

7. Review the Backup Summary that is presented. If it is not correct, click the **Back** icon in the upper-left area, and return to the previous steps.

8. If the proposed schedule is not what you want, click **Change Schedule**. Select how often, what day, and what time you want to do the backup, and click **OK**.

9. Click **Save Settings And Run Backup**. Your next backup will be scheduled and the current backup will begin. You can stop the backup if you wish and change the settings in this window, which replaces the original Backup And Restore window.

10. When the backup is complete, the Backup And Restore window goes into its final form, shown in Figure 3-14. Click the **Close** button to close the Backup And Restore window.

NOTE

System and program files will not be backed up in an automatic scheduled backup.

TIP

The Live File System that lets you use CD-R/DVD-R discs like CD-RW/DVD-RW discs is a super capability that you can use as an additional hard disk.

NOTE

By default, Windows 7 SP1 automatically defragments your drives on a periodic basis, so under most circumstances, you won't need to do it.

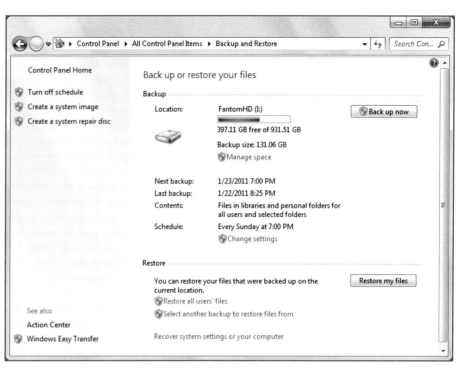

Figure 3-14: The final Backup And Restore window goes through several changes.

Write Files and Folders to a CD or DVD

Windows 7 SP1 allows you to copy ("burn" or record) files to a writable or rewritable CD or DVD. You must have a CD or DVD writing drive and blank media.

1. Place a blank recordable disc in the drive. You will be asked if you want to burn a CD or DVD using Windows Explorer or Windows Media Player, or possibly other programs on your computer.

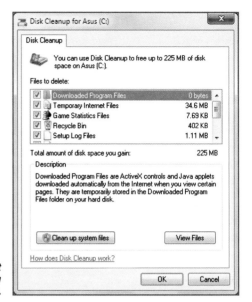

QUICKSTEPS

MANAGING DISKS

Windows 7 SP1 provides three tools to help manage the files and folders stored on hard disks.

CLEAN UP A DISK

Disk Cleanup helps you get rid of old files on your hard disk. Windows looks through your hard disk for types of files that can be deleted and lists them, as shown in Figure 3-15. You can then select the types of files you want to delete.

1. Click **Start**, click **Computer**, right-click a disk drive you want to work on, and click **Properties**.

2. Click **Disk Cleanup**. Windows 7 SP1 will calculate how much space you could save.

3. Select the types of files to delete, and click **OK**. You are asked if you want to permanently delete these files. Click **Delete Files** to permanently delete them.

4. When you are ready, close the Properties dialog box.

CHECK FOR ERRORS

Error Checking tries to read and write on your disk, without losing information, to determine if bad areas exist. If it finds a bad area, that area is flagged so that the system will not use it. Error Checking automatically fixes file system errors and attempts to recover bad sectors.

1. Click **Start**, click **Computer**, right-click a disk drive you want to work on, and click **Properties**.

2. Click the **Tools** tab, and click **Check Now**. Select whether you want to automatically fix errors and/or attempt to recover bad sectors, and click **Start**. You may be told you have to restart Windows to use Error Checking. If so, close any open applications, click **Schedule Disk Check** to do a disk check the next time you start your computer, and then restart your computer. Error Checking will automatically begin when Windows restarts.

Continued . . .

*Figure 3-15: **It is important to get rid of files and folders that you are no longer using.***

2. Click **Burn Files To Disc**. Type a name for the disc. You will be shown two formatting options based on how you want to use the disc:

- **Like A USB Flash Drive**, which is the default. This format, called *Live File System,* can only be read on a computer with Windows XP, Windows Server 2003 or 2008, Windows Vista, or Windows 7 (original or SP1) operating systems. This option allows you to add one file or folder to the CD or DVD at a time, like you would with a hard disk or a USB flash drive. You can leave the disc in the drive and drag data to it whenever you want and delete previously added objects.

- **With A CD/DVD Player.** This format, called *Mastered,* can be read by most computers, including older Windows and Apple computers and most stand-alone CD and DVD players. To use this format, you must gather all the files in one place and then burn them all at one time. Use this format for music and video files that you want to play on automobile or stand-alone devices, such as MP3 and video players.

MANAGING DISKS *(Continued)*

You will be shown the status of the Error Checking operation and told of any problems that could not be fixed. When Error Checking is complete, your computer will finish restarting.

DEFRAGMENT A DISK

When files are stored on a hard disk, they are broken into pieces (or *fragments*) and individually written to the disk. As the disk fills, the fragments are spread over the disk as space allows. To read a file that has been fragmented requires extra disk activity and can slow down the performance of your computer. To fix this, Windows has a defragmentation process that rewrites the contents of a disk, placing all of the pieces of a file in one contiguous area.

1. Click **Start**, click **Computer**, right-click a disk drive you want to work on, and click **Properties**.

2. Click the **Tools** tab, and click **Defragment Now**. The Disk Defragmenter will open, as shown in Figure 3-16. You can choose to turn off the automatic defragmentation or to modify the schedule.

3. If you wish to go ahead manually, such as with an external drive not otherwise defragmented, shown in Figure 3-16, select the drive and click **Analyze Disk** to see if the disk needs defragmenting. If you wish to continue, click **Defragment Disk**. The process can take up to a couple of hours. Some fragments may remain, which is fine.

4. When you are ready, click **Close** to close the Disk Defragmenter window.

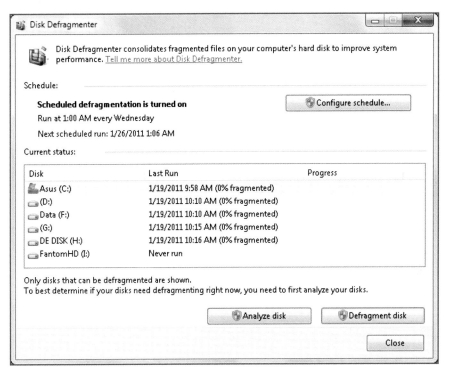

Figure 3-16: Defragmenting brings pieces of a file together into one contiguous area.

3. Click the option you want, and click **Next**. The disc will be formatted and, depending on the option you choose, either Media Player will open or a new AutoPlay dialog box will appear.

4. Open another Windows Explorer window, locate the files and folders you want on the CD or DVD, and drag them to the CD/DVD drive subject pane:

   - If you are using the Live File System format, as you drag the objects to the drive, they will be immediately written on the disc. When you have written all the files you want to the disc, right-click the drive and click **Close Session**. After the "Closing

Session" message above the notification area disappears, you can remove the disc from the drive and insert it at a later time to resume adding or removing files and folders.

- If you are using the Mastered format, drag all the objects you want written on the disc to the drive. When all files and folders are in the drive's subject pane, click **Burn To Disc**. You are asked to confirm or change the title, select a recording speed, and click **Next**. When the burn is complete, the disc will be ejected and you can choose to burn the same files to another disc. In any case, click **Finish**. The temporary files will be erased, which might take a few minutes.

5. When you are done, click **Close** to close Windows Explorer.

Chapter 4
Using the Internet

The Internet provides a major means for worldwide communication between both individuals and organizations, as well as a major means for locating and sharing information. For many, having access to the Internet is the primary reason for having a computer. To use the Internet, you must have a connection to it using one of the many means that are now available. You then can send and receive email; access the World Wide Web; watch movies; and participate in blogs, forums, and newsgroups, among many other things.

Connect to the Internet

You can connect to the Internet using a telephone line, a cable TV connection, a satellite link, or a land-based wireless link. Across these various types of connections there are a myriad of speeds, degrees of reliability, and costs. The most important factor is what is available to you at the location where

QUICKFACTS

UNDERSTANDING INTERNET CONNECTIONS

The following descriptions of Internet connection types give you a starting place for determining the type you want, if it is available to you. The speeds and costs are representative averages and may not be correct for the Internet service provider (ISP) you are considering or for your location. You must get the correct numbers from your local providers.

TELEPHONE DIAL-UP

A dial-up Internet connection is the oldest and slowest type of connection. It requires a modem in or attached to your computer (some computers come with a modem). To use a dial-up connection, the modem must dial the ISP using a regular phone line each time you want to connect to the Internet. This ties up the phone line while you are connected; thus, it cannot be used for other purposes.

- **Speed—Download**: 48 Kbps, **Upload**: 34 Kbps
- **Availability**: Almost anywhere
- **Reliability**: Fair
- **Monthly Cost**: From under $10 to over $20
- **One-Time Cost**: Often none

TELEPHONE DSL

Many phone companies offer a DSL service because it is 20 to 40 times faster than dial-up, does not require a dedicated line (phone conversations and faxes can use the same line at the same time without interference), is always connected, and is not all that expensive. Most DSL is actually ADSL, or asymmetric DSL, meaning that the upload and download speeds are not the same, which is true with almost all service types.

- **Speed—Download**: 512 Kbps to 18 Mbps, **Upload**: 256 Kbps to 2 Mbps

Continued . . .

you want to use it. In an urban area, you have a number of alternatives from landline phone companies, cell phone companies, and cable TV companies, all with many options. As you move away from the urban area, your alternatives will decrease to a telephone dial-up connection and/or a satellite link. With a telephone line, you can connect with a *dial-up* connection, a *DSL* (digital subscriber line) connection, or a high-speed connection of various types. DSL, cable, satellite, and some wireless connections are called *broadband* connections and offer higher speeds and are always on (see the "Understanding Internet Connections" QuickFacts). You must have access to at least one of these forms of communication in order to connect to the Internet. You must also set up the Internet connection itself.

Choose an Internet Connection

With most forms of Internet connections, you have a choice of speed and ancillary services, such as the number of free email accounts and possibly a personal website. Also, depending on the type of connection, you may need dedicated equipment, such as a modem, digital subscriber line (DSL) router, or satellite receiving equipment, which may or may not be included in the price. For any Internet connection service, ask the provider the following questions:

- What is both the best and average experienced download (from the Internet to you) and upload (from you to the Internet) speeds in *Kbps* (kilo or thousands of bits per second) or *Mbps* (millions of bits per second)? (Bits are a series of ones and zeros that represent data.) You will generally do a lot more downloading than uploading.

- What is the total cost per month for a given speed, including all applicable taxes and fees?

- What equipment is needed for this service and how much does it cost, either one time or per month? Does the equipment provide hardwired, wireless, or both types of connections? You might want both so you can have both a desktop computer hardwired and a laptop that you can carry around without plugging it in.

- What installation, setup, and other one-time charges or fees are required? If you pay for six months or a year in advance, are these fees waived?

- How many email accounts are included and how much storage is allowed per account (for example, six accounts and 250MB of storage)? (MB refers to megabytes or millions of bytes, and a byte is eight bits.) How much are additional accounts and storage?

- Are the means for having your own personal or commercial website (called web hosting) included? If so, what are the limits in terms of the amount of storage used by the site and the site activity in terms of the number of bits transferred to and/or from your site per month? For a free personal website, this commonly is 10 to 100MB of storage and 1 to 5GB (gigabits or billions of bits) of activity.

- How long does it take to get the connection up and running?

Set Up Communications

Communications is the link between your computer and the Internet. To set up communications, you must first choose a type of connection link. With a dial-up connection, you must set up a modem. If you are not using dial-up (and that is recommended, if possible), you do not need to install a modem and can skip the following section.

INSTALL A MODEM

If a modem came with your computer, or if one was already installed when you upgraded to Windows 7 SP1, your modem was probably automatically installed and you don't need to do anything more. In that case, or if you are unsure, skip to "Set Up a Dial-Up Connection." Otherwise, if you need to install a modem:

1. Either make sure a modem is physically installed in your computer or, if you have an external modem, that it is connected to your computer, plugged in, and turned on.

2. Click **Start** and click **Control Panel**. On the top-right area, click the **View By** down arrow, and click Large Icons if you are not already in that view.

3. In Large Icons view, click **Phone And Modem**.

4. If this is the first time you've set up a modem, you need to enter location information. Select your country, enter your area or city code, and, if necessary, your carrier code and the number to access an outside line. If needed, click **Pulse Dialing** (with old phone systems only), and click **OK**. The Phone And Modem dialog box will appear.

5. Click the **Modems** tab. If it shows a modem, as you see here, your modem is installed and you can skip to "Set Up a Dial-Up Connection."

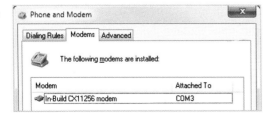

UNDERSTANDING INTERNET CONNECTIONS (Continued)

own private line). In a digital world, this line sharing is not as bad as you might think, but interference can still slow down the actual service, and advertised speeds are seldom attainable for any length of time.

- **Speed—Download**: 3 Mbps to 50 Mbps, **Upload**: 1 Mbps to 10 Mbps
- **Availability**: Urban and most suburban areas
- **Reliability**: Very good
- **Monthly Cost**: From under $40 to over $140
- **One-Time Cost**: Normally have installation fees and equipment charges

CELL PHONE WIRELESS

Most cell phone companies offer a mobile broadband Internet service, which can be used both on "smart phones" and with normal computers with a small plug-in device. Like all cell phone service, it is subject to blind areas where the service cannot be received. Also, just because a company has cell phone service in an area, this does not mean their Internet service extends to that area. This service is developing quickly, and you need to check the latest specifications of those services that are available in your area from carriers such as Verizon, AT&T, Sprint, T-Mobile, and Clearwire.

- **Speed (3G network)—Download**: 600 Kbps to 1.4 Mbps, **Upload**: 500 Kbps to 800 Kbps
- **Speed (4G network)—Download**: 5 Mbps to 12 Mbps, **Upload**: 2 Mbps to 5 Mbps
- **Availability**: Urban and some suburban areas
- **Reliability**: Good

Continued . . .

6. If you don't see a modem but you know you have one installed, close the Phone And Modem dialog box, and return to the Large Icons view of Control Panel. Click **Device Manager**. You'll see a list of all your hardware in alphabetical order. You should not see a Modems listing yet because Windows hasn't fully recognized the device at this point, but hopefully, under Other Devices, you'll see a modem with an exclamation point, as shown in the illustration.

7. If you do not see a modem, it is a good bet that one is not installed and you need to do that. If you do see a modem with an exclamation point, then a device driver needs to be installed. In both of those cases, you need to go outside Windows to locate a solution.

8. If you see the modem listed and have a CD for it, put the CD in the drive. It should automatically start and install the driver. If you need a new modem, talk to the manufacturer of your computer or the store where you bought it.

9. When you are told that your modem has been installed successfully (you should now see your modem listed under a Modems heading), click **Close** twice to close the Device Manager window and Control Panel.

SET UP A DIAL-UP CONNECTION

With a modem installed and working, you can set up a *dial-up connection* that uses the modem to dial and connect to another computer at the other end of a phone line.

1. If your Control Panel isn't open, click **Start** and then click **Control Panel**. In Category view click **Network And Internet**, and then in any view, click **Network And Sharing Center**.

2. Click **Set Up A New Connection Or Network**. The Set Up A Connection Or Network dialog box will appear.

3. Click **Set Up A Dial-Up Connection**, and click **Next**. The Create A Dial-Up Connection dialog box will appear.

4. Enter the phone number to dial, enter the user name and password given to you by your ISP, choose whether to show the password and whether to remember the password or require it to be entered each time you connect, and then enter a name for this connection (see Figure 4-1).

5. Choose whether anyone else can use this user name and password. When you are done, click **Connect**.

UNDERSTANDING INTERNET CONNECTIONS *(Continued)*

- **Monthly Cost**: From under $40 to over $80

- **One-Time Cost**: Normally have activation fees and a device charge

SATELLITE WIRELESS

Satellite Internet service is available in most areas, including those where other services are not available. Satellite service requires a satellite antenna that can "see" the southern horizon, so you need clear southern exposure. Trees, buildings, and hills or mountains close to you on your south side can block reception. Also, heavy weather can cause interruptions. Generally, satellite service is a last resort. One satellite provider is HughesNet, www.hughesnet.com.

- **Speed—Download**: 1 Mbps to 5 Mbps, **Upload**: 128 Kbps to 300 Kbps

- **Availability**: Almost anywhere

- **Reliability**: Fair

- **Monthly Cost**: From under $60 to over $350

- **One-Time Cost**: Purchase or lease of equipment required

TIP

Often, setup, installation, and equipment charges for an Internet connection are waived if you sign a one- or two-year contract and/or prepay for a year or two of service.

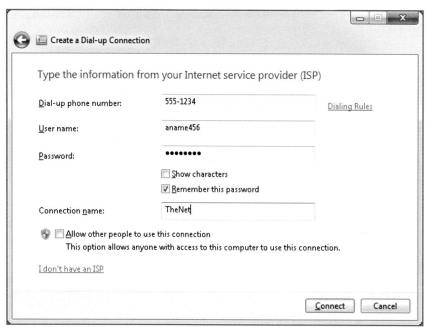

Figure 4-1: You will need a user name and a password, as well as other information from your ISP, in order to connect with them.

6. You will be told when you are connected to the Internet.

7. Click **Browse The Internet Now** to do that. You will be asked if this network is in a home, work, or public location. Click **Public Location**. This will be explained further in Chapter 9. Click **Close**.

8. Internet Explorer (Windows 7 SP1's integral web browser) will open for your use. See "Use the World Wide Web" later in this chapter. Given that you can see sites on the Internet, you have proved that your connection is working. When you are done, click the **Close** button on Internet Explorer.

9. To disconnect, right-click the connection icon in the notification area, click **Disconnect From**, and click the name of your connection. Click **Close** to close the Network And Sharing Center window.

As you perform the steps in this and other chapters, you may see a User Account Control (UAC) dialog box appear and ask if you want to allow a program to make changes to your computer. When you see these dialog boxes, and if you are an administrator and, in fact, want to continue, click **Yes**. If you are not logged on as an administrator, you will need to enter a password. If you don't want to do whatever is being requested, click **No**. The UAC dialog box and its associated steps are not included in the steps here to simplify the process. When you see the UAC dialog box, process it as you want and continue with the instructions. UAC is discussed in Chapter 8.

To connect to the Internet, you need to have an existing account with an ISP and you need to know your ISP's phone number for your modem to dial. You also must have the user name and password for your account. If you want to use Internet mail, you need to know your email address, the type of mail server (POP3, IMAP, or HTTP), the names of the incoming and outgoing mail servers (such as mail.anisp.net), and the name and password for the mail account. This information is provided by your ISP when you establish your account.

Sometimes, a DSL or TV cable connecting device is called a "modem," but it is not an analog-to-digital converter, which is the major point of a **mo**dulator-**dem**odulator. Therefore, that term is not used for those devices in this book. The correct term is "router," which is a bridge between the Internet and your local network/computer.

SET UP A BROADBAND CONNECTION

A broadband connection—made with a DSL phone line, a TV cable, a satellite connection, or a high-speed wireless connection—is normally made with a device that connects to your local area network (LAN) and allows several computers on the network to use the connection. (See Chapter 9 to set up a network.) With a network set up, your computer connected to the network, and a broadband service connected to the network, your computer is connected to the broadband service. There is nothing else you need to do to set up a broadband connection.

Configure an Internet Connection

In the process of establishing either a dial-up or broadband connection, you may have also configured an Internet connection. The easiest way to check that is to try to connect to the Internet by clicking the **Internet Explorer** icon pinned to the left of the taskbar. If an Internet webpage is displayed, like the MSN page shown in Figure 4-2, then you are connected and you need do no more. If you did not connect to the Internet and you know that your dial-up or broadband and network connections are all working properly, you need to configure your Internet connection.

1. If Internet Explorer did not connect to the Internet, click **Start** and click **Control Panel**.

2. In Category view, click **Network And Internet**, and then in any view click **Network And Sharing Center**.

3. In either case, click **Set Up A New Connection Or Network**. The Set Up A Connection Or Network dialog box will appear.

4. Click **Connect To The Internet**, and click **Next**. Click your choice between broadband and dial-up, and click **Next**.

5. Enter a dial-up phone number (if that is your service choice), your user name and password, choose whether to display the password and if it is to be remembered by the system, enter a name for the connection, and choose whether to allow others to use this user name and password. When you are done, click **Connect**.

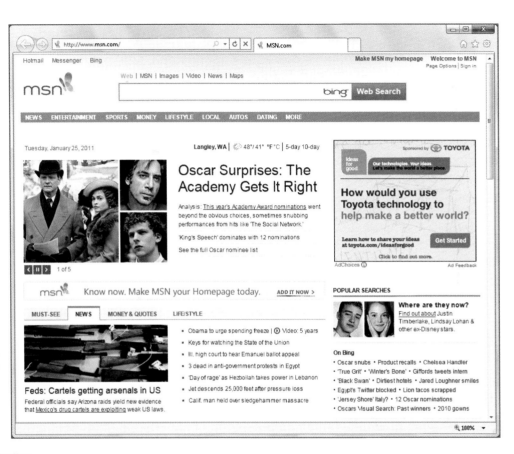

Figure 4-2: The easiest way to see if you have an Internet connection is to try to connect to the Internet.

NOTE

In Figure 4-2 I am using Internet Explorer (IE) 9, which is just becoming available as this book is written. Originally Windows 7 SP1 came with IE 8, but in early 2011 Windows 7 SP1 started including IE 9. If you have an earlier version of Windows 7 SP1 with IE 8, you can download IE 9 from Microsoft.com, which I recommend you do. It is both cleaner and faster, and leaves more room to display a webpage, although the latter is at the expense of some intuitive use. Instructions in this book generally assume you are using IE 9, but will also give the IE 8 steps where there is a difference.

6. Once more, click the **Internet Explorer** icon on the taskbar. If asked, click **Connect** and then click **Dial**. If you still cannot connect to the Internet, you may need to reinstall your modem, in which case you should go to "Install a Modem" earlier in this chapter. If you are using a broadband connection, you may need to go to Chapter 9 and look at potential network problems.

NOTE

If you purchased Windows 7 SP1 or a computer with Windows 7 SP1 in the UK or Europe, when you first start Internet Explorer, a Web Browser Ballot will appear allowing you to choose the web browser you want to use on a recurring basis. Click Install under the browser you want and follow the instructions that are shown. In terms of usage, Mozilla Firefox is in the lead with about 43-percent, Microsoft Internet Explorer and Google Chrome are approximately equal with about 25-percent each, and the balance is approximately split between Safari, which was built for the Apple Mac, and Opera. IE 9, Firefox 4.0 and Chrome are all good choices. I actually use all three. If you want to use more than one, choose one on the Ballot, and then go to the other web sites (microsoft.com/ie9, mozilla.com/firefox, and google.com/chrome) and download their respective products.

NOTE

For the sake of writing convenience and because Windows 7 SP1 comes with Internet Explorer, this book assumes you are using Internet Explorer to access the Internet. Other browsers, such as Mozilla Firefox (mozilla. com) and Google Chrome (google.com), also work fine.

NOTE

Older webpages are shown in Compatibility View as indicated with an additional icon of a broken page at the right end of the address bar.

Use the World Wide Web

The *World Wide Web* (or just the *Web*) is the sum of all the websites in the world—examples of which are CNN, Google, and MSN (which was shown in Figure 4-2). The World Wide Web is what you can access with a *web browser*, such as Internet Explorer, which comes with Windows 7 SP1.

Search the Internet

You can search the Internet in two ways: by using the Microsoft Live Search facility built into Internet Explorer and by using an independent search facility on the Web.

SEARCH FROM INTERNET EXPLORER

To use Internet Explorer's Live Search facility:

1. Click the **Internet Explorer** icon on the taskbar to open it.

2. In IE 8, click in the Search box on the right of the address bar, or in IE 9, click in the address bar. In either case, begin typing what you want to search for. (The first time you search in IE 9 click **Turn On Search Suggestions**.) Click one of the suggestions below the Search box, click **Search** (the magnifying glass in IE 8) on the right end of the Search box or click **Go To** (IE 9), or press ENTER. By default, the Bing search site will open with the results of the search, as you can see in Figure 4-3.

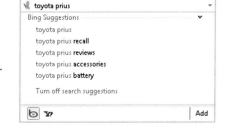

3. Click the link of your choice to go to that site.

SEARCH FROM AN INTERNET SITE

There are many independent Internet search sites. The most popular is Google.

1. In Internet Explorer, click the current address in the address bar, type google.com, and either click **Go To** (the blue arrow) or press ENTER.

QUICKSTEPS

BROWSING THE INTERNET

Browsing the Internet refers to using a browser, like Internet Explorer, to go from one website to another. You can browse to a site by directly entering a site address, navigating to a site from another site, or using the browser controls. First, of course, you have to start the browser.

START A BROWSER

To start your default browser (assumed to be Internet Explorer), click the **Internet Explorer** icon on the left of the taskbar.

ENTER A SITE DIRECTLY

To go directly to a site:

1. Start your browser and click the existing address, or Uniform Resource Locator (URL), in the address bar to select it.

2. Type the address of the site you want to open, as shown, and either click **Go To** (the right-pointing arrow) next to the address bar or press **ENTER**.

USE SITE NAVIGATION

Site navigation uses a combination of links and menus on one webpage to locate and open another webpage, either in the same site or in another site:

- **Links** are words, phrases, sentences, or graphics that always have an open hand displayed when the mouse pointer is moved over them and, when clicked, take you to another location. They are often underlined—if not initially, then when you move the mouse pointer to them.

Continued . . .

Figure 4-3: The results of a search using Internet Explorer's Search box.

2. In the text box, type what you want to search for, and click **Google Search**. The resulting websites are shown in a full webpage, as illustrated in Figure 4-4.

3. Click the link of your choice to go to that site.

QUICKSTEPS

BROWSING THE INTERNET *(Continued)*

- **Menus** contain one or a few words in a horizontal list, vertical list, or both that always have an open hand displayed when the mouse pointer is moved over them and, when clicked, take you to another location.

USE BROWSER NAVIGATION

Browser navigation uses the controls within your browser to go to another location. Internet Explorer has two controls not discussed elsewhere that are used for navigation:

- **Back** and **Forward** buttons take you to the next or previous page in the stack of pages you have viewed most recently. Moving your mouse over these buttons will display a tooltip showing you the name of the page the button will take you to. Also, right-click a *highlighted* **Back** or **Forward** button to open a drop-down menu of recent pages you have visited going in the direction of the button.

- The **Pages recently entered** button displays a drop-down list of webpages that you have recently entered into the address bar, as well as (in IE 9) a list of sites you recently visited.

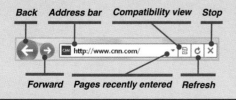

Figure 4-4: The results of a search using Google.

Save a Favorite Site

Sometimes, you visit a site that you would like to return to quickly or often. Internet Explorer has a memory bank called Favorites to which you can save sites for easy retrieval.

ADD A FAVORITE SITE

To add a site to Favorites:

1. In Internet Explorer, open the webpage you want to add to your Favorites list, and make sure its correct address (URL) is in the address bar.

2. In IE 8 click **Favorites** in or above the tab row. In IE 9 click the **Favorites** icon on the right of the tab row.

3. In either case click **Add To Favorites**. The Add A Favorite dialog box appears. Adjust the name as needed in the text box (you may want to type a name you will readily associate with that site), and click **Add**.

OPEN A FAVORITE SITE

To open a favorite site you have saved:

In Internet Explorer 8, click Favorites above the tab row. In IE 9 click the Favorites icon on the right of the tab row. In either case, ensure the Favorites tab is selected, and click the site you want to open.

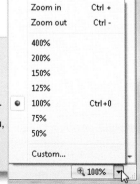

UICKSTEPS

CHANGING YOUR HOME PAGE

When you first start Internet Explorer, a webpage is automatically displayed. This page is called your *home page*. When you go to other webpages, you can return to this page by clicking the **Home** icon on the tab row. When IE starts, you can have it open several pages in addition to the home page, with the additional pages displayed as tabs (see "Use Tabs" in this chapter), which will also be opened when you click the Home Page icon. To change your home page and the other pages initially opened:

1. In Internet Explorer, directly enter or browse to the site you want as your home page. If you want additional pages, open them in separate tabs.

2. In IE 9 right-click the **Home Page** icon, and click **Command Bar**. In either IE 8 or in the IE 9 command bar, click the **Home Page** down arrow, and click **Add Or Change Home Page**. The Add Or Change Home Page dialog box will appear.

3. Click:

   • **Use This Webpage As Your Only Home Page** if you wish to have only a single home page.

   • **Add This Webpage To Your Home Page Tabs** if you wish to have several home pages on different tabs.

Continued . . .

Use Tabs

Internet Explorer 8 and 9 allow you to have several webpages open at one time and easily switch between them by clicking the tab associated with the page. The tabs reside on the *tab row*, immediately above the displayed webpage, which also has the address bar in IE 9, as shown in Figure 4-5.

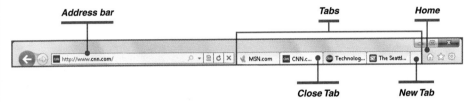

Figure 4-5: Tabs allow you to quickly switch among several websites.

OPEN PAGES IN A NEW TAB

To open a page in a new tab instead of opening the page in an existing tab:

1. Open Internet Explorer with at least one webpage displayed.

2. Click **New Tab** on the right end of the tab row, or press **CTRL+T** and open another webpage in any of the ways described earlier in this chapter.

   –Or–

   Type a web address in the address bar, and press **ALT+ENTER**. (If you just press **ENTER**, you'll open a page in the same tab.)

   –Or–

   Type a search request in the Search box or address bar (in IE 9), and press **ALT+ENTER**. (If you just press **ENTER,** you'll open a page in the same tab.)

   –Or–

   Hold down **CTRL** while clicking a link in an open page. (If you just click the link, you'll open a page in the same tab.) Then click the new tab to open the page.

   –Or–

   In IE 8, click the blue arrow on the right of a site in your Favorites list, or in IE 9, right-click the Favorites site you want to open, and click **Open In New Tab**.

3. Repeat any of the alternatives in step 2 as needed to open additional pages.

QUICKSTEPS

CHANGING YOUR HOME PAGE

(Continued)

- **Use The Current Tab Set As Your Home Page** if you want all the current tabs to appear when you start Internet Explorer or click the Home Page icon (this option is only available if you have two or more tabs open).

4. Click **Yes** to complete your home page selection and close the dialog box.

NOTE

You can also change the home page by clicking the **Tools** menu in IE 8 or the **Tools** icon in IE 9, clicking **Internet Options** in either case, and making the desired changes at the top of the General tab.

TIP

You can open the home page in its own tab instead of replacing the current tab by holding down **CTRL** while clicking the **Home Page** icon.

TIP

Press just the **ALT** key to view Internet Explorer's menus.

SWITCH AMONG TABS

To switch among open tabs:

Click the tab of the page you want to open.

–Or–

Press **CTRL+TAB** to switch to the next tab to the right, or press **CTRL+ SHIFT+TAB** to switch to the next tab to the left.

–Or–

Press **CTRL+*n***, where *n* is a number from one to eight to switch to one of the first eight tabs numbered from the left in the order they were opened. You can also press **CTRL+9** to switch to the last tab that was opened, shown on the right of the tab row. Be sure to use a number key on the top of the main keyboard, *not* on the numeric keypad on the right.

CLOSE TABS

To close one or more tabs:

Right-click the tab for the page you want to close, and click **Close Tab** on the context menu; or click **Close Other Tabs** to close all of the pages except the one you clicked.

–Or–

Press **CTRL+W** to close the current page.

–Or–

Click the tab of the page you want to close, and click the **X** on the right of the tab.

–Or–

Press **ALT+F4** and click **Close All Tabs** to do that; or click **Close Current Tab**; or click **CTRL+ALT+F4** to close all tabs except the currently selected one.

Access Web History

Internet Explorer keeps a history of the websites you visit, and you can use that history to return to a site. You can set the length of time to keep sites in that history, and you can clear your history.

USE WEB HISTORY

To use the Web History feature:

1. In Internet Explorer, click **Favorites** or its icon, and click the **History** tab; or press **CTRL+H** to open the History pane.

UICKSTEPS

ORGANIZING FAVORITE SITES

After a while, you will probably find that you have a number of favorite sites and it is becoming hard to find the one you want. Internet Explorer provides two places to store your favorite sites: a Favorites list, which is presented to you in the form of a menu you can open, and a Favorites bar, which is displayed at all times. There are several ways to organize your favorite sites.

REARRANGE THE FAVORITES LIST

The items on your Favorites list are displayed in the order you added them, unless you drag them to a new location.

In Internet Explorer, click **Favorites** or the icon, locate the site you want to reposition, and drag it to the location in the list where you want it.

CREATE NEW FOLDERS

Internet Explorer (both 8 and 9) comes with several default folders added by Microsoft or by the computer's manufacturer. You can also add your own folders within the Favorites list.

1. In Internet Explorer, click **Favorites** or the icon, click the **Add To Favorites** down arrow, and click **Organize Favorites** to open the Organize Favorites dialog box, shown in Figure 4-6.

2. Click **New Folder**, type the name for the folder, and press **ENTER**.

3. Drag the desired site links to the new folder, drag the folder to where you want it on the list, and then click **Close**.

PUT FAVORITES IN FOLDERS

You can put a site in either your own folders (see "Create New Folders") or the default ones when you initially add it to your Favorites list.

1. Open the webpage you want in your Favorites list, and make sure its correct address or URL is in the address bar.   *Continued . . .*

Figure 4-6: As with files, organizing your favorite websites helps you easily find what you want.

2. Click the down arrow on the History tab bar to select how you want the history sorted. Depending on what you select, you will be able to further specify the type of history you want to view. For example, if you click View By Date, you can then click the day, website, and webpage you want to open, as shown in Figure 4-7.

DELETE AND SET HISTORY

You can set the length of time to keep your Internet history, and you can clear this history.

1. In Internet Explorer, click **Tools** or its icon at the right end of the tab row, and click **Internet Options**.

2. In the General tab, under Browsing History, click **Delete** to open the Delete Browsing History dialog box. If needed, select the **History** check box to delete your browsing history.

ORGANIZING FAVORITE SITES

(Continued)

2. Click **Favorites**, click **Add To Favorites**, adjust the name as needed in the text box, click the **Create In** down arrow, select the folder to use, and click **Add**.

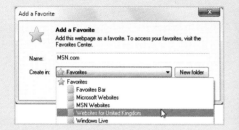

ADD A SITE TO THE FAVORITES BAR

In IE 8, by default, a Favorites bar is displayed on the same row with and to the right of the Favorites menu. In IE 9 you can turn on the Favorites bar by right-clicking any of the three icons (Home, Favorites, and Tools) on the right of the tab row and clicking **Favorites Bar**. By default, the Favorites bar has two sites on it, but you can add others.

Open the site you want to add to the Favorites bar. In either IE 8 or IE 9, if the Favorites bar is open, click the **Add To Favorites Bar** button on the left of the Favorites bar

–Or–

In either IE 8 or 9 click **Favorites**, click the **Add To Favorites** down arrow, and click **Add To Favorites Bar**.

TIP

To delete a favorite site from either the Favorites list or the Favorites bar, right-click it and click **Delete**.

Select any other check box to delete that information, although you should keep the Preserve Favorites Website Data check box selected to *keep* that information (it is a confusing dialog box). Click **Delete**.

–Or–

In the General tab of the Internet Options dialog box, under Browsing History, click **Settings**. Under History, at the bottom of the dialog box, use the **Days** spinner to set the number of days to keep your web history. Click OK.

3. Click **OK** again to close the Internet Options dialog box.

Copy Internet Information

You may occasionally find something on the Internet that you want to copy—a picture, some text, or a webpage.

COPY A PICTURE FROM THE INTERNET

To copy a picture from an Internet webpage to a folder on your hard disk:

1. Open Internet Explorer and locate the webpage containing the picture you want.

2. Right-click the picture and click **Save Picture As**. Locate the folder in which you want to save the picture, enter the filename you want to use and the file type if it is something other than the default .jpg, and click **Save**.

3. Close Internet Explorer if you are done.

Figure 4-7: The Web History feature allows you to find a site that you visited in the recent past.

NOTE

Protected Mode—which you can turn on or off at the bottom of the Security tab (the notice for which you'll see at the bottom of Internet Explorer)—is what produces the messages that tells you a program is trying to run in Internet Explorer or that software is trying to install itself on your computer. In most cases, you can click a bar at the top of the Internet Explorer window if you want to run the program or install the software. You can also double-click the notice at the bottom of Internet Explorer to open the Security tab and turn off Protected Mode (clear the **Enable Protected Mode** check box).

QUICKSTEPS

CONTROLLING INTERNET SECURITY

Internet Explorer allows you to control three aspects of Internet security. You can categorize sites by the degree to which you trust them, determine how you want to handle cookies placed on your computer by websites, and set and use ratings to control the content of websites that can be viewed. These controls are found in the Internet Options dialog box.

In Internet Explorer, click **Tools** or its icon on the right of the tab row, and click **Internet Options**.

CATEGORIZE WEBSITES

Internet Explorer allows you to categorize websites into zones: Internet (sites that are not classified in one of the other ways), Local Intranet, Trusted Sites, and Restricted Sites (as shown in Figure 4-8).

From the Internet Options dialog box:

1. Click the **Security** tab. Click the **Internet** zone. Note its definition.

Continued . . .

COPY TEXT FROM THE INTERNET TO WORD OR EMAIL

To copy text from a webpage to a Microsoft Word document or email message:

1. Open Internet Explorer and locate the webpage containing the text you want.

2. Drag across to highlight the text, right-click the selection, and click **Copy**.

3. Open a Microsoft Word document or an email message in which you want to paste the text. Right-click where you want the text, and click **Paste**.

4. Save the Word document and close Internet Explorer, Microsoft Word, or your email program if you are done with them.

COPY A WEBPAGE FROM THE INTERNET

To make a copy of a webpage and store it on your hard disk:

1. Open Internet Explorer and locate the webpage you want to copy.

2. In IE 8, click **Page** on the tab row, and click **Save As**. In IE 9 click the **Tools** icon, click **File**, and click **Save As**.

3. In the Save Webpage dialog box, select the folder in which to save the page, enter the filename you want to use, and click **Save**.

4. Close Internet Explorer if you are done.

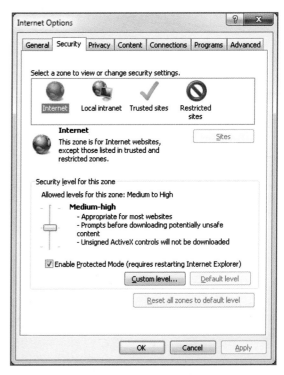

Figure 4-8: Internet Explorer allows you to categorize websites into zones and determine what can be done within those zones.

QUICKSTEPS

CONTROLLING INTERNET SECURITY

(Continued)

2. Click **Custom Level**. Select the elements in this zone that you want to disable, enable, or prompt you before using. Alternatively, select a level of security you want for this zone, and click **Reset**. Click **OK** when you are finished.

3. Click each of the other zones, where you can identify either groups or individual sites you want in that zone.

HANDLE COOKIES

Cookies are small pieces of data that websites store on your computer so that they can remind themselves of who you are. These can save you from having to constantly enter your name and ID. Cookies can also be dangerous, however, letting people into your computer where they can potentially do damage.

Internet Explorer lets you determine the types and sources of cookies you will allow and what those cookies can do on your computer (see Figure 4-9).

From the Internet Options dialog box:

1. Click the **Privacy** tab. Select a privacy setting by dragging the slider up or down.

2. Click **Advanced** to open the Advanced Privacy Settings dialog box. If you wish, click **Override Automatic Cookie Handling**, and select the settings you want to use.

3. Click **OK** to return to the Internet Options dialog box.

Continued . . .

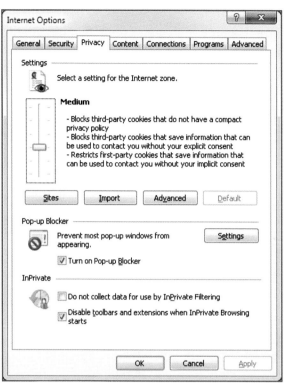

Figure 4-9: Determine how you will handle cookies that websites want to leave on your computer.

Play Internet Audio and Video Files

You can play audio and video files on the Internet with Internet Explorer directly from a link on a webpage. Many webpages have links to audio and video files, such as the one shown in Figure 4-10. To play these files, simply click the links. If you have several audio players installed (for example, Windows Media Player and Real Player), you will be asked which one you want to use. Make that choice, and the player will open to play the requested piece. Chapter 7 discusses working with audio and video files in depth, including how to play these files using Windows Media Player.

CONTROLLING INTERNET SECURITY

(Continued)

4. In the middle of the Privacy tab, you can turn off the pop-up blocker, which is on by default (it is recommended that you leave it on). If you have a site that you frequently use that needs pop-ups, click **Settings**, enter the site address (URL), click **Add**, and click **Close**.

5. At the bottom of the Privacy tab, you can determine how to handle InPrivate Filtering and Browsing. See the Note on InPrivate earlier in this chapter.

CONTROL CONTENT

You can control the content that Internet Explorer displays.

From the Internet Options dialog box:

1. Click the **Content** tab. Click **Parental Controls**. Click the user you want to control to open the User Controls window, shown in Figure 4-11 (there have to be nonadministrative users on the computer in order to set parental controls). Click **On** to turn on parental controls, and configure any other settings you want to use. Click **OK** when you are done, and then close the Parental Controls window.

2. Click **Enable** to open the Content Advisor dialog box. Individually select each of the categories, and drag the slider to the level you want to allow. Detailed descriptions of each area are shown in the lower half of the dialog box.

3. Click **OK** to close the Content Advisor dialog box.

   When you are done, click **OK** to close the Internet Options dialog box. (Other parts of this dialog box are discussed elsewhere in this book.)

Figure 4-10: Play an audio or video file on a webpage by clicking the link.

Use Internet Email

Windows 7 SP1 does not include a mail program, but you can download Windows Live Mail as part of Windows Live Essentials from Microsoft for free. Windows Live Mail allows you to send and receive email and to participate in newsgroups. You can also send and receive email through a web mail account using Internet Explorer. This section will primarily describe using Windows Live Mail. See the "Using Web Mail" QuickSteps for a discussion of that subject.

Get Windows Mail

For email with Windows 7 SP1, this book describes the use of Windows Live Mail because it works well, is freely available from Microsoft, and is designed for Windows 7 SP1. There are a number of other alternatives that you can buy

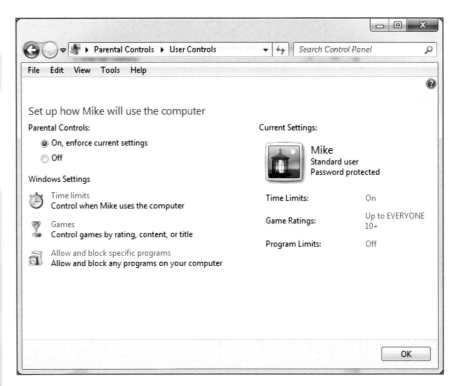

Figure 4-11: You can place a number of controls on what a particular user can do on a computer using the Parental Controls feature.

or get for free, including Outlook from Microsoft, Eudora, Mozilla Thunderbird, and Opera. Conduct an Internet search on "Windows Mail Clients."

To get Windows Live Mail, you must download Windows Live Essentials from Microsoft. To do that:

1. If you have a new computer or new installation of Windows 7, click **Start**, click **Getting Started**, and click **Go Online To Get Windows Live Essentials**.
   If you are using Windows 7 (assumed in this book) and don't see Getting Started, click **Start**, click **All Programs**, click **Accessories**, click **Getting Started**, and double-click **Go Online To Get Windows Live Essentials**, as shown in Figure 4-12.

Figure 4-12: By downloading Windows Live Essentials, Microsoft assures that you have the very latest software and allows other manufacturers the opportunity for you to use their software.

2. Click **Download Now** and in the File Download–Security Warning box at the bottom of IE 9, click **Run**. If a User Account Control dialog box opens, click **Yes** to allow the installation. The Windows Live site will open.

3. Click **Choose The Programs You Want To Install**, choose what you would like (I recommend all, but think it is a good idea to look at what you are installing; see Figure 4-13), and click **Install**. If you are asked to close Internet Explorer and possibly other programs, click **Continue** and the programs will be closed for you.

4. The downloading and installation of Windows Live Essentials will begin and take from 1 to 10 minutes with a broadband Internet connection. When this is completed, you may be asked to restart your computer. If so, make sure all other programs are closed, and click **Restart Now**.

5. When your computer restarts, you are asked to select various settings that tend to lock you into Microsoft's Bing search engine and Microsoft's MSN website. This may be subtle, like telling you that several add-ons are ready to use. Click **Enable** if you want the add-ons or click **Don't Enable** otherwise (my recommendation).

6. If you do not have a Windows Live, Hotmail, Messenger, or Xbox Live account, you will need to create one. Click **Sign Up** and follow the instructions on the screen to establish an account. If you already have one of those accounts, sign in as indicated.

7. If a Windows Live Messenger window has opened, click **Close**. It will be opened and discussed at the end of this chapter.

Establish an Email Account

To send and receive email with Windows Live Mail, you must have an Internet connection, an email account established with an ISP, and that account must be set up in Windows Live Mail.

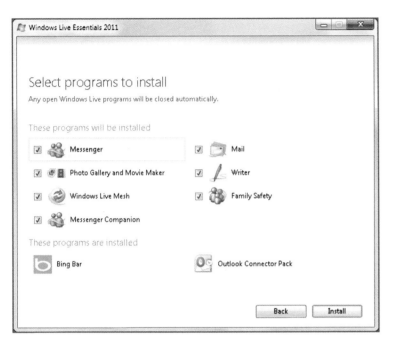

Figure 4-13: Windows Live Essentials includes email, instant messaging, blogging, movie making, and more.

Figure 4-14: You need to get your email address and password from your ISP before you set up an email account.

For an email account, you need:

- Your email address, for example: mike@anisp.com
- The type of mail server the ISP uses (POP3, IMAP, or HTTP—POP3 is the most common)
- The names of the incoming and outgoing mail servers, for example: mail.anisp.com
- The name and password for your mail account

With this information, you can set up an account in Windows Live Mail.

1. Click **Start**, click **All Programs**, and click **Windows Live Mail** if you see it on the Start menu; if not, click the **Windows Live** folder, and then click **Windows Live Mail**.

2. If Windows Live Mail has not been previously set up, the Add Your Email Accounts dialog box will appear (see Figure 4-14); if it doesn't, click the **Accounts** tab, and click **Email** on the left to open it.

3. Enter your email address, press **TAB**, enter your email password, press **TAB**, enter the name you want people to see when they get your email, click the **Manually Configure Server Settings** check box, and click **Next**.

4. Select the type of mail server used by your ISP (commonly POP), enter the name of your ISP's incoming mail server (such as mail. anisp.com), and indicate whether this server requires a secure connection (most don't, but your ISP will tell you if it does and how to handle it). Unless your ISP tells you otherwise, leave the default port number and logon authentication.

5. Enter your logon ID or user name, the name of your ISP's outgoing server (often the same as the incoming server), leave the default port number, and select the relevant check box if your ISP tells you the server requires a secure connection or authentication.

6. When you have completed these steps, click **Next** (if you have other email accounts you want to add, click **Add Another Email Account** and repeat the necessary steps), and then click Finish. Before Windows Live Mail can read messages from certain accounts, it might need to download the existing folders in those accounts. Click **Download** to do that. Windows Live Mail will open. Figure 4-15 shows it after receiving several email messages.

Use the next two sections, "Create and Send Email" and "Receive Email," to test your setup.

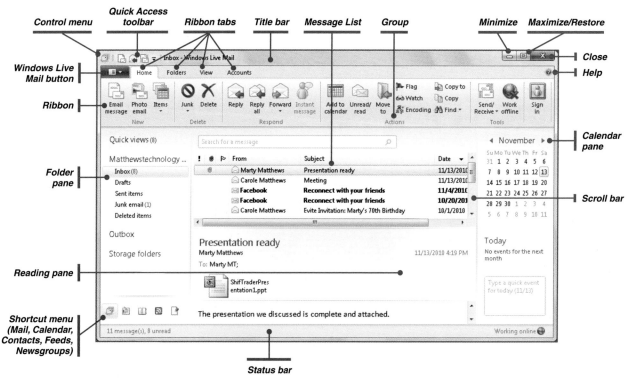

Figure 4-15: Windows Live Mail provides access to email, a calendar, contacts, feeds, and newsgroups.

UNDERSTANDING THE RIBBON

The *ribbon* is the container at the top of both the Windows Live Mail and New Message windows for the tools and features you are most likely to use to accomplish the task at hand (see Figure 4-16). The ribbon collects tools in *groups*—for example, the New group provides the tools to start an email message or add a new event to the calendar. Groups are organized into tabs, which bring together the tools to work on broader tasks. For example, the Folders tab contains groups that allow you to add and work with folders.

The ribbon provides space so each of the tools (or commands) in the groups has a labeled button you can click. Depending on the tool, you are then presented with additional options in the form of a list of commands, a dialog box or task pane, or galleries of visibly accurate choices that reflect what you'll see in your work.

Other features that are colocated with the ribbon include the Windows Live Mail button on the left of the tab row and the Quick Access toolbar on the left of the title bar. The Windows Live Mail button lets you work *with* your mail, as opposed to the ribbon, which centers on working *in* your mail. The Quick Access toolbar provides an always available location for your favorite tools. It starts out with a default set of tools, but you can add to it.

TIP

To quickly start Windows Live Mail with a single click, if it isn't already running, start it as described in "Establish an Email Account," right-click the **Windows Live Mail** icon on the taskbar, and click **Pin This Program To Taskbar**. The icon now will always be available on the taskbar to open the program.

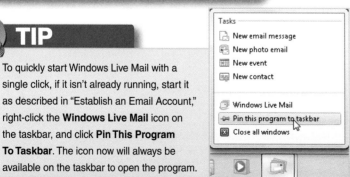

Create and Send Email

To create and send an email message:

1. Open Windows Live Mail as described earlier, and in the Home tab New group, click **Email Message**. The New Message window will open, similar to the one in Figure 4-16.

2. Start to enter a name in the To text box. If the name is in your Contacts list (see the "Using the Contacts List" QuickSteps in this chapter), it will be completed automatically and you can press **ENTER** to accept that name. If the name is not automatically completed, finish typing a full email address (such as billg@ microsoft.com).

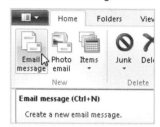

3. If you want more than one addressee, place a semicolon (;) and a space after the first address, and then type a second one as in step 2.

4. If you want to differentiate the addressees to whom the message is principally being sent from those for whom it is just information, click **Show Cc & Bcc**, press **TAB**, and put the second or subsequent addressees in the Cc text box as you did in the To text box.

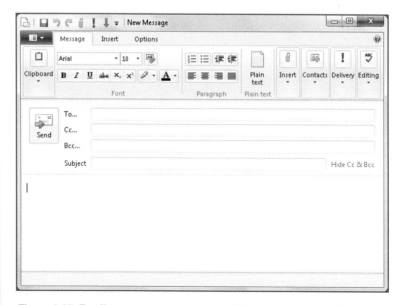

Figure 4-16: Email messages are an easy and fast way to communicate.

5. If you want to send the message to a recipient and not have other recipients see to whom it is sent, click **Show Cc & Bcc**, click in the **Bcc** text box, and type the address to be hidden. (Bcc stands for "blind carbon copy.")

6. Press TAB, type a subject for the message, press TAB again, and type your message.

7. When you have completed your message, click **Send** to the left of the addresses. For a brief moment, you may see a message in your outbox and then, if you look, you will see the message in your Sent Items folder. If you are done, close Windows Live Mail.

Receive Email

Depending on how Windows Live Mail is set up, it may automatically receive any email you have when you are connected to your ISP, or you may have to direct it to download your mail. To open and read your mail:

1. Open **Windows Live Mail**, and click **Inbox** in the Folders list on the left to open your inbox, which contains all of the messages you have received and haven't deleted or organized in folders.

2. If new messages weren't automatically received, in the Home tab Tools group, click the top of the **Send/Receive** area. You should see messages being downloaded.

3. Click a message in the inbox Message List to read it in the reading pane on the bottom or right of the window, as shown in Figure 4-15 (which shows the message on the bottom), or double-click a message to open the message in its own window, as shown in Figure 4-17.

4. Delete a message in either the inbox or its own window by clicking the relevant button on the toolbar. Close Windows Live Mail if you are finished with it.

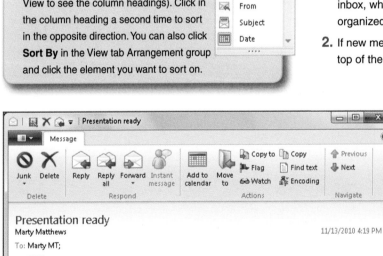

Figure 4-17: Work with a message you have received in the Message List (see Figure 4-15) or in its own window (shown here).

UICKSTEPS

USING THE CONTACTS LIST

The Contacts list, shown in Figure 4-18, allows you to collect email addresses and other information about the people with whom you correspond or otherwise interact.

OPEN THE CONTACTS LIST

Click **Contacts** ▢ in the lower-left area of Windows Live Mail.

ADD A NEW CONTACT

To add a new contact to the Contacts list:

1. With the Contacts Windows Live Mail window open, click **Contact** in the Home tab New group. The Add A Contact dialog box opens.

2. Enter as much of the information as you have or want. For email, you need at least a name and an email address, as shown in the Quick Add category. If you have additional information, such as a nickname, several email addresses, several phone numbers, or a home address for the contact, click the other categories on the left and fill in the desired information.

3. When you are done, click **Add Contact** to close the Add A Contact dialog box.

Continued . . .

Respond to Email

You can respond to messages you receive in three ways. First, click the message in your Message List or open the message in its own window, and then in the Home tab of the inbox or the Message tab of the message, click:

- **Reply** to return a message to just the person who sent the original message.

 –Or–

- **Reply All** to return a message to all the people who were addressees (both To and Cc) in the original message.

 –Or–

- **Forward** (upper half) to relay a message to people not shown as addressees on the original message.

In all three cases, a window similar to the New Message window opens and allows you to add or change addressees and the subject and add a new message.

Figure 4-18: The Contacts list provides a place to store information about the people with whom you correspond.

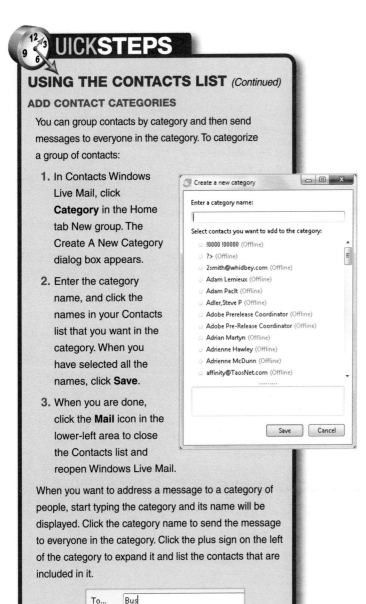

UICKSTEPS

USING THE CONTACTS LIST (Continued)

ADD CONTACT CATEGORIES

You can group contacts by category and then send messages to everyone in the category. To categorize a group of contacts:

1. In Contacts Windows Live Mail, click **Category** in the Home tab New group. The Create A New Category dialog box appears.

2. Enter the category name, and click the names in your Contacts list that you want in the category. When you have selected all the names, click **Save**.

3. When you are done, click the **Mail** icon in the lower-left area to close the Contacts list and reopen Windows Live Mail.

When you want to address a message to a category of people, start typing the category and its name will be displayed. Click the category name to send the message to everyone in the category. Click the plus sign on the left of the category to expand it and list the contacts that are included in it.

Apply Formatting

The simplest messages are sent in plain text without any formatting. These messages take up the least bandwidth and are the easiest to receive. If you wish, you can send messages with formatting using Hypertext Markup Language (HTML), the language with which many websites are created. You can do this for an individual message and for all messages.

APPLY FORMATTING TO ALL MESSAGES

To turn HTML formatting on or off:

1. Click the **Windows Live Mail** button on the left of the tab bar (left of the Home tab), click **Options**, and then click **Mail**.

2. Click the **Send** tab. Under Mail Sending Format, click **HTML** if you want it and it is not selected, or click **Plain Text** if that is what you want (see Figure 4-19).

3. Click **OK** and, if desired, close Windows Live Mail.

SELECT A FONT AND A COLOR FOR ALL MESSAGES

To use a particular font and font color on all of your email messages (you must send your mail using HTML in place of plain text—see "Apply Formatting to All Messages"):

1. Click the **Windows Live Mail** button, click **Options**, and then click **Mail**.

2. Click the **Compose** tab. Under Compose Font, click **Font Settings** opposite Mail.

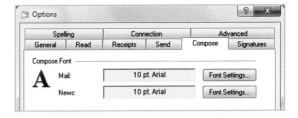

3. Select the font, style, size, effects, and color that you want to use with all your email; click **OK** twice; and then, if desired, close Windows Live Mail.

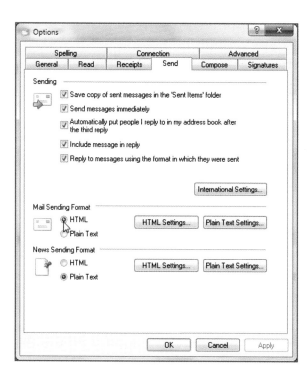

Figure 4-19: *If you send your mail using HTML instead of plain text, you can apply fonts and color and do many other things not available with plain text.*

ATTACH A SIGNATURE

To include a signature (a closing) on all of your email messages:

1. Click the **Windows Live Mail** button, click **Options**, and then click **Mail**.

2. Click the **Signatures** tab, and click **New**. Under Edit Signature, enter the closing text you want to use, or click **File** and enter or browse to the path and filename you want for the closing. The file could be a graphic image, such as a scan of your written signature, if you wished.

3. Click **Add Signatures To All Outgoing Messages**, as shown in Figure 4-20, and click **OK**. Then, if desired, close Windows Live Mail.

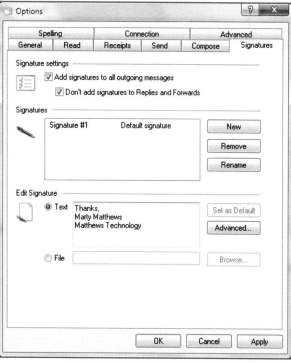

Figure 4-20: *A "signature" in Windows Live Mail is really a closing.*

TIP

If you see an email address in an email message that you want to add to your Contacts list, open the message in its own window, click the address, and click **Add Contact**. This creates a new contact and opens its Add A Contact dialog box so that you can make changes and add other information.

CAUTION

Not all email programs can properly receive HTML messages, which results in messages that are not very readable. However, most programs released in the last 10 years can handle HTML.

QUICKSTEPS

USING WEB MAIL

Web mail is the sending and receiving of email over the Internet using a browser, such as Internet Explorer, instead of an email program, such as Windows Live Mail. There are a number of web mail programs, such as Windows Live Hotmail (hotmail.com), Yahoo! Mail (mail.yahoo.com), and Google's Gmail (gmail.com). So long as you have access to the Internet, you can sign up for one or more of these services. The basic features (simple sending and receiving of email) are often free. For example, to sign up for Windows Live Hotmail:

1. Open Internet Explorer. In the address bar, type hotmail.com and press **ENTER**.

2. If you already have a Windows Live account, enter your ID and password, and click **Sign In**. Otherwise, under Windows Live Hotmail, click **Sign Up**, fill in the requested information, and click **I Accept**.

3. When you are done, the Windows Live Hotmail page will open and display your mail, as shown in Figure 4-21.

4. Click the envelope icon to open and read a message.

5. Click **New** on the toolbar to write an email message. Enter the address, a subject, and the message. When you are done, click **Send**.

6. When you are finished with Hotmail, close Internet Explorer.

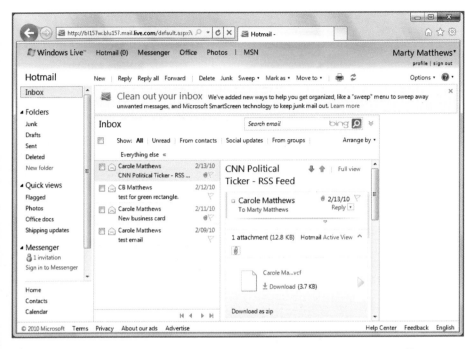

Figure 4-21: Web mail accounts are a quick and free way to get one or more email accounts.

Attach Files to Email

You can attach and send files, such as documents or images, with email messages.

1. Open Windows Live Mail, and click **Email Message** in the Home tab New group.

2. Click **Attach File** in the Message tab Insert group. Select the folder and file you want to send, and click **Open**. The attachment will be shown below the subject.

3. Address, enter, and send the message as you would normally, and then close Windows Live Mail.

TIP

A way to quickly open Windows Live Hotmail is to add it to your Favorites list or Favorites bar. With Hotmail open in Internet Explorer, click the **Favorites** icon ☆ in the upper-right corner of the Internet Explorer window, click the **Add To Favorites** icon, and then click **Add To Favorites** or click the **Add To Favorites** down arrow, and click the **Add To Favorites Bar**. Windows Live Hotmail will appear either in the Favorites list or on the Favorites bar. In either place, click it once to open Windows Live Hotmail.

TIP

With a New Message window open, you can drag a file from Windows Explorer or the desktop to the message, and it will be attached automatically and sent with the message.

Use Calendar

The Windows Live Mail Calendar, which you can use to keep track of scheduled events, is open by default in the right pane, as you have seen in several figures in this chapter, including Figure 4-15.

To close the Calendar or open it if it is closed:

Click the View tab, and click **Calendar Pane** in the Layout group. The calendar pane will either close or open if it was closed.

You can also expand the Calendar to fill the Windows Live Mail window.

Click the **Calendar** icon in the lower-left corner of the Windows Live Mail window. The Calendar opens, as you can see in Figure 4-22.

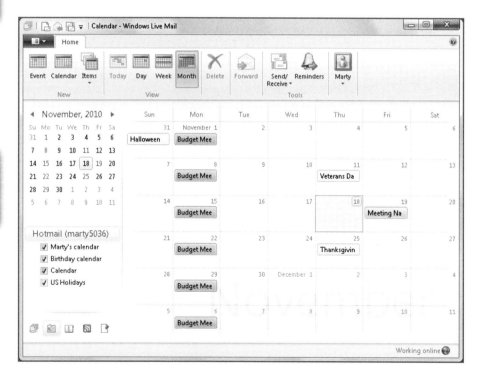

Figure 4-22: The Calendar provides a handy way of keeping track of scheduled events, especially those scheduled through email.

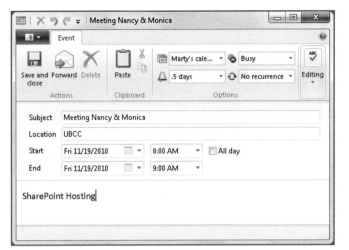

Figure 4-23: The Windows Live Mail Calendar allows you to send scheduled events to others to put on their calendars.

To return from the Calendar to Windows Live Mail:

Click the **Mail** icon in the lower-left corner of the Windows Live Mail window.

DIRECTLY ADD EVENTS TO A CALENDAR

To add an event to a calendar date:

1. With the calendar pane open, right-click a date on the Calendar, and click **Create New Event**. The New Event window will open.

2. Enter the subject, location, dates and times, and a message, as shown in Figure 4-23.

3. If you have multiple calendars, click the **Calendar** down arrow, and select the calendar you want to use. Also, select how you want the calendar to reflect your time during the event.

4. If the event will happen on a repeated basis, click the **Recurrence** down arrow, and click the period for this event.

5. When you have completed the event, click either **Save & Close** to store the event on your calendar or **Forward** to send this to others for their schedules.

6. If you selected Forward, an email message will open. Address it, make any desired changes to the message, and click **Send**.

ADD AN EMAIL MESSAGE TO A CALENDAR

When you receive an email message with scheduling ramifications, you can directly add its information to your calendar.

1. In Windows Live Mail, click the message that has calendar information, and click **Add To Calendar** in the Home tab Actions group.

   –Or–

   Right-click the message and click **Add To Calendar**.

   In both cases, an event window will open. Unfortunately, the subject and the body are the only fields that are filled in for you from the email (the current date is in the Start and End date, but you probably need to change that). You must fill in the location, dates, and times and indicate whether the event is recurring.

2. After filling in the pertinent information, click **Save & Close**. The event will appear on your calendar.

Participate in Newsgroups

Newsgroups are organized chains of messages on a particular subject.
Newsgroups allow people to enter new messages and respond to previous ones.
To participate in one or more newsgroups, you need to set up a newsgroup
account, then locate and open a particular newsgroup, and finally send and
receive messages within the newsgroup.

SET UP A NEWSGROUP ACCOUNT

Setting up a new account for a newsgroup is similar to setting up the account
for your email. To set up a newsgroup account, you need the name of the news
server and, possibly, an account name and password.

1. Open Windows Live Mail, and click the **Newsgroups** icon in the lower-left corner of
   the window. During your initial use of the Newsgroups window you will be asked if you
   want Windows Live Mail to be your default news client.
   If you don't have another newsgroup reader, click **Yes**.

2. To participate in newsgroups, click the **Accounts**
   tab, and click **Newsgroup**. Enter the name you want
   displayed showing from whom your messages are being sent, and click **Next**. Enter
   your email address if not already displayed, and click **Next**.

3. Enter the name of your news server. Your ISP or sponsoring organization will give you
   this. One you can try is news.microsoft.com. If you do not need to enter an account
   name and password, your ISP or sponsoring organization also will tell you this, and
   you can skip to step 6.

4. To enter an account name and password, click **My News Server Requires Me To Log
   On**, and click **Next**. Enter your account name and password, and click **Remember
   Password** (if desired).

5. Click **Next**, click **Finish**, and click **OK** to show available newsgroups. You will see a
   message telling you that you are not subscribed to any newsgroups and asking if you
   would like to see a list of newsgroups. If so, click **View Newsgroups**.

6. A list of newsgroups will appear, as shown in Figure 4-24. If you wish to just view a
   newsgroup, select that newsgroup and click **Go To**. If you wish to view a newsgroup
   over a period of time, click **Subscribe**.
   Newsgroups will be downloaded from your news server. This could take several
   minutes. A new account will appear in the Newsgroup Subscriptions window, and a list
   of newsgroups will be displayed.

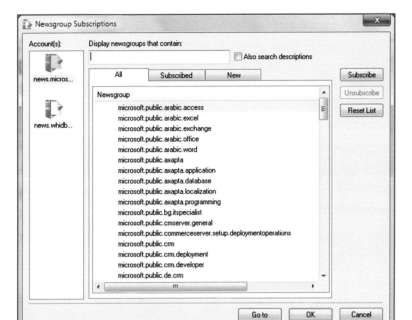

Figure 4-24: *Most ISPs provide a very large list of newsgroups to which you can subscribe.*

SUBSCRIBE TO A NEWSGROUP

Most general-purpose news servers, such as those maintained by ISPs, have a great many newsgroups, probably only some of which might interest you. To subscribe to a newsgroup (meaning to read and reply to messages they contain on a recurring basis):

1. If you have just come from setting up a newsgroup account, skip to step 2. Otherwise, open Windows Live Mail, and click the **Newsgroups** icon.

2. Click the news server you want to use in the left column, and click **View Newsgroups**.

3. To search for a particular newsgroup, type a keyword (such as computers) in the Display Newsgroups That Contain text box, and press **ENTER** (if newsgroups start popping up as you type your search keywords, you may not need to press **ENTER**).

4. Double-click the newsgroups to which you want to subscribe. An icon appears to the left of each newsgroup you double-click. After you have selected the newsgroups, click **OK**. You are returned to Windows Live Mail newsgroups.

READ AND POST MESSAGES IN A NEWSGROUP

For newsgroups to which you have subscribed, you can read and send messages like email messages, but with two differences. You can choose to reply to the newsgroup or to the individual, and a new message is called a *write message*. If someone replies to this message, it is added to the end of the original message, thereby creating a chain, or *thread*, of messages on a given subject.

1. Open Windows Live Mail, open your news server, and click a newsgroup you want to open. A list of messages will be displayed.

2. Click the triangular icon on the left of a message (this identifies that there are replies) to open the related messages.

3. Click a message to display it in the bottom pane, as shown in Figure 4-25 (you may need to click **Click Here** or press **SPACEBAR** to open the message). Or, double-click the message to have it displayed in its own window.

NOTE

To unsubscribe to a newsgroup, right-click the newsgroup name in the list of groups on the left of the newsgroup window, and click **Unsubscribe**. Click **OK** to confirm this action.

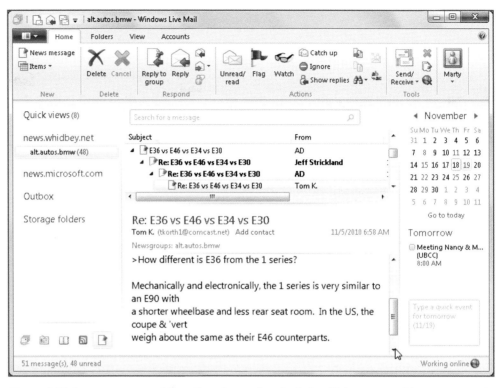

Figure 4-25: A newsgroup provides a thread on a given topic to which you can add your comments.

4. To initiate a newsgroup thread or respond to a newsgroup thread:

- Click **News Message** in the Home tab New group to create a public message that will begin a new thread.

- Click **Reply To Group** in the Home tab Respond group to create a public message in the thread you have selected.

- Click **Reply** in the Home tab Respond group to create a private message to the person who wrote the message you have selected.

- Click **Reply All** in the Home tab Respond group to create individual messages to all who have contributed to the message you have selected.

- Click **Forward** in the Home tab Respond group to send a copy of the message you have selected to one or more individuals.

5. Create and send the message as you would any email message. When you are done, click **Mail** to return to Windows Live Mail.

Use Windows Live Messenger

Windows Live Messenger allows you to send and receive instant messages (or *chat*) with others who are online at the same time as you. This is frequently called "instant messaging" or IM.

Set Up Windows Live Messenger

When you downloaded and installed Windows Live Essentials to get Windows Live Mail, you probably also installed Windows Live Messenger; it is selected by default. If so, its icon 🎔 may be on your taskbar, or at least it is in the Start menu. If you didn't install it and want to now, return to the "Get Windows Mail" section and follow the instructions there.

The use of Windows Live Messenger requires that you first have a Microsoft Live account or an MSN or Hotmail account, which you may have done earlier in this chapter in the "Using Web Mail" QuickSteps. Once you have an account, you are able to set up your contacts and personalize Messenger to your tastes.

ESTABLISH A WINDOWS LIVE ACCOUNT

With Windows Live Messenger installed, open it and establish a Windows Live account.

1. Click **Start**, click **All Programs**, and click **Windows Live Messenger**; or click the **Windows Live** folder, and click **Windows Live Messenger**. The Windows Live Messenger window will open, as you can see to the left.

2. If you already have a Windows Live account, enter your email address and password, and click **Sign In**. Go to the next section, "Add Contacts to Messenger."

3. If you don't have a Windows Live account, click **Sign Up**. Internet Explorer will open and the Windows Live registration will appear. Enter the information requested, click **I Accept**, and when you are told you have successfully registered your email address, close your browser. You will be returned to Windows Live Messenger.

4. Enter your email address and your password, and then click **Sign In**.

ADD CONTACTS TO MESSENGER

To use Windows Live Messenger, you must enter contacts for people you want to "talk" to.

1. If Windows Live Messenger is not already open, click its icon in the taskbar. If the icon isn't there, click **Start**, click **All Programs**, and click **Windows Live Messenger**.

2. The first time you start Windows Live Messenger you will see some introductory screens asking if you want to connect with Facebook and other social media sites. Following that you are asked if you would like either social highlights or MSN news in a side panel of Messenger. Click your choice. If you choose social networks, you are given a choice between Facebook, MySpace, and LinkedIn. Again, click your choice.

3. Click **Add** or its icon in the upper-right corner of the Windows Live Messenger window to open a context menu of choices for IM contacts. Click:

   - **Add A Favorite** to open your list of contacts so that you can select one or more that you want to contact with IM. Click in the **Search Contacts** text box, and type the person's name as best you can. People that fit what you have typed will appear (you can see if that person is online). Double-click the name you want.

   - **Create A Group**. Click **OK** to start a group so you can have group conversations. Type a name for the group, and click **Next**. Click **Select From Your Contact List**, click the contacts you want, and click **OK**. Click **Next** and then click **Done**. After the contacts accept your invitation, they will become members of the group.

   - **Create A Category**. Click **OK** to create a new category, such as "church" or "club," within which you can organize your contacts. Type a name for the category, click to select the contacts you want in the category, and click **Save**.

- **Add A Friend**. Type your friend's email address (this is optional) if you want to send text messages, select a country, type the friend's cell phone number, and click **Next**. If you want to make the person a favorite, click that option and click **Next**. An invitation will be sent to the friend. Depending on the person's status—whether they are online and whether they accept your invitation—you will get a response accordingly. Click **Add More Friends**, if desired, or click **Close**.

- **Search For Someone**. In the Windows Live search page, type the name you want to search for. As you type the name a drop-down list appears with options to search your contacts, your documents, or the Web; or select a few choices. Click your choice. Depending on your choice a Bing search window will open and display a list matching your search or a list of people in your contacts or documents will be displayed. Click the one you want to find.

Figure 4-26: Windows Live Messenger provides a quick way to chat; share photos; and exchange files with family, friends, and associates online.

- **Add People From Other Services**. Type a name or email address, and click **Next** to add people in that way; or click one of the services and follow the instructions to connect that service with Windows Live. If you see a box labeled "Set Up Your Privacy Settings," choose Public, Limited, or Private settings, and click **Save**.

4. When you are done adding contacts, close Internet Explorer. Back in Windows Live Messenger you should now have a list of contacts, as you can see in Figure 4-26. If you want to exit Windows Live Messenger, click **Close**.

CUSTOMIZE MESSENGER

There are several ways to customize Windows Live Messenger.

1. Open **Windows Live Messenger**. Change from full view, shown in Figure 4-26, to compact view, shown on the left, by clicking the **Switch To Compact View** icon in the upper-right corner of the window.

2. Assuming you have connected with social networking sites, click the **Edit Messenger Social Settings** icon. You are presented with a number of options for working with the various services you have selected, as shown in Figure 4-27.

UICKSTEPS

USING WINDOWS LIVE MESSENGER

Using Windows Live Messenger is simple: double-click a contact. If they are online, the Conversation window will open, as shown in Figure 4-28. If they are not online, you will be told the contact will be given the message the next time they are online (you will have fewer options available when sending an offline message).

SEND A MESSAGE

With the Conversation window open (done by double-clicking a contact), send a message by typing it in the bottom pane and pressing **ENTER**. You can add emoticons (smiley faces), change the font, and/or change the message background with the icons below the text box.

RECEIVE A MESSAGE

With a conversation in process, a received message appears in the Conversation window, as you can see in Figure 4-28. If someone sends you an instant message without a Conversation window open, you will see a little pop-up message in your notification area. Double-click this message to open a Conversation window with the sender.

3. When you have chosen the options you want, click **Save** and close Internet Explorer.

4. In Windows Live Messenger, click the down arrow to the right of your name. Here you can choose how you appear to IM users and a number of other options.

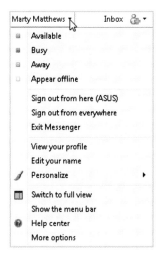

5. Click **More Options** to open the Options dialog box. Here you have a number of options you can use to customize Messenger.

6. Click each of the areas on the left, and review the options and selections on the right. Make the changes that are correct for you, and then click **OK**.

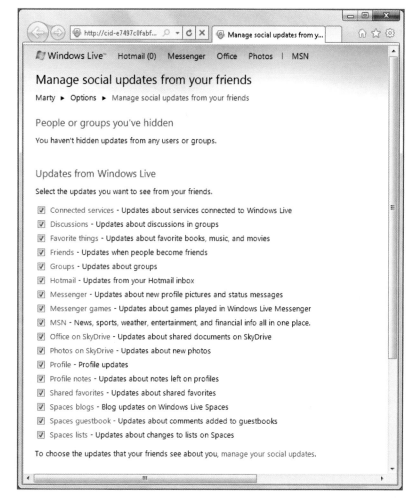

Figure 4-27: *Setting Windows Live Messenger options allows you to customize how your services work with mail.*

Windows Live Messenger does not normally create a permanent record of your conversation unless you specifically choose to do that. To do this, click the down arrow opposite your name, click **More Options**, click **History**, click **Automatically Save My Conversation History**, and click **OK**.

If you want to stop receiving comments permanently from another person (for example, if that person's remarks are getting offensive), click **Close**.

Figure 4-28: *When a conversation is in process, you can see who said what in the Conversation window.*

1 2 3 4 5 6 7 8 9 10

Chapter 5
Managing Windows 7 SP1

Running programs is one of Windows 7 SP1's major functions. The managing of Windows 7 SP1, the subject of this chapter, entails setting up the starting and stopping of programs in a number of different ways. Management also includes the maintenance and enhancement of Windows 7 SP1 and the setting up of Remote Assistance so that you can have someone help you without that person actually being in front of your computer.

Start and Stop Programs

Previous chapters discussed starting programs from the Start menu, through All Programs, through a shortcut on the desktop, and by locating the program with Windows Explorer. All of these methods require a direct action by you. Windows also provides several ways to automatically start programs and to monitor and manage them while they are running.

In many of the steps in this chapter, you will be interrupted and asked by User Account Control (UAC) for permission to continue. So long as it is something you started and want to do, you should click **Continue** or enter a password. To simplify the instructions in this chapter, the UAC instructions have been left out. Chapter 8 discusses UAC in more detail.

You must have administrative privileges and share the Startup folder, giving "Everyone" co-ownership in order to place a shortcut there. See Chapter 8 for a discussion of sharing folders and setting up privileges.

Some programs open automatically when Windows 7 SP1 is started without being in the Startup folder. You can see these programs and manage them using MSConfig, discussed later in this chapter.

Automatically Start Programs

Sometimes, you will want to start a program automatically and have it run in the background every time you start the computer. For example, you might automatically run an antivirus program or a screen-capture program (such as SnagIt, which was used to capture the figures and illustrations you see here). To automatically start a program, open a folder, or open a file in a program:

1. Click **Start**, click **All Programs**, right-click **Startup**, and click **Open All Users**. The Startup folder will open.

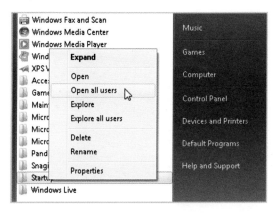

2. Click **Start** and click **Computer** to open Windows Explorer. Position the Explorer window so that you can see both it and the Startup window on the desktop at the same time (right-click the taskbar and click **Show Windows Side By Side** to arrange both windows).

3. In Explorer, open the drive and folders needed to display the program file you want to automatically start, or the folder or disk drive you want to automatically open, or the file you want to automatically start in its program.

4. Hold the right mouse button while dragging (right-drag) the program file, the folder, or the file to the open Startup folder, as you can see in Figure 5-1. When you reach the Startup folder, release the right mouse button, and click **Create Shortcuts Here**.

5. Close the Startup folder and Windows Explorer. The next time you start your computer, the action you want will take place.

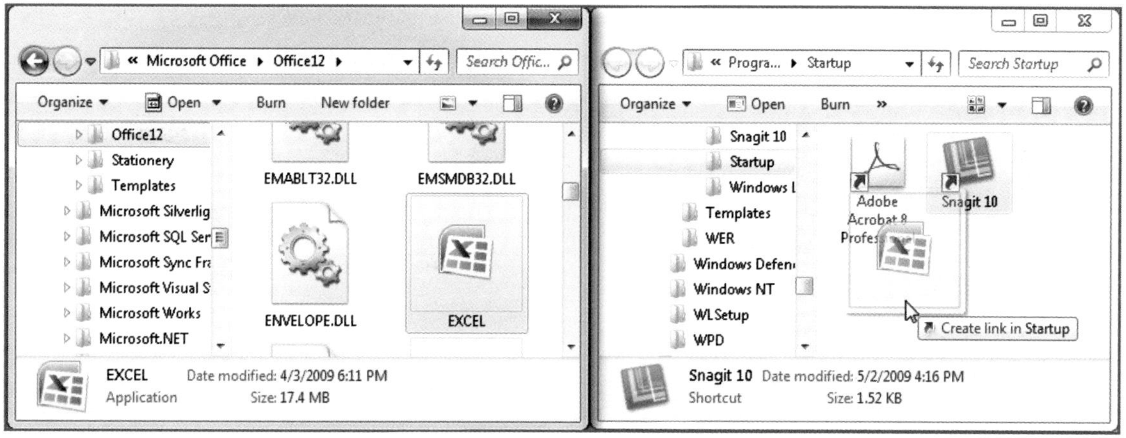

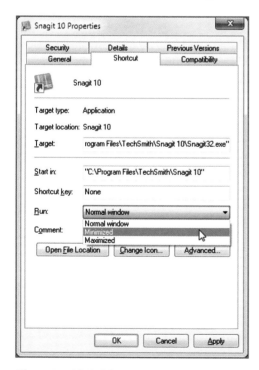

Figure 5-1: Programs in the Startup folder are opened automatically when you start Windows 7 SP1.

Start Programs Minimized

Sometimes, when you start programs automatically, you want them to run in the background—in other words, minimized. To do that:

1. Click **Start**, click **All Programs**, right-click **Startup**, and click **Open All Users** to open the Startup folder.

2. Right-click the program you want minimized, and click **Properties**. Click the **Shortcut** tab.

3. Click the **Run** down arrow, and click **Minimized**, as shown in Figure 5-2.

4. Click **OK** to close the Properties dialog box, and then close the Startup folder.

Schedule Programs

You can schedule a program to run automatically using Windows 7 SP1's Task Scheduler, although you may need to specify how the program is to run using command-line parameters or arguments. See how to use Help in step 2 of "Start

Figure 5-2: Minimizing a program, when it has automatically started, lets it run in the background.

![Task Scheduler window screenshot]

Task Scheduler

File   Action   View   Help

Task Scheduler (Local)
  Task Scheduler Library

Task Scheduler Summary (Last refreshed: 5/24/2009 2:53:

Overview of Task Scheduler

You can use Task Scheduler to create and manage common tasks that your computer will carry out automatically at the times you specify. To begin, click a command in the Action menu.

Task Status

Status of tasks t...   Last 24 hours

Summary: 0 total - 0 running, 0 succeeded, ...

Task Name   Run Res

Last refreshed at 5/24/2009 2:53:17 PM   Refresh

Actions

Task Scheduler (Local)
  Connect to Another Computer...
  Create Basic Task...
  Create Task...
  Import Task...
  Display All Running Tasks
  Enable All Tasks History
  AT Service Account Configuration
  View   ▶
  Refresh
  Help

Figure 5-3: The Task Scheduler is used by Windows 7 SP1 for many of its tasks, but you can also use it to repeatedly perform a task you want.

NOTE

Many programs, such as backup and antivirus programs, use their own scheduler to run automatically on a scheduled basis.

NOTE

The Create Task dialog box, basically identical to the Task Properties dialog box, can be used to set up a scheduled task instead of using the Task Scheduler Wizard. Click **Create Task** instead of Create Basic Task.

Older Programs" later in this chapter to learn what parameters are available for the program you want to run.

1. Click **Start**, click **All Programs**, click **Accessories**, click **System Tools**, and click **Task Scheduler**. The Task Scheduler window will open, as you can see in Figure 5-3.

2. Click **Create Basic Task** in the Actions pane or in the Action menu. The Create A Basic Task Wizard opens. Type a name and description, and click **Next**. Select what you want to use as a trigger, and again click **Next**.

3. Depending on what you choose for the trigger, you may have to select the start date and time and enter additional information, such as the day of the week for a weekly trigger. Click **Next**.

4. Choose whether you want to start a program, send an email, or display a message; and click **Next**.

5. If you want to start a program, either select it from the list of programs or browse to it, add any arguments that are to be passed to the program when it starts, and indicate if you would like the program to be looking at a particular folder when it starts (Start In).

–Or–

If you want to send an email, type the From and To email addresses, the subject, and text; browse to and select an attachment; and type your SMTP email server (this is your outgoing mail server that you entered when you set up Windows Mail—see Chapter 4).

–Or–

If you want to display a message, type a title and the message you want it to contain.

REMINDER

Prepare and distribute the weekly progress report.

OK

6. Click **Next**. The Summary dialog box will appear, as shown in Figure 5-4. Click **Open The Properties Dialog For This Task When I Click Finish**, and click **Finish**. The Task Properties dialog box will appear.

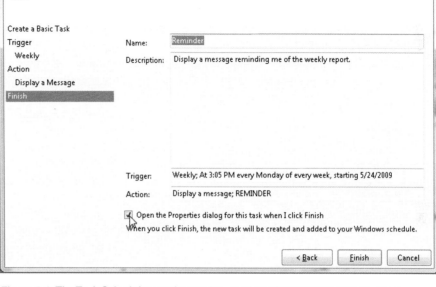

Figure 5-4: The Task Scheduler can be used to send email messages and display a message on your screen, as well as to start a program.

If you don't want tasks grouped on the taskbar, right-click an empty area of the taskbar, click **Properties**, click the **Taskbar Buttons** down arrow, and click **Never Combine**. Click **OK** to close the Properties dialog box. This not only doesn't combine tasks, it also adds a title to each task or icon—taking up a lot of room. This method is not recommended.

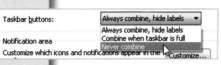

Taskbar buttons:	Always combine, hide labels ▼
	Always combine, hide labels
	Combine when taskbar is full
Notification area	Never combine
Customize which icons and notifications appear in the	Customize...

UICKSTEPS

SWITCHING PROGRAMS *(Continued)*

To select a particular instance of a program when there are multiple instances running, mouse over the icon on the taskbar to open thumbnails of the several instances, and then mouse over the one you want to see enlarged. Finally, when you are ready to fully open one particular instance, click the thumbnail for that instance, as you can see in Figure 5-5.

SWITCH PROGRAMS ON THE TASK LIST

The oldest method of switching programs, which predates Windows 95 and the taskbar, is using the task list.

1. Press **ALT+TAB** and hold down **ALT**. The task list will appear.

2. While continuing to hold down **ALT**, press **TAB** repeatedly until the highlight moves to the program and instance you want or the desktop on the right. Then release **ALT** or click an icon to select the program you want.

7. Look at each of the tabs, review the information you have entered, and determine if you need to change anything.

8. When you are done reviewing the scheduled task, click **OK**. Click **Task Scheduler Library** in the left pane (called the console tree). You should see your scheduled task in the middle pane. Close the Task Scheduler window.

Control Programs with the Task Manager

The Windows Task Manager, shown in Figure 5-6, performs a number of functions, but most importantly, it allows you to see what programs and processes (individual threads of a program) are running and to unequivocally stop both. A display of real-time graphs and tables also shows you what is happening at any second on your computer, as you can see in Figure 5-7. To work with the Task Manager:

1. Press **CTRL+ALT+DELETE** and click **Start Task Manager**. Alternately, you can right-click a blank area of the taskbar, and click **Start Task Manager**.

2. Click the **Applications** tab. You'll see a list of the programs you are running, as shown in Figure 5-6.

3. Click a program in the list. Click **End Task** to stop the program, or click **Switch To** to activate that program.

The Seattle Times | Seattle Times Newspaper - Windows Internet Explorer

QUICKSTEPS

STOPPING PROGRAMS

You may choose to stop a program simply because you are done using it or in an attempt to keep a program from harming your data or other programs.

USE THE CLOSE BUTTON

One of the most common ways to close a program is to click the **Close** button on the upper-right corner of all windows.

USE THE EXIT COMMAND

Almost all programs have an Exit command in a menu on the far left of the menu bar; often, this is the File menu (in Microsoft Office 2010, the File tab is the "menu" and the exit command is located in the lower-right corner). Open this menu and click **Exit**.

CLOSE FROM THE TASKBAR

There are two ways to close a program from the taskbar.

Mouse over the icon, move the mouse to the red X that will appear in the upper-right corner of the thumbnail, and click.

–Or–

Right-click a task on the taskbar, and click **Close Window**.

CLOSE FROM THE KEYBOARD

With the program you want to close open and selected, press **ALT+F4**.

If none of these options work, see "Control Programs with the Task Manager."

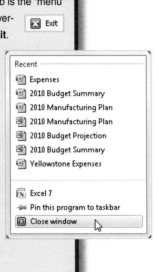

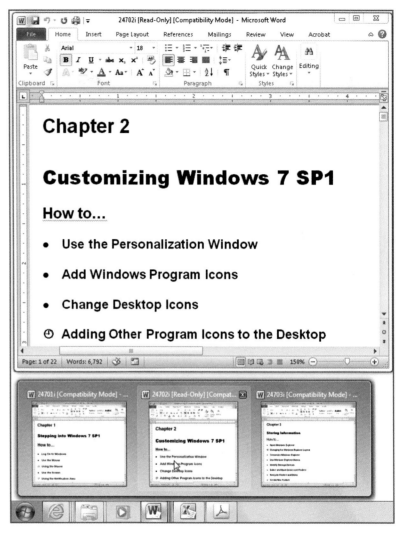

Figure 5-5: You can select one of several instances of a running program by mousing over the taskbar icon or the thumbnails and then clicking the thumbnail you want.

Figure 5-6: The Task Manager shows you what programs are running and allows you to stop them.

4. Click **New Task** to open the Run command, where you can enter a program you want to start. See "Start a Program in Run," next.

5. Click the **Processes** tab. Here you see a list of all the processes that are currently running and their CPU (percentage) and memory (KB) usage. Most of these processes are components of Windows 7 SP1.

6. Click the **Services** tab. This is a list of the Windows 7 SP1 services that are active and their status. There is nothing that you can do here except observe.

7. Click the **Performance** tab. This tab graphically shows the central processing unit (CPU) and memory usage (see Figure 5-7), while the Networking tab shows the computer's use of the network. The Users tab shows the users that are logged on to the computer. You can disconnect them if they are coming in over the network or log them off if they are directly logged on.

8. When you are done, close the Windows Task Manager.

NOTE

It could be that none of the options mentioned in the "Stopping Programs" QuickSteps will work if the program is performing a task or has some fault. In that case, if you want to force the program to stop, shut down Windows itself, and click **Force Shut Down**.

CAUTION

It is generally not a good idea to end a process. Instead, end the task in the Applications tab that is generating the process (see Figure 5-6).

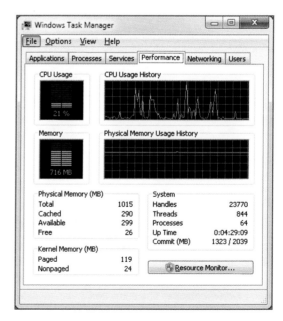

Figure 5-7: Under most circumstances, on a personal computer, only a small fraction of the computer's resources are being used.

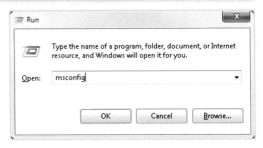

Start a Program in Run

The Start menu has an option called "Run" that opens the Run dialog box. This
is the same dialog box that is opened by clicking New Task in the Task Manager
(see "Control Programs with the Task Manager" earlier in this chapter). From
this dialog box, you can start most programs if you know the path to the
program and its name and don't mind typing all that information.

1. Click **Start**, click **All Programs**, click **Accessories**, and click **Run**.

   –Or–

   Click **Start**, type run in the Search Programs And Files box, and press **ENTER**.

2. In either case, the Run dialog box will appear. Type the path and filename of the
program you want to run, and press **ENTER**.

Start Older Programs

While you can start most programs from the desktop or Start menu,
older, less sophisticated programs require that they be run in their own
isolated window named Command Prompt (also called a DOS, or Disk
Operating System, window). Here, you can type DOS commands at
the flashing underscore, which is called the *command prompt.*

1. Click **Start**, click **All Programs**, click **Accessories**, and click **Command
Prompt**. The Command Prompt window will open.

2. Type help and press **ENTER**. A list of commands that can be used at the
command prompt will be displayed, as shown in Figure 5-8 (the colors of
the background and text have been switched for printing purposes; see
the accompanying Note).

3. To run a program in the Games folder on the C: drive (if you have one—it
is not there by default), type cd c:\games (change directory to c:\games),
press **ENTER**, type dir /p (display the contents of the directory), press
ENTER to see the name of the program, type the name of the program
executable, and press **ENTER**. The program should run, although not all
programs will run in Windows 7 SP1.

4. When you are done with the Command Prompt window, type exit and
press **ENTER**.

*Figure 5-8: **At the command prompt, you can type DOS commands, which
Windows 7 SP1 will carry out.***

NOTE

If you open the Command Prompt window, you will see white text on a black background. For Figure 5-8, the text and background colors have been reversed by clicking the control menu in the upper-left corner, clicking **Properties**, clicking the **Colors** tab, and selecting black in the Screen Text field and white in the Screen Background field. Click **OK** to close the Properties dialog box.

CAUTION

Unless you are trying to diagnose a problem and have some experience doing this, you normally do not want to change the settings in the System Configuration dialog box. However, you can safely stop obvious known Windows-related programs without harm.

Control Automatic Programs

Sometimes, when you install a program, it sets up itself or other programs to run in perpetuity, even if that is not what you had in mind. Many of these programs are not started from the Startup folder. To control these programs and prevent them from running, Windows 7 SP1 has a program named MSConfig, and the easiest way to start it is from the Run dialog box.

1. Click **Start**, click **All Programs**, click **Accessories**, and click **Run**.

   –Or–

   Click **Start**, type run in the Search Programs And Files box, and press **ENTER**.

2. Type msconfig and press **ENTER**. The System Configuration dialog box appears.

3. Click the **Startup** tab. You will see a list of all the programs that start when Windows 7 SP1 starts, as shown in Figure 5-9.

4. Clear the check box to deselect a program so that it is not started the next time Windows 7 SP1 starts. When you are done, click **OK** to close the System Configuration dialog box. A System Configuration message box will appear. Click **Restart** to restart your computer and reflect the changes you have made.

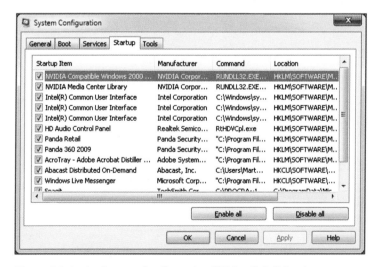

Figure 5-9: *In the System Configuration (MSConfig) dialog box, you can stop from running all of the programs that Windows 7 SP1 starts automatically.*

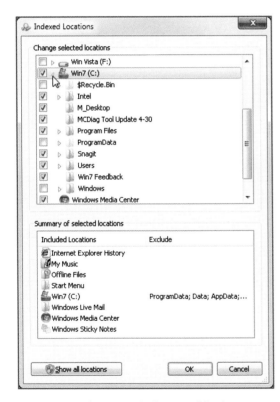

Figure 5-10: *Windows Indexing uses idle time to index your files and folders.*

Control Windows Indexing

Windows 7 SP1 automatically indexes the files that are stored on a computer to substantially speed up your searches of files and folders.

1. Click **Start**, click **Control Panel**, select **Large Icons** view if it is not already selected, and click **Indexing Options** to open the Indexing Options dialog box.

2. If you want to change what is being indexed, click **Modify**, click the triangle icon to open the drives on your computer, and click the folders, as shown in Figure 5-10. Then click **OK**.

3. If you want to change the types of files being indexed, click **Advanced**. Choose if you want encrypted files indexed, or if you want similar words that have different marks (diacritics such as the accent, grave, and umlaut) that change the sound and meaning of the word indexed differently. Click the **File Types** tab, and select the types of files you want included. When you are done, click **OK**.

4. Close the Indexing Options dialog box.

RUNNING ACCESSORY PROGRAMS

Windows 7 SP1 comes with a number of accessory programs. You can open these by clicking **Start**, clicking **All Programs**, and choosing **Accessories**. Many of these programs are discussed elsewhere in this book, but Calculator, Character Map, Notepad, and Paint will be briefly looked at here. You should also explore these on your own.

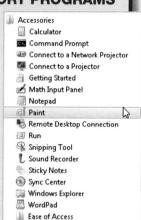

CALCULATOR

The Calculator, started from Accessories, has four alternative calculators, each with its own view:

- Standard desktop calculator
- Scientific calculator, shown in Figure 5-11
- Programmer calculator
- Statistics calculator

A unit converter; a date calculator; and four worksheets for calculating a mortgage, a vehicle lease, and fuel economy in both mpg and L/100 km are included that are extensions to the current view. To switch from one view to the other, click **View** and click the other view. To use a calculator, click the numbers on the screen or type them on the keyboard.

CHARACTER MAP

The Character Map, which is in System Tools, allows you to select special characters that are not available on a standard keyboard.

Continued . . .

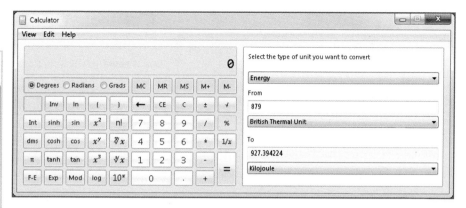

*Figure 5-11: **The Scientific view of the Calculator provides a number of advanced functions, including several extensions such as the unit converter shown here.***

Maintain Windows 7 SP1

Windows 7 SP1 maintenance consists of periodically updating fixes and new features, restoring Windows 7 SP1 when hardware or other software damages it, getting information about it, and installing new hardware and software.

Update Windows 7 SP1

Microsoft tries hard to encourage you to allow Windows 7 SP1 to update itself, from the point of installation, where you are asked to establish automatic updates, to periodically reminding you to do that. If you turn on Automatic Updates, on a regular basis, Windows will automatically determine if any updates are available, download the updates (which come from Microsoft) over the Internet, and install them. If Automatic Updates was not turned on during installation, you can do that at any time and control the updating process once it is turned on.

RUNNING ACCESSORY PROGRAMS

(Continued)

1. Click the **Font** down arrow, and click the font you want for the special character.

2. Scroll until you find it, and then double-click the character; or click the character and click **Select** to copy it to the Clipboard.

3. In the program where you want the character, right-click an open area, and click **Paste** or press **CTRL+V**.

NOTEPAD

Notepad is a simple text editor you can use to view and create unformatted text (.txt) files. If you double-click a text file in Windows Explorer, Notepad will likely open and display the file. If a line of text is too long to display without scrolling, click **Format** and click **Word Wrap**. To create a file, simply start typing in the Notepad window, click the **File** menu, and click **Save**. Before printing a file, click **File**; click **Page Setup**; and select the paper orientation, margins, header, and footer.

PAINT

Paint lets you view, create, and edit bitmap image files in .bmp, .dib, .gif, .ico, .jpg, .png, and .tif formats. Several drawing tools and many colors are available to create simple drawings and illustrations (see Figure 5-12).

*Figure 5-12: **Paint allows you to make simple line drawings or touch up images.***

TURN ON AUTOMATIC UPDATES

To turn on, off, and control Windows Update:

1. Click **Start** and click **Control Panel**. In Category view, click **System And Security**, and in any view, click **Windows Update**.

2. Click **Change Settings**, determine the amount of automation you want, and click one of the following four choices after clicking the **Important Updates** down arrow (see Figure 5-13):

   • The first and recommended choice, which is the default, automatically determines if updates are available, downloads them, and then installs them on a frequency and at a time you specify.

- The second choice automatically determines if updates are available and downloads them; it then asks you whether you want to install them.

- The third choice automatically determines if updates are available, asks you before downloading them, and asks you again before installing them.

- The fourth choice, which is not recommended, never checks for updates.

3. Choose whether to include recommended updates when you are otherwise online with Microsoft, whether all users can install the updates, and whether to use Microsoft Update Service to receive updates for other Microsoft products you have installed, like Microsoft Office.

4. Click **OK** when you are finished, and close Windows Update.

APPLY UPDATES

If you choose either the second or third option for handling updates, you will periodically see a notice that updates are ready to download and/or install.

When you see the notice:

1. Click the notice. The Windows Updates dialog box will appear and show you the updates that are available.

2. Click the individual updates to see detailed information for the updates being proposed.

3. Select the check boxes for the updates you want to download and/or install, and then click **OK**.

4. After you have selected all the updates you want, click **Install Updates**. You will see a notice that the updates are being installed.

5. When the updates have been downloaded and installed, Windows Update will reopen, tell you of this fact, and often ask to restart your computer.

6. Close any open programs, and click **Restart Now**.

*Figure 5-13: **Automatic Updates determines which updates you need and can automatically download and install them.***

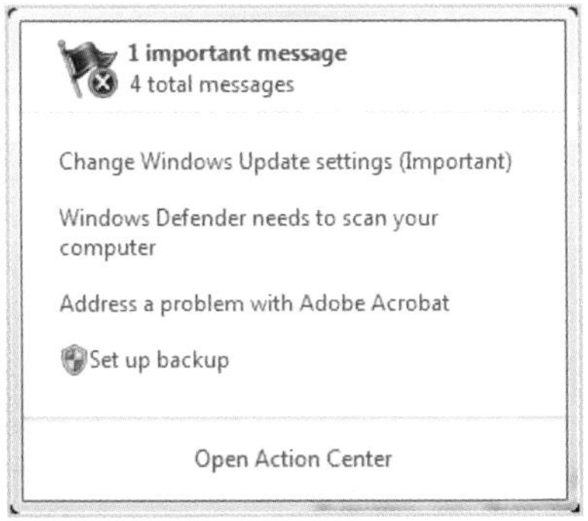

Use the Action Center

The Windows Action Center contains messages that have been sent to you from Windows and other programs that, at least from the viewpoint of the program, you need to respond to. When a message is sent to you by a program, a flag with a red X appears in the notification area.

Click the notification area Action Center flag to open the Action Center jump list. Click any option on the jump list to go directly to the window or dialog box, where you can view the message and possibly take corrective actions.

–Or–

1. Click **Open Action Center** to review recent messages and resolve problems, as you can see in Figure 5-14.

2. Click the relevant item to address the issue, and when you are ready, close the Action Center.

CHANGE ACTION CENTER SETTINGS

You can change how the Action Center informs you of an alert message.

1. From the Action Center, click **Change Action Center Settings**.

2. Select the security and maintenance messages you want to see. Open any of the related settings that seem pertinent, returning to the Action Center when you are ready.

3. When your Action Center settings are the way you want them, click **OK** and close the Action Center.

Restore Windows 7 SP1

System Restore keeps track of the changes you make to your system, including the software you install and the settings you make. If a hardware change, a software installation, or something else causes the system not to load or not to run properly, you can use System Restore to return the system to the way it was at the last restore point.

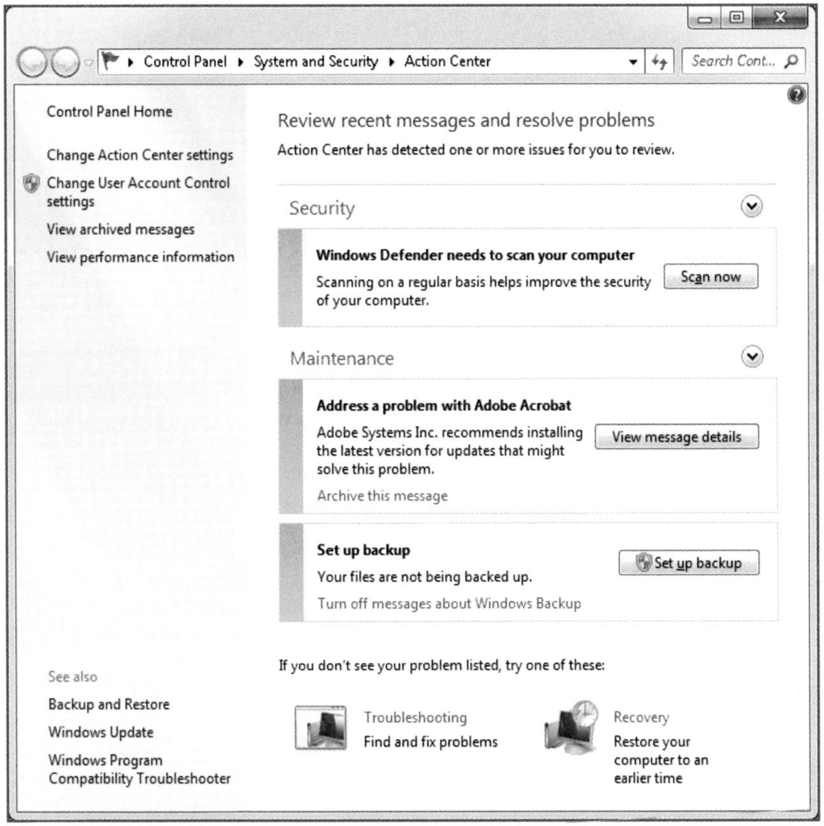

Figure 5-14: **The Action Center consolidates and maintains alert messages that are sent to you by the programs you run.**

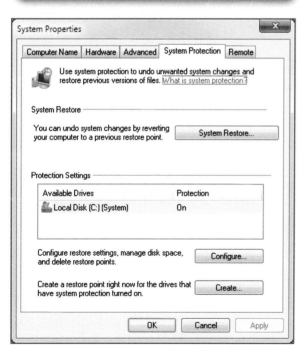

NOTE

System Restore does not restore or make any changes to data files, only to system and application program files. Data files must be backed up, using either the Windows 7 SP1 backup program or a third-party backup program, and then restored from a backup.

NOTE

System Restore actually needs at least 300MB on each hard drive that has the feature turned on, and may use up to 15 percent of each drive. If a drive is smaller than 1GB, System Restore cannot be used.

Figure 5-15: System Restore returns the system to a previous time when it was functioning normally.

SET UP SYSTEM RESTORE

In a default installation of Windows 7 SP1, System Restore is automatically installed. If you have at least 300MB of free disk space after installing Windows 7 SP1, System Restore will be turned on and the first restore point will be set. If System Restore is not enabled, you can turn it on and set a restore point.

1. Click **Start** and click **Control Panel**. In Category view, click **System And Security**, click **System**, and click **System Protection** in the left pane. The System Properties dialog box will appear with the System Protection tab displayed, as you can see in Figure 5-15.

2. By default, the disk on which Windows 7 SP1 is installed should have system protection turned on, indicating that System Restore is automatically operating for that disk. Again by default, your other hard drives are not selected.

3. If any drive does not have protection on and you want it on, select the disk, click **Configure**, click **Restore System Settings And Previous Versions Of Files**, adjust the disk space usage as desired, and click **OK**.

4. When you have made the adjustments you want, click **OK**.

CREATE RESTORE POINTS

A *restore point* is an identifiable point in time when you know your system was working correctly. If your computer's settings are saved at that point, you can use those settings to restore your computer to that time. Normally, Windows 7 SP1 automatically creates restore points for the system drive on a periodic basis. But if you know at a given point in time that your computer is operating exactly the way you want it to, you can create a restore point.

1. Click **Start** and click **Control Panel**. In Category view, click **System And Security**, click **System**, and click **System Protection** in the left pane. The System Properties dialog box will appear with the System Protection tab displayed.

2. Click **Create** and type a name for the restore point. The date and time are automatically added, and you cannot change the name once you create it.

3. Click **Create** again. You will be told when the restore point is created. Click **OK** and click **Close** to close the System Properties dialog box.

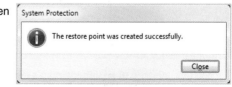

RUN SYSTEM RESTORE FROM WINDOWS

If you can start and operate Windows 7 SP1 normally, try to execute the following steps. If you can't make it through these steps without Windows 7 SP1 crashing, go to the next section.

1. Click **Start** and click **Control Panel**. In Category view, click **System And Security**, click **System**, and click **System Protection** in the left pane. The System Properties dialog box will appear with the System Protection tab displayed.

2. Click **System Restore**; a message explains the restore. Click **Next** to open the System Restore dialog box shown in Figure 5-16.

3. Select the restore point you want to use, and click **Scan For Affected Programs**. This will tell you if any programs have been updated or had a driver installed after the restore point. If you go ahead with the restore, these programs will be restored to their state before the update.

4. Click **Close** and click **Next**. You are asked to confirm the restore point the system will be returned to and given information about that point. If you do not want to restore to that point, click **Back** and return to step 3.

5. System Restore will need to restart your computer, so make sure all other programs are closed. When you are ready to restore to the described point, click **Finish**.

6. A confirmation dialog box appears, telling you that the restore process cannot be interrupted or undone until it has completed. Click **Yes** to continue. Some time will be spent saving files and settings for a new restore point, and then the computer will be restarted.

7. When the restore is completed, you will be told that it was successful. Click **Close**.

RUN SYSTEM RESTORE FROM SYSTEM RECOVERY

Windows 7 SP1 has a System Recovery mode that allows you to start Windows in a minimal way and fix many problems. You can start System Restore in this mode.

1. If your computer is turned on, turn it off (use Shut Down and make sure the power is off), and let it sit for at least two full minutes. This allows all of the components to fully discharge and will give you a clean restart.

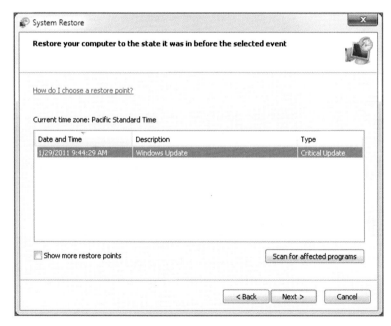

Figure 5-16: **You can do a system restore at any of the restore points on the computer and return all of the Windows 7 SP1 settings and registry to that point in time.**

2. After your computer has sat for at least two minutes without power, remove any disks in the floppy, CD or DVD drives (which you have to do before you turn the computer off), or any flash or USB drives, and turn the computer on. As soon as the memory check is complete, hold down the **F8** key. After a moment, the Advanced Boot Options menu will appear.

3. If necessary, use the **UP ARROW** key to go to the top choice, **Repair Your Computer**, and then press **ENTER**. Windows 7 SP1 will begin loading.

4. Select the type of keyboard you want to use, and click **Next**. Select and/or type your user name and password, and click **Next**.

5. Click **System Restore**. The System Restore window will open, as you saw earlier. Click **Next**.

6. Follow the instructions in "Run System Restore from Windows" earlier in this chapter from step 3 on.

7. The restoration process will begin, and Windows 7 SP1 will restart. The System Restore dialog box will appear, telling you that the restoration was successful. Click **OK**.

Get System Information

When you are working on a computer problem, you, or possibly a technical support person working with you, will want some information about your computer. The two primary sources are basic computer information and advanced system information.

BASIC COMPUTER INFORMATION

Basic computer information provides general system information, such as the Windows edition, the processor and memory, and the computer name and workgroup (see Figure 5-17). To see the basic computer information:

Click **Start** and click **Control Panel**. In Category view, click **System And Security**, and click **System**. The System window will open. After you have reviewed the information, click **Close**.

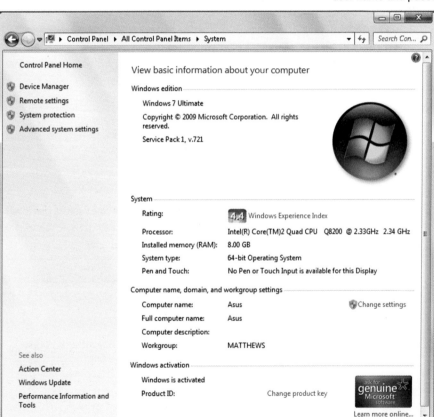

*Figure 5-17: **Basic computer information provides an overview of the computer and its operating system.***

ADVANCED SYSTEM INFORMATION

Advanced system information provides detailed system information and lets you look at services that are running, Group Policy settings, and the error log. To see the advanced system information:

Click **Start** and click **All Programs**. Click **Accessories**, click **System Tools**, and click **System Information**. The System Information window will open. Click any of the topics in the left pane to display that information in the right pane. Figure 5-18 shows the summary-level information that is available. Click **Close** when you are done.

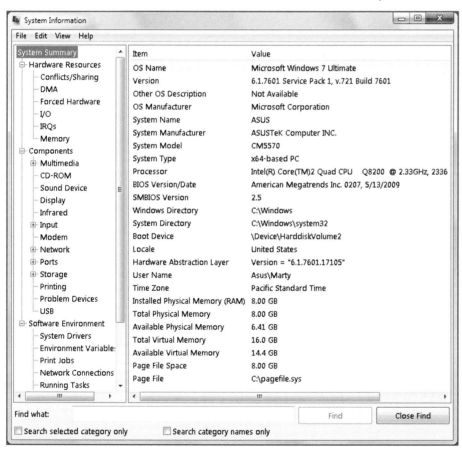

Figure 5-18: *Advanced system information provides a great depth of information useful in troubleshooting.*

Set Power Options

Setting power options is important on laptop and notebook computers that run at least some of the time on batteries. It can also be useful on desktop computers to conserve power. The Windows 7 SP1 Power Options feature provides a number of settings that allow you to manage your computer's use of power.

1. Click **Start** and click **Control Panel**. In Category view, click **System And Security**, and click **Power Options**.

2. Choose one of the power plans, depending on whether you want to emphasize battery life (energy savings on desktops) or performance (see Figure 5-19). You can also reduce the screen brightness on a laptop or notebook computer to reduce the power drain.

3. To see a more detailed setting, click **Choose When To Turn Off The Display**. If you are using a laptop or notebook computer, your power options will look like those in Figure 5-20. (A desktop computer won't have the battery or brightness settings.)

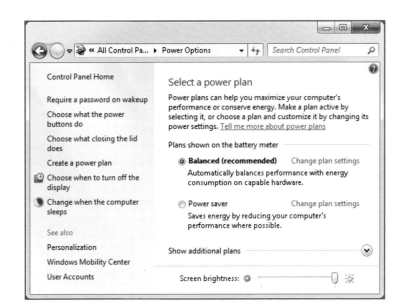

Figure 5-19: *Windows 7 SP1 has two preferred power plans that let you emphasize either performance or energy consumption.*

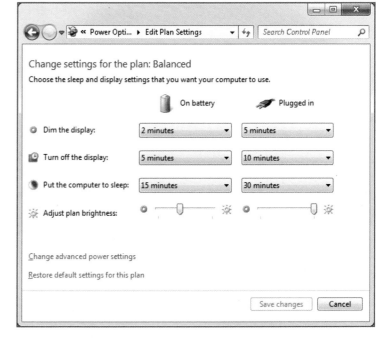

Figure 5-20: *You can set the amount of idle time before the display and/or the computer are turned off or put to sleep, respectively.*

NOTE

See Chapter 1 for a discussion of the differences between shutting down a computer and putting it to sleep.

NOTE

In medium to larger organizations, application software might be available over the local area network (LAN) on a server. Generally, it is better to download the software and then do the installation from your computer than to do the installation over the network in case the network connection is lost during installation (the same can be said for online software; better to download and then install rather than installing directly through an Internet connection).

4. Click each of the drop-down lists, select the setting that is correct for you, and adjust the screen brightness. If you would like to control individual pieces of hardware (disk drives, USB ports, and so on), click **Change Advanced Power Settings**, click the plus signs to open the lists, click the action you want to change, and click the spinners to adjust the values. Click **OK** when you are finished.

5. When you are ready, click **Save Changes** to accept the changes you have made to your power options settings.

Add and Remove Software

Today, almost all application and utility software comes in one of two ways: on a CD or DVD, or downloaded over the Internet.

INSTALL SOFTWARE FROM A CD

If you get software on a CD and your computer is less than 10 years old, all you need to do is put the CD in the drive, wait for the install program to automatically load, and follow the displayed instructions, of which there are usually only a few. When the installation is complete, you may need to acknowledge that by clicking **OK** or **Finish**. Then remove the CD from its drive. That is all there is to it.

INSTALL SOFTWARE FROM THE INTERNET

To download and install a program from the Internet:

1. Click the **Internet Explorer** icon on the taskbar. In the address bar, type the URL (uniform resource locator, also called the address) for the source of the download, and press **ENTER**. (For this example, I'm downloading the Firefox web browser whose URL is mozilla.com.)

2. Locate the link for the download, and click it, as shown in Figure 5-21. You may need to approve the downloading in Internet Explorer by clicking the bar at the top of the window (IE 8) or at the bottom of the window (IE 9) and clicking **Download File**.

3. A dialog box will appear, asking if you want to run or save the program. Click **Run** (this is an exception to the "Save" rule mentioned earlier in the chapter, because every time you install Firefox, you want to get the latest program). Click **Yes** in the User Account Control dialog box to continue to install the program.

4. In the Welcome dialog box, click **Next** and follow the program's installation instructions, making the choices that are correct for you.

5. When the installation is complete, you will be asked if you want to launch (start) the program. Click **Finish** and you will see Firefox open on your screen and a shortcut to the application.

Figure 5-21: Mozilla's Firefox is a good alternative browser to Internet Explorer.

REMOVE SOFTWARE

There are at least two ways to get rid of a program you have installed and one way not to do it. You do not want to just delete the program files in Windows Explorer. That leaves files in other locations and all the settings in the registry. To correctly remove a program, you need to use either the uninstall program that comes with many programs or Windows 7 SP1's Uninstall Or Change A Program feature. To do the latter:

1. Click **Start** and click **Control Panel**. In Category view, click **Programs** and click **Programs And Features**. The Uninstall Or Change A Program window will open.

2. Right-click the program you want to uninstall, and click **Uninstall**, as you can see in Figure 5-22. Follow the instructions as they are presented, which vary from program to program.

3. When the uninstall has successfully completed, close the Uninstall Or Change A Program window.

Figure 5-22: **Programs are removed through the Uninstall Or Change A Program feature.**

NOTE

The "change" part of the Uninstall Or Change A Program window is used to install updates and patches to programs. It requires that you have either a CD with the changes or have downloaded them. With some programs, you will get a third option: Repair.

Add Hardware

Most hardware today is *Plug and Play*. That means that when you plug a device in, Windows recognizes it and installs the necessary driver software automatically and you can immediately begin using it. Often, when you first turn on the computer after installing the hardware, you see a message telling you that you have new hardware or that Windows is installing the device driver. Frequently, you need do nothing more;

Installing device driver software
Click here for status.

Figure window contents

Control Panel ▸ All Control Panel Items ▸ Programs and Features

Control Panel Home

View installed updates

Turn Windows features on or off

Uninstall or change a program

To uninstall a program, select it from the list and then click Uninstall, Change, or Repair.

Organize ▾   Uninstall   Repair

Name	Publisher	Installed On	Size	Version
Adobe Acrobat 9 Pro Extended - English, Fra...	Adobe Sys...	2/16/2011		9.0.0
Adobe AIR	Adobe Sys...	2/16/2011		1.1.0.5790
Adobe Dreamweaver CS3	Adobe Sys...	2/16/2011	858 MB	9.0
Adobe Flash Player 10 ActiveX	Adobe Sys...	2/16/2011	6.00 MB	10.2.152.26
Adobe Flash Player 10 Plugin	Adobe Sys...	2/16/2011	6.00 MB	10.1.102.64
Adobe Media Player	Adobe Sys...	2/16/2011		1.1
Adobe Reader X (10.0.1)	Adobe Sys...	2/10/2011	111 MB	10.0.1
AI Manager	ASUSTeK	2/16/2011		1.04.00
Amazon Games & Software Downloader	Amazon	12/20/2009		2.0.2.0
AnswerWorks 5.0 English Runtime	Vantage S...	9/23/2010		5.0.7
APEX 64-bit Add-On	Adobe Sys...	8/24/2009	33.0 KB	9.0.0
Aptana Studio	Aptana, Inc.	2/16/2011		1.2.0
ASUSUpdate		2/16/2011		
Azurewave Wireless LAN Card	Azurewave	5/12/2009		1.0.7.0
Bonjour	Apple Inc.	1/1/2011	1.74 MB	2.0.4.0
Core... (emove only)		2/16/2011		
Core...		2/16/2011		
CorelDRAW(R) Graphics Suite X4	Corel Corp...	2/16/2011		
CorelDRAW(R) Graphics Suite X4 - Extra Con...	Corel Corp...	2/16/2011		
CorelDRAW(R) Graphics Suite X4 - Windows...	Corel Corp...	2/16/2011	2.92 MB	
EPU-4 Engine		2/16/2011		1.00.19

Uninstall
Repair

Apple Inc. Product version: 2.0.4.0
Help link: http://www.apple.com/support/

1
2
3
4
5
6
7
8
9
10

the installation will complete by itself. With other equipment, you must click the message for the installation to proceed. In either case, you are told when it has successfully completed.

Problems may occur when you have older hardware and the programs that run it, called *drivers,* are not included with Windows 7 SP1. In that case, you will see a dialog box saying you must locate the drivers. Here are some options for locating drivers:

- Let **Windows 7 SP1** see what it can do by itself by clicking **Locate And Install Driver Software** in the Found New Hardware dialog box. Windows 7 SP1 will scan your computer and see what it can find. The original dialog box appears only because a driver wasn't in the standard Windows 7 SP1 driver folder. It may well be in other locations.

- **Microsoft** has drivers for the most popular and recent devices and, as a part of Windows Update (discussed earlier in this chapter), the ability to scan your system and see if it has any drivers to help you. The first step is to look at Windows Update by clicking **Start**, clicking **All Programs**, and clicking **Windows Update**. Click **Check For Updates** in the upper-left area, and see if a driver for your device is found.

- The **manufacturer of the device** is generally a good source, but as hardware gets older, manufacturers stop writing new drivers for more recent operating systems. The easiest way to look for manufacturer support is on the Internet. If you know the manufacturer's website, you can enter it; or you may have to search for it. If you must search, start out by typing the manufacturer's name in the Internet Explorer address bar. This uses Windows Live Search and gives you a list of sites.

- **Third-party sources** can be found using search engines like Google (google.com) and searching for "device drivers." You should find a number of sources, as you can see in Figure 5-23. Some of these sources charge you for the driver; others are free. Make sure the driver will work with Windows 7 SP1.

Use Remote Assistance

Remote Assistance allows you to invite someone to remotely look at your computer and control it for the purposes of assisting you. The other person must be using Windows 7 SP1, Windows Vista, Windows XP, or Windows Server 2003 or 2008, and it will be helpful if both of you have an email account. To use Remote Assistance, you must set it up, and then you can be either the requester or the helper.

NOTE

If you are using Windows 7 SP1 and want to use Remote Assistance with someone using Windows XP or Windows Server 2003, you must be on the receiving end of the assistance and you cannot use Windows 7 SP1's Pause feature. Also, the person using Windows XP/Server 2003 cannot use Start Talk for voice capability.

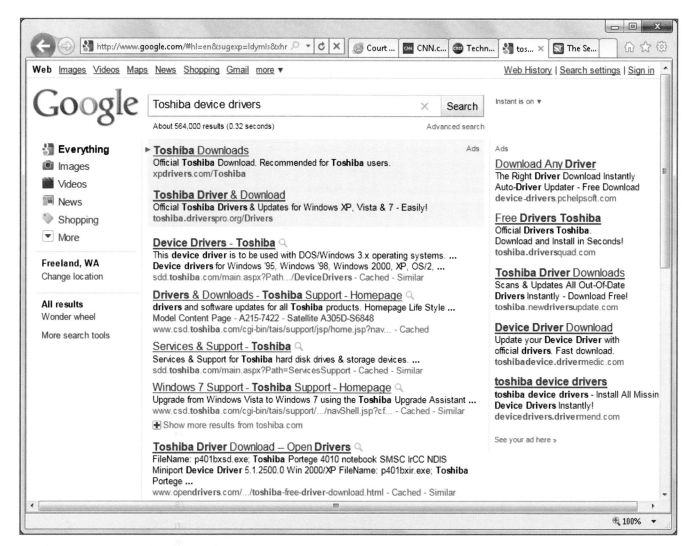

Figure 5-23: Many device drivers can be found by searching the Internet, although you may have to pay for them.

System Properties

| Computer Name | Hardware | Advanced | System Protection | Remote |

Remote Assistance

☑ Allow Remote Assistance connections to this computer

What happens when I enable Remote Assistance?

Advanced...

Remote Desktop

Click an option, and then specify who can connect, if needed.

◉ Don't allow connections to this computer

○ Allow connections from computers running any version of Remote Desktop (less secure)

○ Allow connections only from computers running Remote Desktop with Network Level Authentication (more secure)

Help me choose   Select Users...

OK   Cancel   Apply

*Figure 5-24: **Before using Remote Assistance, it must be turned on.***

NOTE

If you're not using Windows 7 Professional, Enterprise, or Ultimate editions, you won't see the Remote Desktop section shown in Figure 5-24.

SET UP REMOTE ASSISTANCE

Although Remote Assistance is installed with Windows 7 SP1, you must turn it on and set your firewall so that Windows 7 SP1 will allow it through. Both of these tasks are done in Control Panel.

1. Click **Start** and click **Control Panel**. In Category view, click **System And Security**, click **System**, and click **Remote Settings** in the left pane. The System Properties dialog box will appear with the Remote tab displayed (see Figure 5-24).

2. Select **Allow Remote Assistance Connections To This Computer**, if it isn't already, and click **Advanced**.

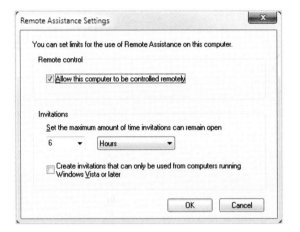

3. Determine if you want a person to control your computer, and select the check box under **Remote Control** accordingly. Set the time an invitation for Remote Assistance is to remain open.

4. Click **OK** twice to close the two open dialog boxes. In Control Panel, click **Control Panel** in the address bar, click **System And Security**, and click **Windows Firewall**.

5. Click **Allow A Program Or Feature Through Windows Firewall**. The Allow Programs To Communicate Through Windows Firewall window will open and show the programs and features that are allowed through the firewall.

6. Click **Change Settings** toward the top of the window, then scroll through the list until you see **Remote Assistance**, and click it, if it isn't already selected (see Figure 5-25).

7. Click **OK** to close the dialog box, close the Windows Firewall window, and then close Control Panel.

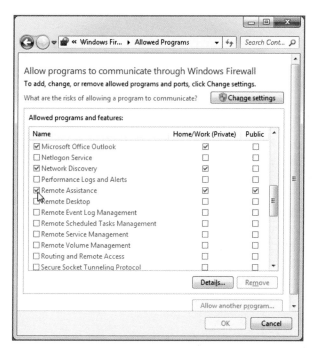

Figure 5-25: *Before you can use Remote Assistance, you must make sure that your firewall will let it through.*

![NOTE]

Remote Desktop, which is discussed in Chapter 10, is different from Remote Assistance, even though, when enabled, it is on the same Remote tab of the System Properties dialog box. Remote Desktop lets you sit at home and log on and use your computer at work as though you were sitting in front of it.

REQUEST REMOTE ASSISTANCE

To use Remote Assistance, first find someone willing to provide it and request the assistance. Besides the obvious invitation text, the request for assistance message will include a password to access your computer and the code to allow the encryption of information to be sent back and forth. All this is provided for you with Windows Remote Assistance. To begin a Remote Assistance session:

1. Click **Start**, click **All Programs**, click **Maintenance**, and click **Windows Remote Assistance** to open the Windows Remote Assistance dialog box.

2. Click **Invite Someone You Trust To Help You**, and then click one of the following methods:

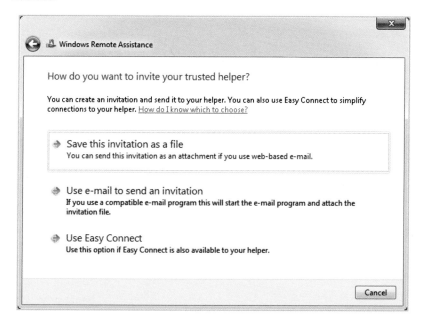

- **Save This Invitation As A File** that you can transfer as an attachment to an email message using any email program or web-based email such as Google's Gmail, or via a CD or USB flash drive.

- **Use E-mail To Send An Invitation** if you are using Windows Live Mail or Microsoft Office Outlook or another compatible email package.

- **Use Easy Connect** if the other computer is using Windows 7 SP1.

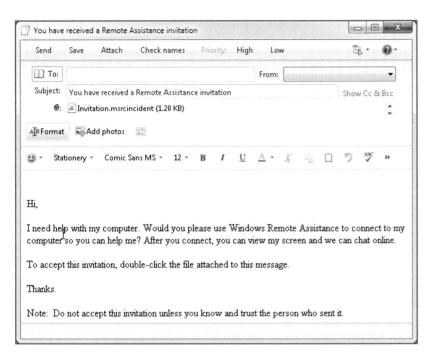

Figure 5-26: *You need to send an invitation that asks a person for assistance and gives him or her the means to communicate in an encrypted manner.*

3. If you choose **Use E-mail To Send An Invitation**, your email program will open and display a message to your helper and contain the invitation as an attachment, as shown in Figure 5-26. Address the email and click **Send**. Skip to step 6.

4. If you choose **Save This Invitation As A File**, select the drive and folder where you want to store the invitation—it may be across a network on your helper's computer. Click **Save**.

5. Attach the saved file to an email message or store it on a CD or flash drive, and send or deliver it to your helper.

6. If you choose **Easy Connect**, or in either of the other two cases, a Windows Remote Assistance window will open, providing you with the password you must also communicate to your helper, say, via phone. This window will wait for your helper to answer.

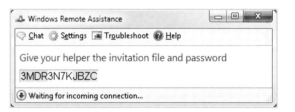

7. When your helper answers, you will be asked if you want to allow the person to see your computer. Click **Yes** if you do. Your computer screen will appear on your helper's computer.

8. Click **Chat**, click in the text box at the bottom, and type a message to the other person, who can see everything on your computer (see "Provide Remote Assistance," next). Click **Send**.

NOTE

You are protected from misuse of Remote Assistance in five ways: Without an invitation, the person giving assistance cannot access your computer; you can limit both the time the invitation remains open and the time the person can be on your computer; you can determine whether the person can control your computer or just look at it; you can click **Stop Sharing** or press **ALT+T** at any time to immediately terminate the other person's control; and you can click **Close** to instantly disconnect the other person.

9. If the other person requests control of your computer, you'll see a message asking if that is what you want to do. If you do, select the check box, and then click **Yes**. If you become uncomfortable, you can click **Stop Sharing** or press **ALT+T** at any time.

10. To end the session, send a message to that effect, and close the Remote Assistance window.

PROVIDE REMOTE ASSISTANCE

If you want to provide remote assistance:

1. Upon receiving an invitation as a file, drag it to the desktop, and double-click it.

2. If you are using Easy Connect, click **Start**, click **All Programs**, click **Maintenance**, and click **Windows Remote Assistance**. Click **Help Someone Who Has Invited You**. It may take a couple of minutes to connect.

3. Enter the password you have been given, click **OK**, and, if the other person approves, you are shown his or her screen and can request control of the other person's computer. You can view the screen in its actual size or scale it to fit your screen, as shown in Figure 5-27.

4. To request control of the other computer, click **Request Control**. Click **Stop Sharing** to give up control.

5. Click **Close** to end the session and close the Remote Assistance window.

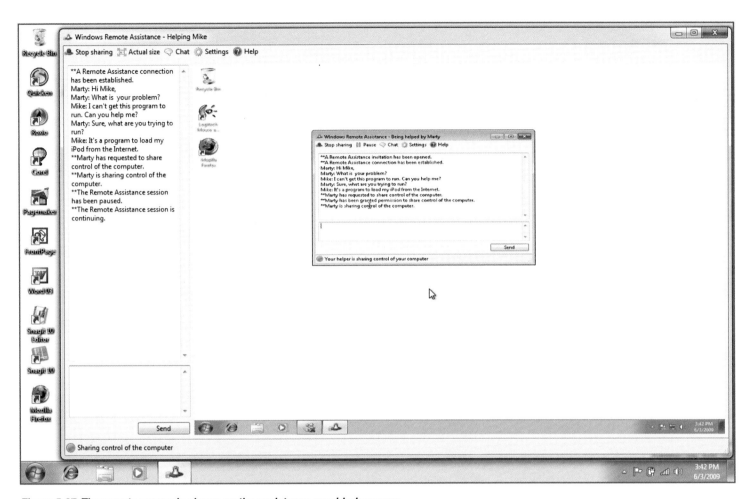

Figure 5-27: *The remote screen is shown on the assistance provider's screen.*

Chapter 6
Working with Documents and Pictures

In this chapter you will discover many aspects of creating documents and pictures, installing and using digital cameras and scanners, and installing and using printers and their fonts with documents and pictures.

Create Documents and Pictures

Creating documents and pictures is primarily done with programs outside of Windows 7 SP1, although Windows has simple programs to do this. Windows 7 SP1 also has facilities to bring documents and pictures in from other computers, from the Internet, and from scanners and cameras.

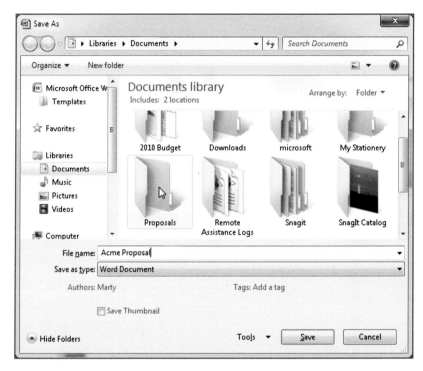

As in other chapters, in the steps here, you may be interrupted and asked by User Account Control (UAC) for permission to continue. So long as it is something you started, click **Continue** or enter a password. To simplify the instructions in this chapter, the UAC instructions have been left out. Chapter 8 discusses UAC in more detail.

QUICKSTEPS

ACQUIRING A DOCUMENT

The documents in your computer got there because they were created with a program on your computer, or they were brought to the computer on a disk, transferred over a local area network (LAN), or downloaded from the Internet.

CREATE A DOCUMENT WITH A PROGRAM

To create a document with a program:

1. Start the program. For example, start Microsoft Word by clicking **Start**, clicking **All Programs**, clicking **Microsoft Office**, and clicking **Microsoft Word**.

2. Create the document using the facilities in the program. In Word, for example, type the document and format it using Word's formatting tools.

3. In Word, save the document by clicking the **File** button. Then click **Save As**, if needed; click **Browse Folders**; and select the disk drive and folder in which to store the document. Enter a filename and click **Save**, as shown in Figure 6-1.

4. Close the program used to create the file.

Continued . . .

Figure 6-1: *Most document-creation programs let you choose where you want to save the files you create.*

Create a Picture

Pictures are really just documents that contain an image. They can be created or brought into your computer in the same way as any other document (see the "Acquiring a Document" QuickSteps). For example, to create and save a picture in Microsoft Paint:

1. Click **Start**, click **All Programs**, click **Accessories**, and click **Paint**.

2. Create a picture using the tools in Paint. For example, click the **Pencil** tool, choose a color, and create the drawing.

3. Save the document by clicking the **Paint** menu (next to the Home tab). Then click **Save As**, select the disk drive and folder in which to store the document, enter a filename, select a Save As type, and click **Save**. Close Paint.

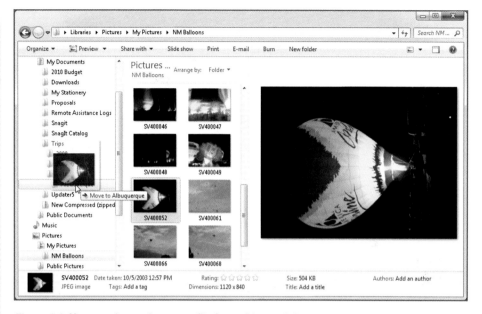

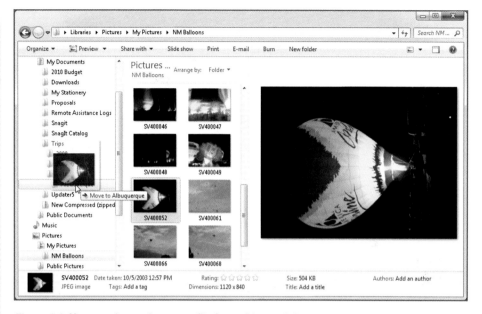

Figure 6-2: *You can drag a document file from either a disk on your computer or from another computer on your network.*

QUICKSTEPS

ACQUIRING A DOCUMENT *(Continued)*

BRING IN A DOCUMENT FROM A DISK

Use Windows Explorer to bring in a document from a disk or other removable storage device.

1. Click **Start** and click **Computer**.

2. Double-click the drive from which you want to retrieve a document (this could be another hard drive, floppy disk, CD, DVD, flash drive, or other device), and double-click to open any necessary folders to locate the document file and display it in the subject (middle) pane (assuming your Windows Explorer window displays a three-pane view: navigation, subject, and preview).

3. In the navigation pane, display (but do not select or open) the drive and folder(s) in which you want to store the file by clicking their respective triangles on the left.

4. Drag the document file to the displayed folder, as illustrated in Figure 6-2. When you are done, close Windows Explorer.

DOWNLOAD A DOCUMENT ACROSS A NETWORK

Use Windows Explorer to bring in a document from another computer on your network (the folder on the other computer will need to be shared; see Chapter 8 for more information on sharing files and folders).

1. Click **Start**, click **Computer**, and click **Network** in the left column.

2. Double-click the other computer from which you want the document, and double-click to open any necessary drives, folders, and subfolders to locate the document file.

Continued . . .

Install Cameras and Scanners

Installing cameras and scanners depends a lot on the device—whether it is Plug and Play (you plug it in and it starts to function), what type of connection it has, and so on. Most recent cameras and scanners are Plug and Play devices. To use them:

1. Plug the device into the computer, and turn it on. If it is Plug and Play, the first time you plug it in, you will see a message that a device driver is being installed and then that it is ready to use. Finally an AutoPlay or specific device dialog box may appear, as you see in Figure 6-3, and allow you to choose what you want to do. If this happens for you and you plugged in a scanner, skip to "Scan Pictures" later in this chapter. If you plugged in a camera, skip to "Import Camera Images" later in this chapter. Otherwise, continue to step 2.

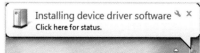

Installing device driver software
Click here for status.

QUICKSTEPS

ACQUIRING A DOCUMENT *(Continued)*

3. In the navigation pane, display (but do not select or open) the drive and folder(s) in which you want to store the file by clicking their respective triangles on the left.

4. Drag the document file to the displayed folder. When you are done, close Windows Explorer.

DOWNLOAD A DOCUMENT FROM THE INTERNET

Use Internet Explorer to bring in a document from a site on the Internet.

1. Click the **Internet Explorer** icon on the taskbar.

2. Type an address, search, or browse to a site and page from which you can download the document file.

3. Use the links and tools on the website to select and begin the file download. For example, right-click a picture and click **Save Picture As**.

4. In the Save Picture dialog box, select the disk and open the folder(s) in which you want to store the file on your computer.

5. Type or edit the filename, and press **ENTER** to complete the download. When you are done, close your browser.

Figure 6-3: **Most recent Plug and Play cameras and scanners are automatically detected and installed.**

2. Click **Start** and click **Devices And Printers**. If you see your device, installation is complete, and you can skip the remainder of these steps.

3. Click **Add A Device**. The Add A Device wizard starts. Click the device you want to install, and click **Next**. Scroll through the manufacturer and model lists, and see if your device is there. If so, select it and click **Next**. Confirm the name you want to use, click **Next**, and then click **Finish** to complete the installation.

4. If you don't see your device on the lists and you have a disk that came with it, place the disk in the drive, and click **Have Disk**. If a driver appears, complete the installation and close the Add A Device wizard. If you cannot find the driver, close the Add A Device wizard and the Devices And Printers window, and use the manufacturer's installation program on the disk.

Scan Pictures

Scanners allow you to take printed images and convert them to digital images on your computer. The scanner must first be installed, as described in "Install Cameras and Scanners" earlier in this chapter. If you ended up using the manufacturer's software to install the scanner, you might need to use it to scan images, too. If you used Windows to install the scanner, use the following steps to scan an image:

1. Turn on your scanner, and place what you want to scan onto the scanning surface.

2. Click **Start**, click **All Programs**, and click **Windows Fax And Scan**. The Windows Fax And Scan window opens.

3. Click **New Scan** on the toolbar. The New Scan dialog box appears. The scanner you installed should be displayed in the upper-left area. Change the scanner if you wish.

4. Choose the color, file type, and resolution you want to use; and click **Preview**. The image in the scanner will appear in the dialog box.

5. Adjust the margins around the page by dragging the dashed lines on the four sides, as shown in Figure 6-4. When you are ready, click **Scan**.

6. The scanned image will appear in the Windows Fax And Scan window (see Figure 6-5). Select the image in the list at the top of the window, and, using the toolbar, choose to:

- **Forward As Fax** using the Windows fax capability described later in this chapter

- **Forward As E-mail** using your default email application

- **Save As** using Windows Explorer to save the image as a file on one of the storage devices available to you

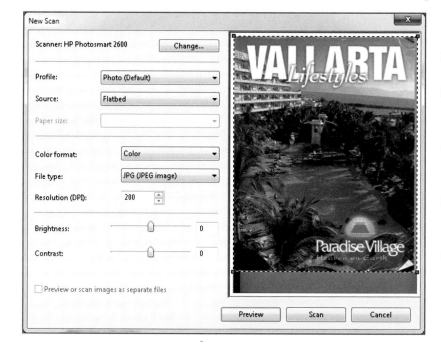

Figure 6-4: In the Windows 7 SP1 scanning software, you can change several of the parameters, including the margins of what to include, and see the results in the preview pane.

Figure 6-5: *Images that you scan can be faxed, emailed, saved, and printed.*

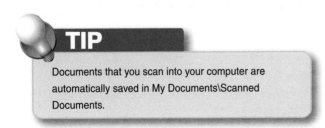

TIP

Documents that you scan into your computer are automatically saved in My Documents\Scanned Documents.

- **Print** using a printer available to you
- **Delete** the image

7. Work through the related dialog box(es) that appear to complete the scanning process. When you are ready, close the Windows Fax And Scan window.

Import Camera Images

When most digital cameras or their memory cards are plugged into the computer (see "Install Cameras and Scanners" earlier in this chapter), the device-specific dialog box (shown previously in Figure 6-3) or the AutoPlay dialog box should automatically appear. The AutoPlay dialog box, shown next, calls the camera a removable disk and asks if you want to:

- **Import Pictures And Videos**, in essence, copying them to your hard disk
- **View Pictures** in your camera using Windows Photo Viewer

- **Import Pictures And Videos** in your camera using Windows Live Photo Gallery
- **View Pictures** in your camera using Windows Live Photo Gallery
- **Open Folder To View Files** to look at your camera as if it were a disk and the pictures as files using Windows Explorer

1. Click **Import Pictures And Videos Using Windows Live Photo Gallery**. The Import Photos And Videos dialog box should appear.

2. Choose if you want to review and organize your photos first or import them all immediately.

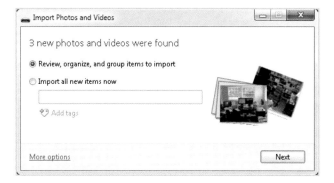

3. If you choose to review and organize, click **Next**. A window opens that allows you to select the photos you want imported. You can group photos by date, add names to groups, and add tags to groups that will form the basis of photo names (the date is already a part of the name). When you are ready, click **Import**.

4. If you choose to import all items at once, select that option, enter a name, if desired click **Add Tags** and type a tag to add to the filename of all the pictures, and click **Import**.

   The first time you do this, you will see a message box asking if you want to use Windows Live Photo Gallery to open picture file types instead of the default Windows viewer. Click **Yes**.

5. In either case, you will see each of the pictures as they are imported. When the process is completed, the Windows Live Photo Gallery will open and show thumbnails of the pictures, as you can see in Figure 6-6.

6. The ribbon at the top of the window, which was discussed in Chapter 4, provides a number of tools to help you categorize, organize, edit, and view the photos in the gallery. Hover the mouse pointer over each tool to get a screen tip describing what the tool does.

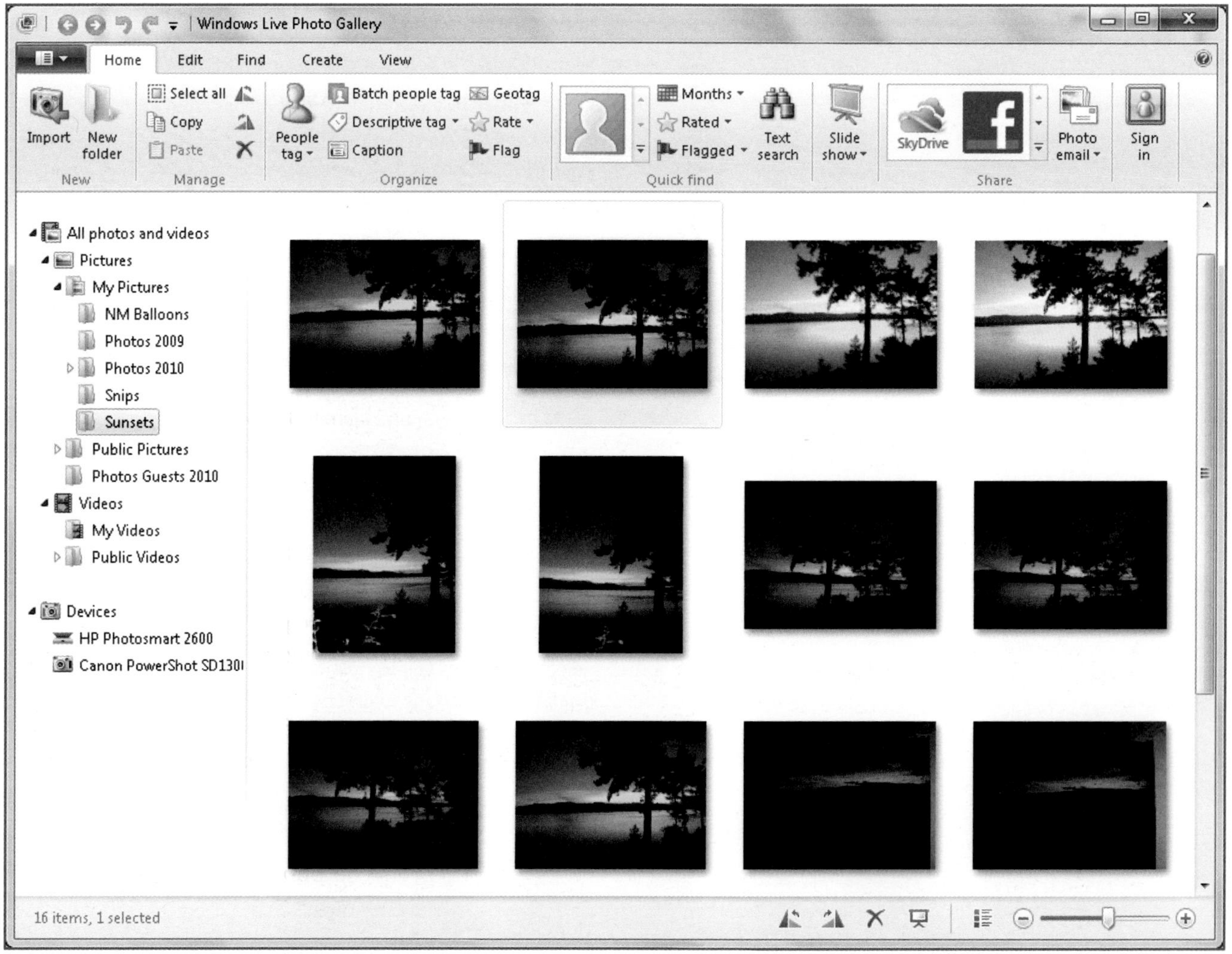

Figure 6-6: *The Windows Live Photo Gallery gives you a quick way to organize and work with your pictures.*

A great feature of Photo Gallery is its ability to select the head shots of individuals from a photo, list them separately in the pane on the right, and then tag the person with his or her name. Click **Tag Someone** in the right pane, click in the upper-left area just outside of someone's head, drag the selection box so it encompasses their head, type a name or caption, and press **ENTER**.

VIEWING OTHER PICTURES

If your pictures are not in the Photo Gallery, to locate and view them:

1. Click **Start**, click **Computer**, and open the drive and folders necessary to locate your pictures.

2. Click the **Change Your View** menu down arrow, and click **Extra Large Icons**; or adjust the slider so that you can adequately see the thumbnail images.

3. Double-click the picture you want to view in a larger size. The Windows Live Photo Gallery will open without the ribbon and display the picture. Click **Edit, Organize, Or Share** to open the full Photo Gallery so you can work with the picture.

Work with Photo Gallery Pictures

Once you have brought pictures into your computer from a camera, a scanner, an Internet download, or a removable disk, you can look at them on your computer screen. Assuming that you brought your pictures into Photo Gallery as discussed in "Import Camera Images" or "Scan Pictures" earlier in this chapter:

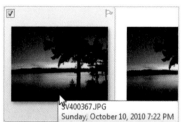

1. Click **Start**, click **All Programs**, and click **Windows Live Photo Gallery**. The Windows Live Photo Gallery will open.

2. Select the tag you assigned or date your pictures were taken to open the category that contains them, as was shown in Figure 6-6. In effect you are opening a subfolder.

3. To see a larger image, double-click its thumbnail. The image will expand to fit the Photo Gallery window, similar to what is shown in Figure 6-7. The controls at the bottom of the window allow you to cycle through a number of pictures and work with them.

4. If you have several pictures you want to view, click the right and left arrows on the bottom of the window to go through them sequentially. You can also use the other controls at the bottom of the window or in the ribbons at the top to perform their stated functions.

5. When you are done, click **Close File** on the right of the ribbon to return to the gallery and view the photo thumbnails, or click **Close** to leave Windows Live Photo Gallery.

Capture Snips

Windows 7 SP1 includes the Snipping Tool to capture images of the screen, called "screen shots" or "snips." This can capture four areas of the screen:

- **Full screen** captures the entire screen.
- **Window** captures a complete window.
- **Rectangular area** captures a rectangle you draw around objects.
- **Free-form area** captures any area you draw around objects.

Once you have captured an area, it is temporarily stored on the Clipboard and displayed in the mark-up window where you can write and draw on the snip to

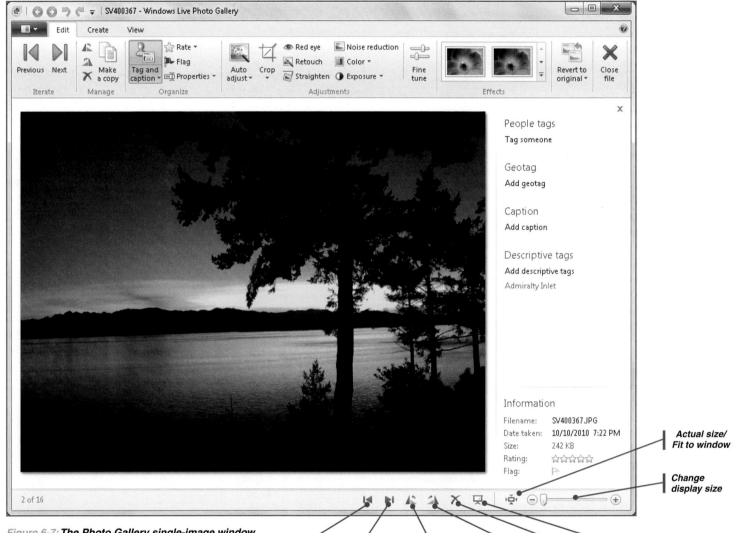

Figure 6-7: *The Photo Gallery single-image window offers a great way to view pictures in a set individually and work on them.*

Previous picture

Next picture

Rotate counterclockwise

Rotate clockwise

Delete picture

Play slide show

Actual size/ Fit to window

Change display size

annotate it and, when you are ready, save the snip where you want it. To do all of that:

1. Display the windows or other objects on the screen whose images you want to capture (see the Tip on capturing a menu).

2. Click **Start**, click **All Programs**, click **Accessories**, and click **Snipping Tool**. The screen will be dimmed, the Snipping Tool dialog box will appear, along with a cross-hair to use to outline the area to be captured—by default, you will see a rectangle (see Figure 6-8).

3. If you want to capture a rectangular area, drag the cross-hair from one corner of the rectangle to the opposite corner. To capture a different type of area, click the **New** down arrow, and click one of the other three types of areas. Then, with:

   - **Free-Form Snip**, drag the cross-hair around the area to be captured
   - **Window Snip**, click the window to be captured
   - **Full-Screen Snip**, the screen is automatically captured

TIP

To capture a snip of a menu, open the Snipping Tool, press **ESC**, display the menu to be captured, press **CTRL+PRINT SCREEN**, click the **New** down arrow, select the type of area to be captured (Free-Form, Rectangle, and so forth), and delineate that area as you would otherwise.

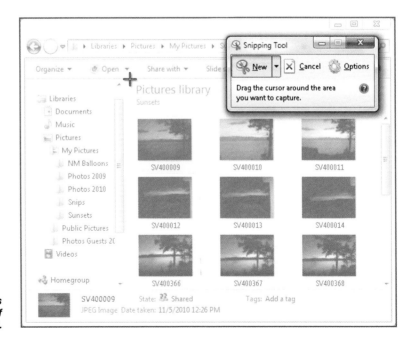

*Figure 6-8: **The Snipping Tool allows you to capture an image of an area of the screen for future reference or use.***

QUICKSTEPS

USING STICKY NOTES

Sticky Notes are exactly what the name implies: little notes to yourself that you can place anywhere on your screen. You can type messages on these notes; change their color; cut, copy, and paste the text on them with the Clipboard to and from other programs; create additional notes; and delete the note.

+   ×

Meeting With Paul S.
at 3:30 on Thursday
the 18th

1. Click **Start**, click **All Programs**, click **Accessories**, and click **Sticky Notes**. If you don't already have a note on your desktop, one will appear.

2. If you already have one or more notes on the desktop, the most recent one will be selected. If you want a new note, click **New Note** (the plus sign in the upper-left corner).

3. On the new note, type the message you want it to contain; or, having copied some text from another source, right-click the note and click **Paste**.

   (You can resize a note like a window.)

4. Right-click the note, click the color you want it to be, and then drag the note to where you want it.

5. When you no longer want the note on the desktop, click **Delete Note** (the X in the upper-right), and click **Yes**.

4. In all cases, the mark-up window opens, showing you the area that was captured, as you can see in Figure 6-9, and allowing you to use the pen, highlighter, and eraser to annotate the snip.

5. From the mark-up window, you can also directly email the snip to someone by clicking **Send Snip**, which opens an email message with the snip in it; save the snip by clicking **Save Snip**, select a folder, enter a name, select a file type, and click **Save**.

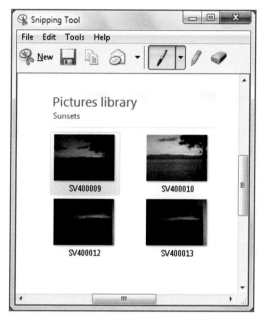

*Figure 6-9: **The Snipping Tool mark-up window allows you to annotate, email, and save a snip.***

Print Documents and Pictures

It is important to be able to install and fully use printers so that you can transfer your digital documents to paper.

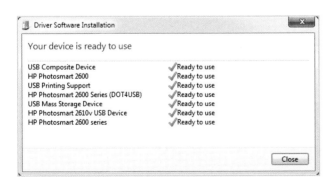

Some laptop computer-and-printer combinations are connected through an infrared beam or other wireless connection. In this case, "plugging the printer into the computer" means to establish that wireless connection.

Install a Printer

All printers are either automatically installed or done so using the Devices And Printers window. Because there are differences in how the installation is done, look at the sections in this chapter on installing local Plug and Play printers, installing other local printers, installing network printers, and selecting a default printer. Also, if you are installing a local printer, first consider the following checklist.

PRINTER INSTALLATION CHECKLIST

A local printer is one that is attached to your computer with a cable or wireless connection. Make sure that your printer meets the following conditions *before* you begin the installation:

- It is plugged into the correct port on your computer (see manufacturer's instructions).
- It is plugged into an electrical outlet.
- It has fresh ink, toner, or ribbon, which, along with the print heads, is properly installed.
- It has adequate paper.
- It is turned on.

INSTALL A LOCAL PLUG AND PLAY PRINTER

Installing Plug and Play printers is supposed to be fairly automatic, and, for the most part, it is.

1. With your computer and printer turned off, connect the devices to each other. Then make sure the other points in the previous checklist are satisfied.

2. Turn on your computer, let it fully boot, and then turn on your printer. Your computer should find and automatically install the new printer and briefly give you messages to that effect.

3. Click **Start** and click **Devices And Printers**. The Devices And Printers window will open, and you should see your new printer. Hover the mouse pointer over that printer, and you should see "Status: Ready," as shown in Figure 6-10. (If you don't see your printer, it was not installed. Go to the next section.)

4. Right-click the new printer, click **Printer Properties**, and click **Print Test Page**. If the test page prints satisfactorily, click **Close**. Otherwise, click **Get Help With Printing**, follow the suggestions, and close the Help and printer windows when you are done. When you are ready, click **OK** to close the printer Properties dialog box.

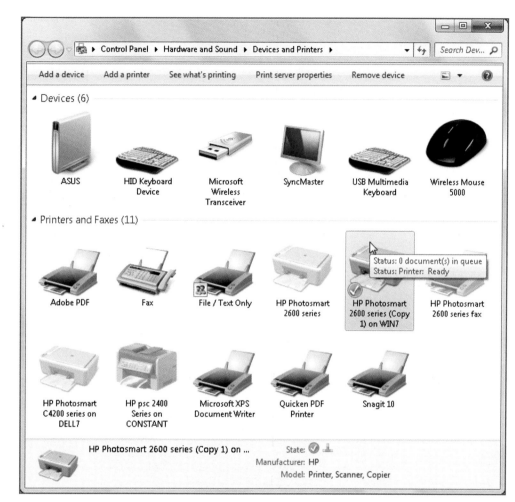

Figure 6-10: *When you connect a Plug and Play printer, it should be recognized by the computer and automatically installed.*

5. If you want the new printer to be the default printer used by all applications on the computer, right-click the printer and click **Set As Default Printer**.

6. Close the Devices And Printers window.

INSTALL A LOCAL PRINTER MANUALLY

If a printer isn't automatically installed in the process of using steps 1 through 3 in the previous section, you must install it manually.

1. If a CD came with your printer, providing it says that it is for Windows 7, place that CD in the drive, and follow the on-screen instructions to install the printer. When this is complete, go to step 3 in "Install a Local Plug and Play Printer," and determine if the printer will print a test page. If so, skip to step 7.

2. If you don't have a manufacturer's CD, click **Start** and click **Devices And Printers**. The Devices And Printers window should open.

3. Click **Add A Printer** on the toolbar, and click **Add A Local Printer**.

4. Click **Use An Existing Port:**, open the drop-down list, and select the correct port (on newer printers, it is probably USB001; on the majority of older printers, it is LPT1), and click **Next**.

Choose a printer port

A printer port is a type of connection that allows your computer to exchange information with a printer.

◉ Use an existing port: LPT1: (Printer Port)

○ Create a new port:

   Type of port: Local Port

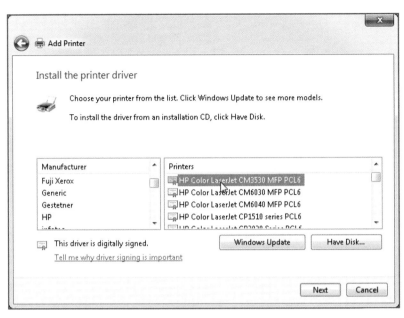

Figure 6-11: **Manually installing a printer requires that you know some facts about the printer.**

TIP

If your printer was automatically installed but a CD came with your printer and you wonder if you should install using the CD, the general answer is no. Most printer drivers in Windows 7 SP1 originally came from the manufacturers and have been tested by Microsoft, so they should work well. Unless the printer came out after the release of Windows 7 SP1 (spring 2011), the driver in Windows 7 SP1 should be newer, and in the installation dialog boxes, you can choose to update the drivers.

5. Select the manufacturer and model of the printer you want to install (see Figure 6-11). If you can't find your printer, click **Windows Update** to download the latest printer drivers. Then, once more, search for the manufacturer and model. When you find the correct printer, click **Next**.

6. Confirm or change the printer name, and click **Next**. Determine if you want to share this printer; if so, enter its share name, location, and comments. Click **Next**.

7. Choose whether you want this printer to be your default printer. Click **Print A Test Page**. If the test page prints satisfactorily, click **Close**. Otherwise, click **Get Help With Printing**, follow the suggestions, and close the Help and Printer windows when you are done. When you are ready, click **Finish** to close the Add Printer dialog box, and close the Devices And Printers window.

INSTALL A NETWORK PRINTER

Network printers are not directly connected to your computer, but are available to you as a result of your computer's connection to a network and the fact that the printers have been shared. There are three types of network printers:

● Printers connected to someone else's computer, which are shared

● Printers connected to a dedicated printer server, which are shared

● Printers directly connected to a network (which, in effect, have a built-in computer)

The first two types of network printers are installed with the Network Printer option in the Add Printer dialog box and will be described here. The third option is installed with the Local Printer option, often automatically.

1. Click **Start** and click **Devices And Printers**. The Devices And Printers window will open.

2. Click **Add A Printer** on the toolbar, and click **Add A Network, Wireless Or Bluetooth Printer**. Windows will search for network printers, as shown in Figure 6-12.

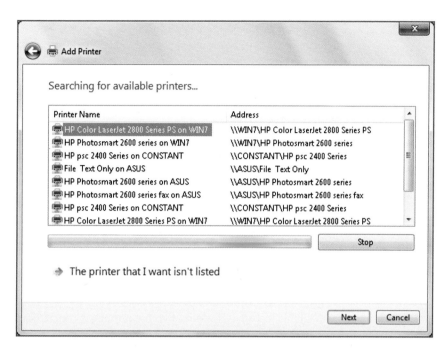

*Figure 6-12: **A printer on another computer must be shared by that computer before you can use it.***

NOTE

The search for network printers will find those printers that: (1) have been published to Active Directory—normally in larger organizations; (2) are attached to computers on the network; (3) use a Bluetooth wireless system and a Bluetooth transceiver is connected to the computer doing the search; and (4) are directly connected to the network (not through another computer) and have their own IP address (probably automatically assigned).

3. Scroll through the printers to locate the one you want. Click that printer and click **Next**. Skip to step 5.

4. If the search did not find the network printer you were looking for, click **The Printer That I Want Isn't Listed**. Click **Browse For A Printer**, and click **Next**. Double-click the computer to which the printer is attached, double-click the printer, and click **OK**.

5. Adjust the name of the printer if you want, and click **Next**. Click **Set As The Default Printer**, if you want to do that. Click **Print A Test Page**. If the test page prints satisfactorily, click **Close**. Otherwise, click **Get Help With Printing**, follow the suggestions, and close the Help window when you are done. When you are ready, click **Finish** to close the Add Printer dialog box and close the Devices And Printers window.

IDENTIFY A DEFAULT PRINTER

If you have several printers available to you, one must be identified as your default printer—the one that will be used for printing whenever you don't select another one. To change your default printer:

1. Click **Start** and click **Devices And Printers**. The Devices And Printers window will open.

2. Right-click the printer you want to be the default, and click **Set As Default Printer**.

3. Close the Devices And Printers window when finished.

SHARE A PRINTER

If you have a printer attached to your computer and you want to let others use it, you can share the printer.

1. In the Devices And Printers window, right-click the printer you want to share, and click **Printer Properties**. The printer's Properties dialog box will appear.

PRINTING

Most printing is done from a program. Using Microsoft Office Word 2010, whose Print window is shown in Figure 6-13, as an example:

PRINT DOCUMENTS

To print the document currently open in Word:

Click **Quick Print** on Word's Quick Access toolbar to immediately print using the default settings.

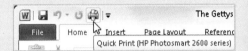

CHOOSE A PRINTER

To choose which printer you want to use:

Click the **File** button, and click **Print** to open Word's Print window shown in Figure 6-13. Click the **Printer** drop-down list, and choose the printer you want.

DETERMINE SPECIFIC PAGES TO PRINT

In the first section of the Print window under Settings, by clicking the down arrow on the right, you can select:

- **Print All Pages** to print the entire document

- **Print Selection** to print the text that has been selected

- **Print Current Page** to print only the currently viewed page

- **Print Custom Range** to print a series of individual pages and/or a range of pages by specifying the individual pages separated by commas and specifying the range with a hyphen. For example, typing 4,6,8-10,12 will cause pages 4, 6, 8, 9, 10, and 12 to be printed.

2. Click the **Sharing** tab, click **Share This Printer**, enter a share name, and click **OK**.

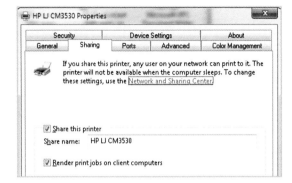

3. Close the printer's Properties dialog box.

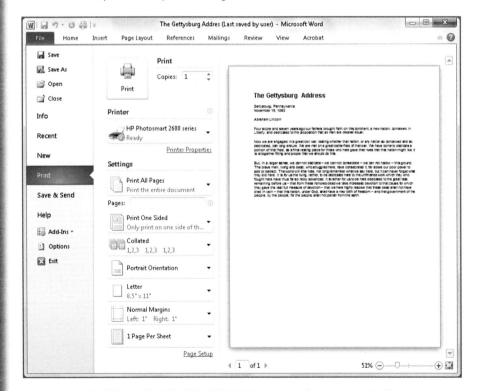

Figure 6-13: **The Microsoft Office Word 2010 Print window has options similar to many other programs.**

Print Pictures

Printing pictures from a program is exactly the same as described in the "Printing" QuickSteps. In addition, Windows has a Print Pictures dialog box used to print pictures from either Windows Explorer or the Photo Gallery.

1. Click **Start** and click **Pictures** to use Windows Explorer; or click **Start**, click **All Programs**, click **Windows Live**, and click **Windows Live Photo Gallery** to use that program.

2. In either program, select the picture(s) you want to print. To select one, click it. To select a contiguous set of pictures, click the first one, hold down **SHIFT**, and click the last picture. To select noncontiguous pictures, hold down **CTRL** while clicking the pictures you want.

3. Click the **File** tab, and click **Print** on the left. To print on a local or network printer, click **Print** again; alternately, you can order prints online. Using the selected printer, the Print Pictures dialog box will appear, as shown in Figure 6-14.

4. Select the printer, paper size, quality, paper type, number to print on a page, number of copies, and whether to fit the picture to a frame. You can also click **Options** above the Cancel button to look at, and possibly change, several print settings. Click **OK** after looking at (and possibly selecting) the options.

5. When you are ready, click **Print**. The pictures will be printed. When you are done, close Windows Explorer or Windows Live Photo Gallery, whichever you have open.

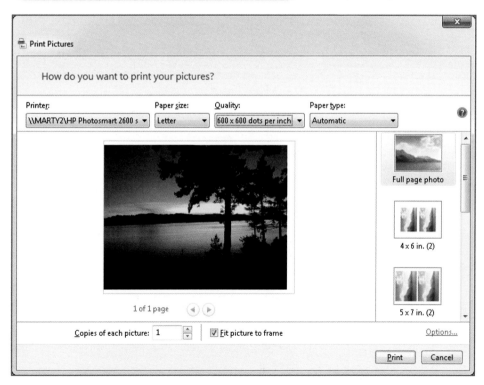

*Figure 6-14: **If you use high-quality photo paper and a newer color printer, you can get almost professional-grade pictures.***

Print to a File

There are two primary reasons to print to a file: to have a file you can take to a remote printer, and to get information out of one program and into another. The first requires formatting the information for a printer and then sending it to a file. The actual printer must be installed on your computer even though it is not physically connected to your computer. In the second case, you must create a "printer" to produce unformatted generic text. The following sections explain first how to create a text file printer and then how to print to a file.

CREATE A TEXT FILE PRINTER

1. Click **Start** and click **Devices And Printers**. The Devices And Printers window will open.

2. Click **Add A Printer** on the toolbar, and click **Add A Local Printer**. Click the **Use An Existing Port** down arrow, and click **File (Print To File)**.

3. Click **Next**. In the Install The Printer Driver dialog box, scroll down and click **Generic** as the manufacturer and **Generic/Text Only** as the printer.

4. Click **Next**. Enter a name for the printer, and click **Next**. Determine if you want to share this printer and, if so, enter a share name. Click **Next**.

5. Click **Set As The Default Printer** (if you want to do that), skip printing a test page, and click **Finish**. A new icon will appear in your Devices And Printers window. Close the Devices And Printers window when you are done.

SELECT PRINT TO FILE

Whether you want to print to a file so that you can print on a remote printer or so that you can create a text file, the steps are the same once you have created a text file printer.

1. In the program in which you are printing, click the **File** menu (or the **File** button in Microsoft Office 2010), and click **Print**.

2. Click the **Printer** down arrow, and select the ultimate printer or the generic text file printer. Click the **Printer** down arrow a second time, and click **Print To File**. Select the print range, number of copies, and other settings; and click **OK** or **Print** depending on your program. Select the folder, type the filename to use, and click **OK**.

Print Webpages

Printing webpages is little different from printing any other document.

1. Click the **Internet Explorer** icon on the taskbar to open your browser (assumed to be Internet Explorer).

2. Browse to the page you want to print, and in either IE 8 or IE 9, right-click the page and click **Print**. Or, if you have turned on the menu bar, press **ALT**, click the **File** menu, and click **Print**. The Print dialog box will open. Select the printer and other options, and click **Print** again.

3. Close your Internet browser.

Configure a Printer

Configuring a printer is usually done for special purposes and often isn't required. Nevertheless, all configuring is done from the printer's Properties dialog box.

1. Click **Start** and click **Devices And Printers**. The Devices And Printers window will open.

2. Right-click the printer you want to configure, click **Printer Properties** and, if needed, select your printer. The printer's Properties dialog box will appear (you cannot change most settings for networked printers).

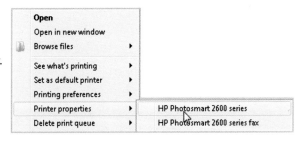

In the General tab (shown in Figure 6-15), you can change the printer name, its location, and enter a comment. In the Ports tab, you can specify the port used by the printer, configure ports, and set up printer pooling. In the Device Settings tab, you can set what is loaded in each paper tray, how to handle font substitution, and what printer options are available (your printer may be different). Though most printer configurations are self-explanatory, several items are worthy of further discussion and are explained in the following sections.

ENABLE PRINTER POOLING

Printer pooling allows you to have two or more physical printing devices with the same print driver assigned to one printer. When print jobs are sent to the

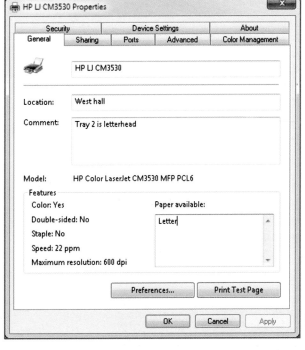

*Figure 6-15: **Printers, while having many settings, are often run without ever changing the default settings.***

printer, Windows determines which of the physical devices is available and routes the job to that device.

1. In the Properties dialog box for the printer to which all work will be directed, click the **Ports** tab, and click **Enable Printer Pooling**.

2. Click each of the ports with a printing device that is to be in the pool. When all the ports are selected, click **OK** to close the Properties dialog box.

3. If the printer that contains the pool isn't already selected as the default printer, right-click the printer and click **Set As Default Printer**.

SET PRINTER PRIORITY

Assigning several printers to one printing device allows you to have two or more settings used with one device. If you want to have two or more priorities automatically assigned to jobs going to a printer, create two or more printers that all point to the same printer port but that have different priorities. Then have high-priority print jobs printed to a printer with a priority of 99 and low-priority jobs printed to a printer with a priority of 1.

1. Install all printers as previously described in "Install a Printer," all with the same port. Name each printer to indicate its priority, such as "High-Priority Printer" and "Low-Priority Printer."

2. In the Devices And Printers window, right-click the high-priority printer, and click **Printer Properties**.

3. Click the **Advanced** tab, type a priority of <u>99</u>, and click **OK**.

4. Similarly, right-click the other printers, open their Properties dialog boxes, click the **Advanced** tab, and set the priority, from 1 for the lowest priority to 98 for the second-highest priority.

Jobs with the highest priority will print before jobs with a lower priority if they are in the *queue* (waiting to be printed) at the same time.

ASSIGN PAPER TRAYS

Some printers have more than one paper tray, and each tray can have different types or sizes of paper. If you assign types and sizes of paper to trays in the printer's Properties dialog box and a user requests a specific type and size of

---

TIP

If you have a program that automatically prints certain tasks, such as incoming orders, you might want to assign that automatic task a lower priority than a word-processing task, such as a new proposal.

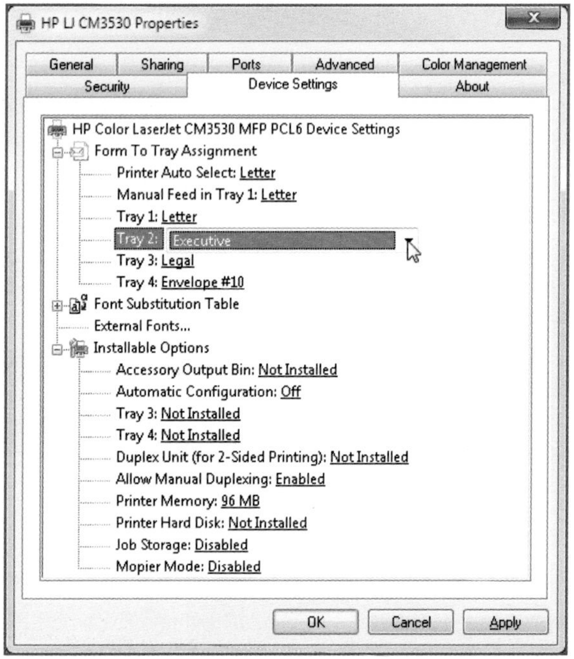

paper when printing, Windows 7 SP1 automatically designates the correct paper tray for the print job.

1. In the printer Properties dialog box for the printer whose trays you want to assign, click the **Device Settings** tab.

2. Click the type of paper in a tray, open the drop-down list, and select the type and size of paper in that tray, similar to what you see in Figure 6-16.

3. When you have set the paper type and size in each tray, click **OK**.

CONFIGURE SPOOL SETTINGS

The time it takes to print a document is normally longer than the time it takes to transfer the information to the printer. *Printer spooling* temporarily stores information on disk, allowing Windows to feed it to the printer as it can be handled. Under most circumstances, you want to use printer spooling and not tie up the program waiting for the printer. The printer's Properties Advanced tab lets you choose to spool or not, and gives you two options if you spool:

Figure 6-16: **You can set the paper type and size in each paper tray.**

- **Start Printing After Last Page Is Spooled** waits to print until the last page is spooled, allowing the program to finish faster and the user to get back to the program faster, but it takes longer to finish printing.

- **Start Printing Immediately** allows printing to be done sooner, but the program will be tied up a little longer.

The default, Start Printing Immediately, provides a middle ground between getting the printing done and getting back to the program.

USE SEPARATOR PAGES

If you have several jobs on a printer, it might be helpful to have a separator page between them. A separator page can also be used to switch a printer between PostScript (a printer language) and PCL (Printer Control Language) on Hewlett-Packard (HP) and compatible printers. Four sample SEP separation

NOTE

The Print Spooled Documents First check box, located below the spool options, is selected by default. Normally, you want to keep it that way.

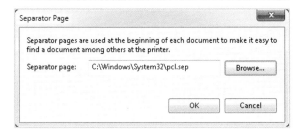

files come with Windows 7 SP1 and are located in the \Windows\System32\ folder:

- **Pcl.sep** prints a separation page before the start of each print job on PCL-compatible printers. If the printer handles both PostScript and PCL, it will be switched to PCL.

- **Pscript.sep** does *not* print a separation page, but printers with both PostScript and PCL will be switched to PostScript.

- **Sysprint.sep** prints a separation page before the start of each print job on PostScript-compatible printers.

- **Sysprtj.sep** is the same as Sysprint.sep, but in the Japanese language.

You can choose to have a separator page added at the beginning of each print job by clicking **Separator Page** on the Advanced tab of the printer's Properties dialog box, browsing for and selecting the page you want, clicking **Open**, and clicking **OK** twice.

Control Printing

To control printing means to control the process as it is taking place, whether with one print job or with several in line. If several print jobs are spooled at close to the same time, they form a *print queue*, waiting for earlier jobs to finish. You may control printing in several ways, as described next. These tasks are handled in the printer's window, which is similar to that shown in Figure 6-17, and is opened by selecting a printer and clicking **See What's Printing** in the Devices And Printers window, or by double-clicking the printer icon in the notification area of the taskbar and then clicking **See What's Printing**.

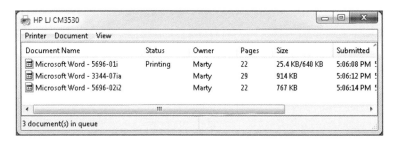

Figure 6-17: *Controlling printing takes place in the printer's window and allows you to pause, resume, restart, and cancel printing.*

NOTE

You cannot change the order in which documents are being printed by pausing the current document that is printing. You must either complete printing the current document or cancel it. You can, however, use Pause to get around intermediate documents that are not currently printing. For example, suppose you want to immediately print the third document in the queue, but the first document is currently printing. You must either let the first document finish printing or cancel it. You can then pause the second document before it starts printing, and the third document will begin printing when the first document is out of the way.

PAUSE, RESUME, AND RESTART PRINTING

While printing, a situation may occur (such as needing to add toner) where you want to pause and then resume printing, either for one or all documents:

- **Pause all documents**   In the printer's window, click the **Printer** menu, and click **Pause Printing**. "Paused" will appear in the title bar, and, if you look in the Printer menu, you will see a check mark in front of Pause Printing.

- **Resume printing all documents**   In the printer's window, click **Printer** and click **Pause Printing**. "Paused" disappears from the title bar and the check mark disappears from the Pause Printing option in the Printer menu.

- **Pause a document**   In the printer's window, select the document or documents to pause, click **Document**, and click **Pause**. "Paused" will appear in the Status column of the document(s) you selected.

- **Resume printing a paused document where it left off**   In the printer's window, select the document, click **Document**, and click **Resume**. "Printing" will appear in the Status column of the document selected.

- **Restart printing at the beginning of a document**   In the printer's window, select the document, click **Document**, and click **Restart**. "Restarting" and then "Printing" will appear in the Status column.

CANCEL PRINTING

Canceling printing can be done either at the printer level for all the jobs in the printer queue or at the document level for selected documents. A canceled job is deleted from the print queue and must be restarted by the original program.

- **Cancel a job**   In the printer's window, select the job or jobs that you want canceled. Click **Document** and click **Cancel**. Click **Cancel** a second time to confirm the cancellation. The job or jobs will disappear from the window and the queue.

- **Cancel all the jobs in the queue**   In the printer's window, click **Printer** and click **Cancel All Documents**. You are asked whether you are sure you want to cancel all documents. Click **Yes**. All jobs will disappear from the queue and the printer window.

REDIRECT DOCUMENTS

If you have two printers with the same print driver, you can redirect all the print jobs that are in the queue for one printer to the other, where they will be

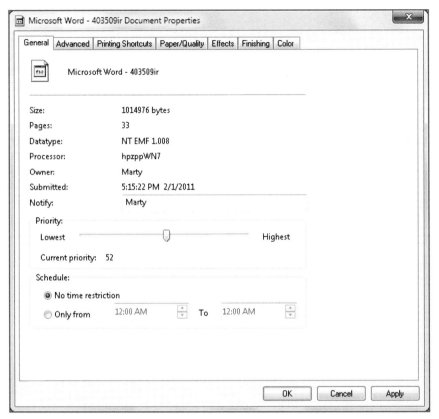

Figure 6-18: *Setting the properties of a document in the print queue can change its priority and when it prints.*

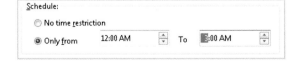

printed without having to be resubmitted. You do this by changing the port to which the queue is directed.

1. In the printer's window, click **Printer**, click **Properties**, and click the **Ports** tab.

2. If the second printer is in the list of ports, select it. Otherwise, click **Add Port** to open the Printer Ports dialog box. Click **Local Port** and click **New Port**, which opens the Port Name dialog box.

3. Enter the UNC (Uniform Naming Convention) name for the printer (for example, \\Server3\HPLJ9050 for an HP printer to the Server3 computer), and click **OK**.

4. Click **Close** and then click **OK**. The print queue will be redirected to the other printer.

CHANGE A DOCUMENT'S PROPERTIES

A document in a print queue has a Properties dialog box, shown in Figure 6-18, which is opened by right-clicking the document and selecting **Properties**. The General tab allows you to change a number of things:

- **Priority**   To change a document's default priority of 1, the lowest priority, so that the document can be printed before another that hasn't started printing yet, set the document's priority in the document's Properties dialog box to anything higher than the other document by dragging the **Priority** slider to the right.

- **Who to notify**   To change who is optionally notified of any special situations occurring during printing, as well as when a document has finished printing, put the name of another person (the individual's user name on a shared computer or network) in the **Notify** text box of the document's Properties dialog box.

- **Set print time**   To change when a job is printed, open a document's Properties dialog box, click **Only From** at the bottom under Schedule, and then enter the time range within which you want the job printed. This allows you to print large jobs, which might otherwise clog the print queue, at a time when there is little or no load.

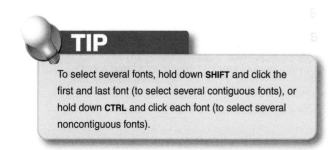

Figure 6-19: *Windows 7 SP1 comes with a large number of fonts, but you can add others.*

TIP

To select several fonts, hold down **SHIFT** and click the first and last font (to select several contiguous fonts), or hold down **CTRL** and click each font (to select several noncontiguous fonts).

Handle Fonts

A *font* is a set of characters with the same design, size, weight, and style. A font is a member of a *typeface* family, all with the same design. The font 12-point Arial bold italic is a member of the Arial typeface with a 12-point size, bold weight, and italic style. Windows 7 SP1 comes with a large number of fonts, a few of which are shown in Figure 6-19.

ADD FONTS

To add fonts to those that are installed by Windows 7 SP1:

1. Click **Start**, click **Control Panel**, click **Appearance And Personalization** in Category view, and click **Fonts**. The Fonts window opens as shown in Figure 6-19.

2. Either use Windows Explorer to locate a font (or fonts) on your computer (this can be a flash drive, a CD/DVD, or a hard disk) or on your network; or use Internet Explorer to download a font to your computer and then, with Windows Explorer, locate it so you can see and then select the actual font(s) you want to install.

3. Right-click the selected fonts, and then click **Install**. A message will tell you the fonts are being installed. When you are done, the new fonts will appear in the Fonts window.

DELETE FONTS

Remove fonts simply by selecting them in the Fonts window and pressing **DELETE** or by right-clicking the font(s) and clicking **Delete**. In either case, you are told that if the font is deleted some text might not appear as you intended and asked whether you are sure you want to do that. Click **Yes** if you are. The fonts will be deleted *permanently* and *cannot* be retrieved from the Recycle Bin.

USE FONTS

Fonts are used or specified from within a program. In Microsoft Word, for example, you can select a line of text and then open the Font drop-down list on the Formatting toolbar (in versions prior to Office 2007) or in the Font group (in Office 2007/2010). Every program is a little different. One nice feature in recent versions of Word is that the list shows what the fonts look like.

How To...

- *Play CDs*
- *Control the Volume*
- *Access Online Media*
- *Finding Your Music Online*
- *Buy Media Online*
- *Copy (Rip) CDs to Your Computer*
- *Organize Music*
- *Make (Burn) a Music CD*
- *Displaying Visualizations in Windows Media Player*
- *Copy to (Sync with) Music Players*
- *Play DVDs*
- *Preparing to Make a Movie*
- *Import Video from a Camcorder*
- *Make a Movie*
- *Complete a Movie*
- *Exploring Windows Media Center*

Chapter 7
Enjoying Multimedia

Multimedia is the combination of audio and video, with the term *media* referring to either audio or video. As an operating system, Windows 7 SP1 has to handle audio and video files and accept their input from a number of different devices. It has four major programs—Windows Media Player, Windows DVD Maker, Windows Media Center, and Windows Live Movie Maker—that enable you to work with multimedia files and read and write them onto CDs, DVDs, flash drives, and music players, as well as *stream* them to other computers (streaming sends audio or video files to another computer in such a way that the other computer can display the files as they are being sent). We'll look first at sound by itself, then at video with sound.

Work with Audio

Audio is sound. Windows 7 SP1 works with and uses sound in several ways, the simplest being to alert you of various events, like an incoming email message or closing down the system. Chapter 2 shows you how to customize the use of sounds for these purposes.

The other use of sound is to entertain or inform you—be it listening to music or lectures from CDs, Internet radio, or another Internet site. It is this use of sound that is the subject of this section.

Play CDs

Playing a CD is as easy as inserting a disc in the drive. When you do that, by default, Windows Media Player opens and starts playing the CD. The other alternative is that you will be asked if you want Windows Media Player to play the disc. In that case, if you click **Play Audio CD Using Windows Media Player**, Media Player will open and begin playing the disc. Initially, the on-screen view, called "Now Playing," is a small window, as shown in Figure 7-1. If you click **Switch To Library** in the upper-right corner under the Close button 🗗, a larger, more comprehensive window will open, as you can see in Figure 7-2. The Media Player library window has a variety of controls that enable you to determine how it functions and looks. These controls are located either in the functional controls and option menus at the top of the window or in the playback controls at the bottom.

Figure 7-1: *Windows Media Player Now Playing view shows you its controls when you move the mouse over it.*

Menu options   **Functional controls**

Media Guide   **Playback controls**

*Figure 7-2: **Windows Media Player Library view gives you access to a wide range of audio and video entertainment.***

- **Menu options** includes facilities to:
  - **Organize** the Media Player window.
  - **Stream** media from your computer.
  - **Create a playlist** of selected tracks.
- **Functional controls** allow selection of the primary Media Player functions:
  - **Rip CD** copies audio CDs to the Media Library.
  - **Rip settings** for audio being copied from a CD.
  - **Play** plays selected tracks and creates a playlist.
  - **Burn** copies playlists from the library to writable CDs and DVDs.
  - **Sync** synchronizes content between portable music devices and your PC.
- **Media Guide** opens the Windows Media Guide, an online media source for music, movies, TV, and radio.
- **Playback controls** provides CD player–like controls to play/pause, stop, go to a previous track, go to the next track, and adjust volume, as well as randomly play tracks (shuffle) and repeat a specific track.

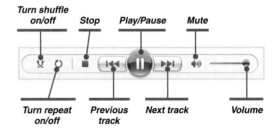

When you click any of the three tabs for the functional controls in the upper-right area, the list pane opens. The Play tab initially lists what is currently being played, but can be cleared and used to build your own playlist. The parts of the Media Player in Play mode are shown in Figure 7-3, and include:

- List options hides (closes) the list pane and manipulates the list.
- **Play to** starts an audio or video stream to a media device.
- **Clear list** stops what is being played and prepares the pane for creating a playlist.
- **Save list** saves the current playlist to your media library.
- **Shop for CD/DVD** enables you to buy the item you are listening to or watching.
- **Previous and Next** let you cycle through the playlists in your library.
- **Switch to Now Playing** collapses the window to just the small window shown in Figure 7-1.

Figure 7-3: *The list pane shows what is currently playing and is where playlists are created.*

Control the Volume

You can control your computer's audio volume from several places, including the physical volume control on your speakers or on your laptop computer, the volume control on the bottom-right of the playback controls of the Media Player, and the volume icon in the notification area on the right of the taskbar .

Clicking the **Volume** icon in the notification area opens a small Volume slider that you can drag for louder or softer sound, or you can click **Mute** (the blue speaker at the bottom of the slider) to do just that. Click anywhere on the desktop to close the Volume slider.

Access Online Media

If you have a broadband Internet connection (as described in Chapter 4) of at least 512 Kbps (more will improve your experience) and sound capability, you can find a large amount of media, including music, movies, and TV. Windows Media Player gives you access to this media through the Media Guide, whose icon is in the lower-left corner of the Media Player and opens the window shown in Figure 7-4.

To use the Media Guide to locate media from a closed Media Player:

1. Click the **Windows Media Player** icon on the taskbar (it is pinned there by default). If you don't have a Media Player icon on the taskbar, click **Start**, click **All Programs**, and click **Windows Media Player**.

2. Click the **Media Guide** icon in the lower-left corner of the Media Player. It may be that the Media Guide icon has been replaced by the Online Stores icon because that is what was last used. In that case, click the **Online Stores** down arrow, and click **Media Guide**.

3. Click in the **Search** text box; type the name of the piece, the performer, or the genre; and either press **ENTER** or click the **Search** magnifying glass. The search results list will appear.

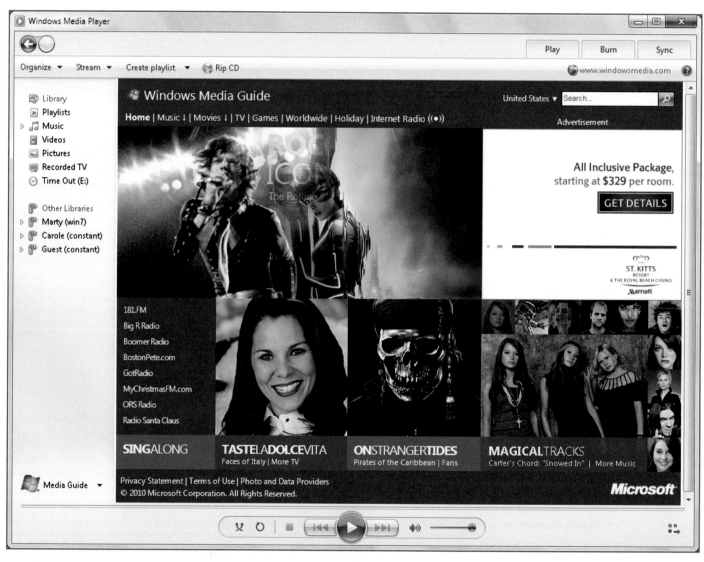

Figure 7-4: *The Media Guide facilitates locating music, movies, and TV media.*

TIP

Doing direct searches from your Internet browser may help you find what you want.

QUICKSTEPS

FINDING YOUR MUSIC ONLINE

Having spent my adolescent youth in the late 1950s, many of my favorite songs from that era are by The Platters and include *Unchained Melody*, *Smoke Gets in Your Eyes*, and *Twilight Time*. You can easily find and listen to your favorite music and most other popular songs by simply typing a song's name into either the Google or Bing search text box. For example, I might type <u>Platters – Unchained Melody</u>. This produces a list of links to sites where you can listen to, download, and buy the song, as you can see on the left of Figure 7-5. Many of the links that are found are on YouTube. Clicking one of these links opens YouTube and begins playing the song. On the page that opens there are links to either other songs by the same artist or other artists performing the same song, as you can see on the right of Figure 7-5.

4. Select your choice within the results list, or if you don't find what you want, try a different search. From the results, you often are able to listen to or view a segment and find out where you can buy the entire piece.

5. Close the Media Player when you are ready.

Buy Media Online

There are many sources of media on the Internet. Two paths to buying media are through the Online Stores in the Media Player and through the very popular iTunes.

USE MEDIA PLAYER

The Online Stores in the Media Player provides links to several stores—links that you can follow to locate and buy media.

1. Click the **Windows Media Player** icon on the taskbar. If you don't have a Media Player icon on the taskbar, click **Start**, click **All Programs**, and click **Windows Media Player**.

2. Click the **Online Stores** icon if it is displayed; otherwise, click the **Media Guide** down arrow, and click **Browse All Online Stores**. The Online Stores page will open and display several stores that sell music, videos, and audio books, all of which can be downloaded.

3. Click a store that looks promising and follow the instructions to use that store and download the media to your computer and into your music or video library.

4. Close the Media Player when you are ready.

USE ITUNES

iTunes is an online media store operated by Apple, Inc. and claims to be the world's number-one music store. Apple also offers the iTunes Player, which you can download for free and which is a competitor to the Windows Media Player.

1. Click the **Internet Explorer** icon on your taskbar to open it. Click in the address bar, and type <u>itunes.com</u>.

2. Click the **What Is iTunes**, **What's On iTunes**, and **How To** links to learn more about iTunes. If needed, download QuickTime, a video player, to view the video on installing iTunes. Follow the online instructions, clicking the various QuickTime and Windows controls as needed.

*Figure 7-5: **Finding music online is simply a matter of typing the name of the performer and/or the song in a search text box and then selecting the one you want to hear, as shown on the left. You can then go on to related songs as you see on the right.***

CAUTION

iTunes and many other online stores make it *very easy to buy from them,* and you can quickly run up a sizable bill. You need to create an account with the store and provide your name, address, email, and credit card info. Once you do this, it is almost too easy to buy in the future!

3. When you are ready, download and install iTunes, following the instructions and clicking the appropriate controls as needed.

4. After the installer has restarted your computer, double-click the **iTunes** icon on your desktop [icon]. iTunes will start, ask you a series of set-up questions, and then open.

5. If it isn't already selected, click **iTunes Store** to open the window shown in Figure 7-6. Use the various links and the search box to select and possibly download the media you want.

6. Close iTunes when you are finished.

Figure 7-6: *iTunes is both a media player and a popular site for downloading media.*

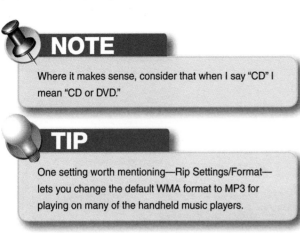

Copy (Rip) CDs to Your Computer

Media Player gives you the ability to copy (or "rip") CD tracks that you like to your hard disk so that you can build and manage a library of your favorite music and copy this material to a recordable CD or DVD, or to a music player. To copy from a CD (see Figure 7-7):

1. Insert the CD from which you want to copy tracks. If it doesn't automatically start playing, click **Play Audio CD Using Windows Media Player** to open Windows Media Player.

2. Click **Switch To Library** in the upper-right corner. In the details pane, select the tracks you want to copy to your hard disk by clicking the check boxes to the left of each track. Click **Play** in the playback controls to listen to the tracks and to make sure your choices are correct.

3. If you wish, click **Rip Settings** and review the settings that are available to you. For the most part, the default settings provide the best middle ground between high quality and file size.

4. When you are satisfied that you have selected the correct tracks and settings, click **Rip CD**. The selected tracks will be copied to your hard disk. When you are done, remove the CD and close Media Player.

Organize Music

Once you have copied several CDs and have downloaded other music to your hard disk, you will likely want

Figure 7-7: *Media Player can be used to build a music library from your CDs.*

this material organized. When music and videos are copied to the library, the contents are automatically indexed alphabetically by album, artist, and genre. You may want to combine selected tracks into a *playlist* that allows you to play pieces from several albums. To build a new playlist:

1. Open Media Player and click **Create Playlist** in the menu options area. Type the name you want for the new playlist, and press **ENTER**. A new playlist will appear in the list of playlists in the navigation pane.

2. Open an album, artist, or genre; and select a piece or the pieces (hold down **CTRL** as you click multiple pieces) that you want in the new playlist. Drag the piece(s) to the playlist title in the navigation pane.

3. Select other pieces you want to add, and drag them to the playlist title in the navigation pane. Click the playlist to display the contents in the detail pane, or double-click the playlist to display it in the Play tab in the list pane and begin to play it.

   –Or–

1. Open Media Player and click the **Play** tab to open it in the list pane. Select and display in the details pane the music you want in the playlist. Drag the piece(s) you want to the list pane, as you can see in Figure 7-8.

2. When you have added all the pieces that you initially want (you can always add more later), click **Save List**, type a name, and press **ENTER**.

3. Listen to the playlist by clicking the play button in the playback controls. When you are done, click **Clear List**, click the **Play** tab to close the list pane, and close Media Player.

Make (Burn) a Music CD

Once you have created a playlist (see "Organize Music" earlier in this chapter), you can write (or "burn") it to a writable CD using Media Player's Burn feature.

*Figure 7-8: **Media Player provides a way to manage the media you store on your computer, including building playlists.***

TIP

When listening to a playlist, you can randomize the order in which the pieces will play by clicking **Turn Shuffle On** in the playback controls, which is the first button on the left. Click it a second time to return to normal play.

This creates an "audio" CD that works in a portable or car CD player. This is not the same as simply making a copy of the digital files as explained in step 4 below.

1. Put a blank recordable disc in the CD recording drive. The AutoPlay dialog box will appear and ask what you want to do. Click **Burn An Audio CD** to open Windows Media Player with the Burn functional area displayed.

2. Open your playlists in the navigation pane, and drag a playlist (or individual songs from an open playlist) that you want on the CD to the Burn List on the right. Do this in the order you want the songs played. You can see how much of the CD is being used and the amount of time remaining just above the Burn List, as shown in Figure 7-9.

3. You can make corrections to the Burn List by dragging additional songs there until you use up the remaining time, or by right-clicking a song on the Burn List and clicking **Remove From List** in the context menu that opens. You can also clear the Burn List and start over.

Figure 7-9: *Burning a playlist to a writable CD allows you to create a disc that has just your favorite songs.*

Cancel burn Clear list

CD Drive (J:)
Audio CD
CD R
Burning: 16% completed
Next drive ▸

4. When you are sure you have the list of pieces you want to burn, click **Start Burn**. The digital files will first be converted to analog music files and then written to a CD or DVD. You can see the progress in the thermometer bar near the top of the list pane (it is not very fast!). When the burn is complete and if no one has changed the default settings, the disc will be ejected from the drive. Write the title on the disc with a soft felt-tip marker, or use a LightScribe drive to burn a label on the special discs you use for this purpose.

The resulting CD should be playable in most CD players.

Copy to (Sync with) Music Players

Windows Media Player allows you to plug in a digital music device, such as an MP3 player, and transfer music to and from (sync with) the device.

1. Start Windows Media Player, and click **Sync** in the Windows Media Player functional controls. You will be told to connect your device.

2. Start your device and then plug it into your computer. The first time you do that, Windows will install a driver for it, and then the AutoPlay dialog box will appear.

AutoPlay

IPOD (L:)

General options

Open folder to view files
using Windows Explorer

Speed up my system
using Windows ReadyBoost

View more AutoPlay options in Control Panel

You can manually select playlists and songs that you want copied to the device, as shown in Figure 7-10.

3. In the Devices Setup dialog box, click **Finish** or **Cancel**, depending on your situation. If you click **Cancel**, drag the playlists and/or songs you want on the device to the Sync Lists on the right. If you wish, you can play the Sync List by double-clicking the first playlist or song.

4. When you are certain that you have all the music in the Sync List that you want on your device, click **Start Sync**. The music will be copied to the device.

UICKSTEPS

DISPLAYING VISUALIZATIONS IN WINDOWS MEDIA PLAYER

The Media Player's Now Playing window, shown in Figure 7-1, can display a graphic visualization of the music that is playing instead of the album cover. Several visualizations come with Media Player, and you can download more. To display a visualization:

1. Right-click the **Now Playing** window, click **Visualizations**, select one of the three types of visualizations (Album Art and Info Center View are static displays), and then click the visualization you want to use.

2. If you want to download additional visualizations, right-click the **Now Playing** window, click **Visualizations**, and click **Download Visualizations**. Then follow the instructions on the websites you will visit.

NOTE

If you choose to sync your entire library, consider the Shuffle Music option. With this option selected, Windows will put the music on the device such that songs will randomly play. Each time you plug your device into your computer, a new random order will be established and copied to the device.

*Figure 7-10: **A digital music device can mirror your Media Player library if it has enough room and that is what you want.***

Work with Video

Windows 7 SP1 lets you watch videos from a DVD, from live or recorded TV, or downloaded from the Internet using Windows Media Player or Windows Media Center. It also allows you to capture videos and still images from a digital camcorder or digital camera using Windows Live Photo Gallery and then edit those into your own movie using Windows Live Movie Maker.

Play DVDs

Playing DVDs is as easy as playing CDs: Simply insert a DVD into its drive. When you do that, the AutoPlay dialog box will appear, and you will be asked if you want to play the DVD using Windows Live Media Player. We'll discuss Media Center later in this chapter, but if you click **Play DVD Movie** using Windows Media Player, the player will open and play the disc. The Media Player controls are virtually the same for DVDs as they are for CDs, as you can see in Figure 7-11, except the View Full Screen option enlarges the movie or video you are watching to fit the full screen, and the DVD menu has options for viewing menus and special features on the DVD.

Figure 7-11: *Watching movies, or in this case a concert, is increasingly popular, especially with a laptop on a trip.*

PREPARING TO MAKE A MOVIE

Making a movie with a computer takes more hardware than any other task. The faster your CPU, the more memory it has, the better your video display adapter, and the larger your disk, the more smoothly the task will go. The beauty is that most recent computers have what you need by default.

REQUIREMENTS CHECKLIST

The recommended hardware requirements for making movies are as follows:

COMPONENT	RECOMMENDED HARDWARE
CPU	2.4 GHz dual core
RAM memory	2GB
Hard drive free space	60GB
Optical drive	DVD±R
Video display card	Supports DirectX 9.0c, WDDM driver, Windows Aero, Pixel Shader 2.0, 32 bits/pixel, 128MB dedicated video memory or more
Video recording from DV camcorders	IEEE 1394 FireWire card, OHCI-compliant
Video capture from analog VCR/camera/TV	Windows 7 SP1–compatible video capture card
Audio capture from microphone, tape	Windows 7 SP1–compatible audio card and microphone

Continued . . .

Import Video from a Camcorder

Importing video directly from your camcorder to your hard disk is done using the Windows Live Photo Gallery.

1. Click **Start**, click **All Programs**, and click **Windows Live Photo Gallery**. In the Home tab click **Import**.

2. Plug your camcorder into an OHCI-compliant FireWire port on your computer, and turn it on. Windows 7 SP1 will detect it, install the necessary driver software, and open the AutoPlay dialog box. Click **Close** in the AutoPlay dialog box.

3. In the Import Photos And Videos dialog box, click **Refresh**. Select your digital video camera, and click **Import**. The Import Video dialog box will appear. Type the name you want for the video, click either **Import The Entire Video** or **Choose Parts Of The Video**, and click **Next** (you can also burn the entire video to a DVD, but here we want to make a movie from the video).

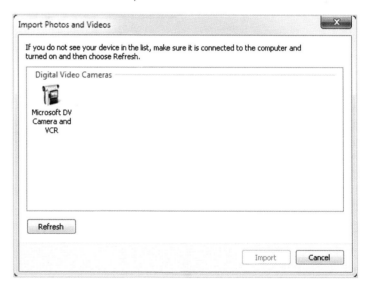

If you chose to import the entire video and your camcorder uses tape, the tape will be rewound, and then the capture will begin playing and importing the video without controls to pause, rewind, or fast-forward it. When the end of the video is reached, the importation will stop, the Import Video dialog box will close, and you will see a message telling you it is finished. Click **OK**.

UICKSTEPS

PREPARING TO MAKE A MOVIE

(Continued)

NOTES ON REQUIREMENTS

- Memory is most important. The more, the better.
- CPU capability is a close second in importance. To work with full-motion video, you need a lot of it. A 2.4 MHz dual core is really the minimum.
- The initial capture of video from a camcorder to your computer can use approximately 12GB per hour captured in disk space.
- The video display card has become quite important to Windows Live Movie Maker. It will not work without the minimum shown in the table. See the Note on how to check this.
- With a digital video (DV) camcorder and an IEEE 1394 FireWire interface, get an Open Host Controller Interface (OHCI)–compliant FireWire card for your computer, if one isn't built in.
- A video capture card can bring in a video signal from a TV, a VCR, an analog camcorder, and (in most cases) a DV camcorder; however, the result is not as good as a digital recording.

TIP

If you are using Movie Maker to record an analog signal coming from a video capture card and are having problems—which is common—don't fight it. Use the software that comes with the video capture card to create a file on your hard disk, and then import that file into Movie Maker.

–Or–

If you chose to import portions of the video, the camcorder will not be rewound and you can use its controls to position the video. Also, you are given controls in the Import Video dialog box. Position the video in your camcorder to a little before where you want to start recording using either its controls or those in the Import Video dialog box, and click the **Stop** icon. Then, in the dialog box, click the **Play** icon. When you are at the spot you want start importing, click **Import**. You can import some of the video, stop it, reposition the video, and again click **Play** and **Import**. When you are done with the importation, click **Finish** to close the Import Video dialog box.

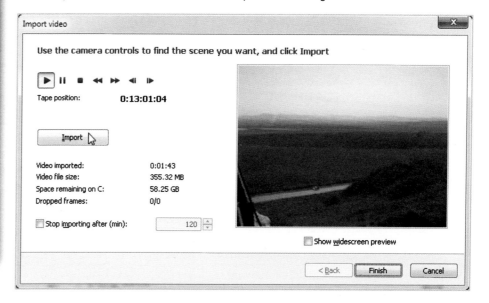

Windows Live Photo Gallery will show you where your video is stored. From either Photo Gallery or Windows Media Player, you can play the captured video by locating and double-clicking it.

Make a Movie

Making a movie out of the imported camcorder video and other material involves selecting and editing the available material; assembling it into the order in which you want it; adding narration, titles, and special effects; and

NOTE

There can be some copyright issues when using music from professionally recorded CDs, DVDs, and tapes. If you are making a movie solely for your own use and are not going to put it on the Internet, sell it, or otherwise distribute it, then there are no issues. If you are going to use your movie in any of the prohibited ways and it contains someone else's copyrighted material (either audio or video), you need to get permission from the copyright holder.

TIP

It is better to import a longer video in smaller chunks or clips that you can then blend together into a movie.

NOTE

In Chapter 4, when I suggested you install Windows Live, Movie Maker was not selected by default so you may not have installed it at that time. Therefore, it may not be in your Windows Live list and you will need to go back to the Windows Live site and install it. See Chapter 4 for more information.

finally publishing the finished product. Windows Live Movie Maker provides the means to do that. While working in Movie Maker, you are working on what Movie Maker calls a "project," which is a fluid collection of video clips, still pictures, titles, audio clips, narration, and special effects that you have added and laid out along a timeline. So long as you are in the project and have not published the movie, you can change almost anything. Projects can be saved and reopened for as long as you like.

To begin making a movie using the imported camcorder video and other material:

1. Click **Start**, click **All Programs**, and click **Windows Live Movie Maker**. Movie Maker opens with a new project tentatively named "My Movie." Start the project by adding content.

2. Click **Add Videos And Photos** in the Home tab Add group. In the Add Videos And Photos dialog box that appears, locate and select the video footage you want to work with, and click **Open**.

3. Repeat step 2, as shown in Figure 7-12, adding video footage, still pictures, and music (click **Add Music** in the Add group) that you want to use. Most audio, video, and picture file types are supported. When you have all the material you want, drag it around the content (right) pane until it is in the order that you want.

You can continue to add, remove (right-click and click **Remove**), and rearrange elements in your project throughout its creation. You can also:

- **Trim** video clips
- **Add transitions** between pictures
- **Adjust the duration** for which a still image is shown
- **Add titles** to the video
- **Adjust the mix** between the sound on a video and the added music

TRIM VIDEO CLIPS

You can remove unwanted frames by *trimming*, or deleting, frames from the beginning or end of a video clip.

1. Select the video clip you want to trim.

2. Click the **Video Tools Edit** tab, and click **Trim Tool** in the Editing group. The Trim Tool will appear superimposed upon the progress slider below the preview window.

Figure 7-12: *The process of making a movie entails selecting and editing video, audio, and still images.*

3. If you want to trim the beginning of the clip, play the clip to the point at which you want to trim, and then drag the left trim handle to that point, dragging it back and forth until it is correctly placed.

4. To trim the right end of the clip, drag the right trim handle to the left until you get to the point where you want to trim off the rest of the clip.

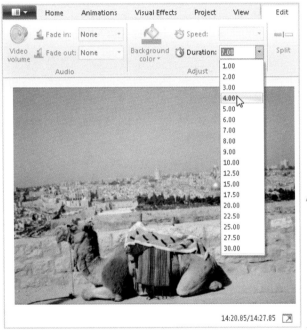

5. When the trim handles are positioned at both ends where you want them, click **Save Trim** in the Trim tab Trim group to save the trim positions and close the Trim operation.

ADD TRANSITIONS

When you bring in or drag a clip or a still image to the workspace, it simply abuts the preceding clip. The last frame of the preceding clip plays or a still image is displayed, and then the first frame of the new clip plays or the next still image is displayed. Movie Maker provides several transitions that you can add to smooth out the progression from one element to the next.

1. Click the rightmost clip or image of a pair where you want a transition.

2. Click the **Animations** tab, and click the transition you want to use. The focus will shift back to the left member of the pair so you can click the **Play** icon to see the transition.

ADJUST DURATION OF STILL IMAGES

By default, still images that are used in a movie are displayed for 7 seconds. You can adjust this to anything from 1 to 30 seconds.

1. Select the still image whose duration you want to change.

2. Click the **Video Tools Edit** tab, click the **Duration** down arrow in the Adjust group, and click the duration (in seconds) you want to use.

ADD TEXT

Windows Live Movie Maker provides the means to add titles and text to movies you create. You have three choices of text that can be added from the Home tab Add group:

- **Title**, which is text in its own set of frames before the currently selected frame
- **Caption**, which is text that is displayed on the current set of frames or on a still photo
- **Credits**, which are added at the end of either a selected set of frames or still picture(s) and can have headings of "Credits," "Director," "Starring," and "Location" by clicking the down arrow

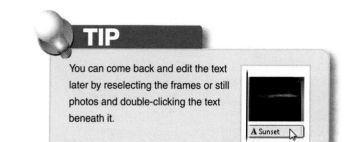

TIP

You can come back and edit the text later by reselecting the frames or still photos and double-clicking the text beneath it.

To add, for example, a caption:

1. Select the video or still image where you want the text, and in the Home tab Add group, click **Caption**. A text box with eight sizing handles will appear on the selected image with "[Enter text here]" selected, as you can see in Figure 7-13.

2. In the Text Tools Format tab, select the font, its size, whether it is bold and/or italic, and its color in the Font group, as well as the transparency and alignment within the text box in the Paragraph group.

3. Type the text you want in the title. When you are finished, use the sizing handles to size the box to position the text. Use **SHIFT+ENTER** to create a line break.

Figure 7-13: Movie Maker gives you a number of options for adding text and how that text is handled.

4. Point on an edge of the text box to get a four-headed arrow, and then drag the text box to where you want it in the image.

5. Try out the various effects to see if you want to use any of them (too much can be annoying).

6. When you are ready, click another image to close the text box and leave the text.

ADD MUSIC

You can add background music to your video by including an existing music track.

1. In the Home tab Add group, click the **Add Music** icon (not the down arrow).

2. In the Windows Explorer window that opens, navigate to and double-click the music track you want to include. The Music Tools Options tab will appear and you'll see the music track appear above the frames over which it plays.

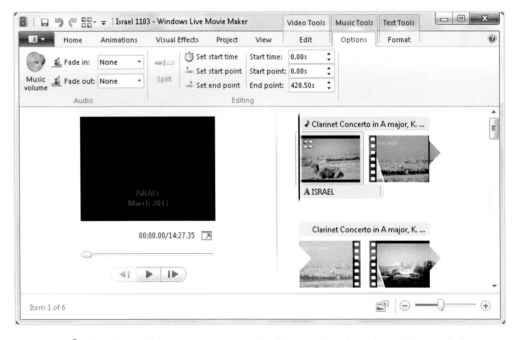

3. Click **Music Volume** and then drag the slider to adjust the volume. Click the **Fade In** or **Fade Out** down arrows, and select how you want the music to fade in and out. Similarly, set the **Start Time**, **Start Point**, and **End Point** by either entering the number in seconds or by clicking the **Set** commands and dragging the positioning bar in the clips.

MIX SOUND

After adding a music track you have two soundtracks—one that was on the original video and one that you have added. By default, the volume level of both tracks is the same. You can adjust the relative level between the two soundtracks in the Project tab by clicking **Audio Mix**. The Mix slider will appear. Dragging the slider to the left increases the relative level of the video soundtrack; dragging it to the right increases the relative level of the music you have added. In both cases, the change is for the entire project. When you complete a change, close the slider by clicking anywhere below it.

Complete a Movie

The final step in making a movie is to create a movie file that you can upload to the Internet or output, either for a DVD or a portable device.

SAVE THE MOVIE FILE

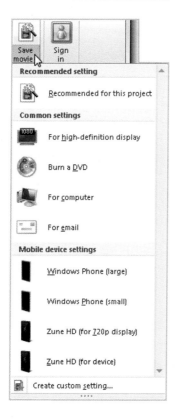

If you want to save your movie to replay on your computer or put it on a DVD:

1. In the Home tab, click the **Save Movie** down arrow, and review the choices for saving this movie, as shown in Table 7-1.

2. Click how you want to save the movie (the Recommended Setting is a good middle ground).

3. In the Save Movie dialog box that appears, select the drive and folder in which you want to save your movie, enter a name for it, and click **Save** (this will take several minutes).

SETTING	DISPLAY	FILE SIZE/MINUTE
Recommended	640 × 480 pixels	50.98 MB
High Definition	1440 × 1080 pixels	173.03 MB
Burn A DVD	720 × 480 pixels	21.39 MB
For Computer	640 × 480 pixels	40.71 MB
For Email	320 × 240 pixels	11.97 MB

Table 7-1: *Settings for Saving a Movie*

EXPLORING WINDOWS MEDIA CENTER

With the right equipment, Windows Media Center allows you to view, record, and play back live TV. It also provides an enhanced playback and viewing experience with DVDs, CDs, and the music and photographic libraries you have on your computer. It connects you to web services from Microsoft and other vendors. Windows Media Center is available in Windows 7 SP1 Home Premium, Professional, Enterprise, and Ultimate editions.

To effectively use and get the full benefit from Windows Media, you need all the recommended computer components discussed in the "Preparing to Make a Movie" QuickSteps, and, if you want live TV, a TV tuner card in your computer and a connection to TV media. The tuner cards are available for moderate amounts from several companies. Look for compatibility with Windows Media Center.

To use Media Center:

1. Click **Start**, click **All Programs**, and click **Windows Media Center**. The first time you do that, you will go through an initial setup.

2. Click **Continue** and then click the **Express** arrow. Windows will look at the hardware that is available on your computer. If you have a TV tuner card, you will then need to click **Live TV Set Up**, and Media Center will be configured for the type of TV signal you have (antenna, cable, or satellite).

3. Then you will be asked questions about your ZIP code so that you can receive an online TV guide tailored to your local area. When you are done with the setup, you will see the main Media Center window shown below.

Continued . . .

With the DVD choice, Movie Maker will save the project, which may take a considerable amount of time if your video is of any length, and you will be told when it is complete.

4. Click **Open Folder** to open the folder in Windows Explorer that contains your new video. Leave this window open; you will be using it again in a minute.

SAVE A MOVIE TO DVD

You can burn your new movie file onto a DVD, which you could also have done in the previous set of steps.

1. Click **Start**, click **All Programs**, and click **Windows DVD Maker**. If this is the first time you have used Windows DVD Maker, click **Choose Photos And Videos**.

2. Position the Windows DVD Maker window and the Windows Explorer window with your video so you can see them both.

3. Drag your video from Windows Explorer to DVD Maker. Type a name for the DVD title, and click **Next**.

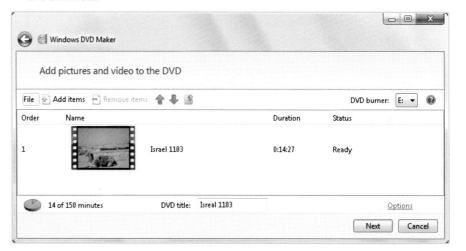

QUICKFACTS

EXPLORING WINDOWS MEDIA CENTER *(Continued)*

At this point, you can use your mouse, the keyboard, or the TV remote control that came with your TV tuner card to navigate (move your mouse to see its controls) and watch TV, either in a window on your screen or in the default full screen. If you don't have a tuner card, you can play Internet and recorded TV. The possibilities of what you can do are significant.

TIP

Saving a movie is equivalent to printing a document: You still have the original content to rebuild the movie, but the movie itself can't be edited.

NOTE

Opening a *project* opens the media in Movie Maker, where it can be edited. Opening a *movie* sets it up for playback in Media Player or other video display programs and devices.

4. If you wish to see your video, click **Preview**, use the player controls, and when you are done, click **OK**. Review the text, customization, and style alternatives to add a menu to your DVD, including being able to select among multiple videos.

5. When you are ready, click **Burn**. Put a blank DVD in your drive, and the process will begin. It will take a bit of time, depending on how long your movie is and the speed of your computer and DVD drive.

6. When the DVD is created, it will be ejected from the drive and you'll be asked if you want to make another. Remove and label the disc using a soft felt-tip marker.

7. If you want to make another copy, click that option and insert another blank disc; otherwise, click **Close** and click **Close** again to close Windows DVD Maker. Click **Yes** to save your DVD project, enter a name, and click **Save**.

SHARE ON THE INTERNET

If you want, you can save your movie on the Internet.

1. In the Home tab Share group, click one of the Internet sites on which you want to save your video.

2. Depending on the site you select, you may have to register and enter an ID and password.

3. Follow the instructions to enter such things as a title, description, and other information. Movie Maker will then make the movie (a slow process), and it will be uploaded to the Internet. You will see a message when the process is complete.

Chapter 8
Controlling Security

Controlling computer security is a complex subject because of the many different aspects of computing that need protection. In this chapter you'll see how to control who uses a computer, control what users do, and protect data stored in the computer.

Control Who Is a User

Controlling who uses a computer means identifying the users to the computer, giving them a secure way of signing on to the computer, and preventing everyone else from using it. This is achieved through the process of adding and managing users and passwords.

With Windows 7 SP1, like previous versions of Windows, the first user of a computer is, by default, an administrator; however, the administrator operates like a standard user until there is a need to be an administrator. Then a Windows feature called *User Account Control* (UAC) pops up and asks if you want to allow a program to make changes. If so, click **Yes** to proceed. A person who is not an administrator in the same circumstance would have to enter an administrator's password to continue.

NOTE

This book talks about setting up *local* user accounts, which are those that are set up on and use a local computer, as well as a workgroup local area network (LAN). If your computer is part of a domain (generally found in larger organizations—see Chapter 9 for a discussion of domains), it is important to use domain user accounts that are set up on a domain controller rather than local user accounts, since local user accounts are not recognized by the domain.

NOTE

There are three views of the Control Panel: the Category view, which is the default; the Large Icons view; and the Small Icons view. The Category view is a hierarchical one in which you first select a category and then the control. In the two icon views, you directly select the control. To change the view, click the **View By** down arrow and then click the view you want. This book assumes you are looking at the Category view, unless otherwise mentioned.

TIP

If your personal account on your computer is currently set up as an Administrator account, it is strongly recommended that you create a new Standard User account and use that for your everyday computer use. Only use the Administrator account for installing software, changing and adding user information, and performing other tasks requiring an administrator.

Even though you may initially be an administrator, *it is strongly recommended that your normal everyday account be as a standard user.* The reason for this is that if you are signed on as an administrator and a hacker or malevolent software (called "malware") enters your system at the same time, the hacker or software might gain administrator privileges through you. The best solution is to use a separate administrator account with a strong password just for installing software, working with users, and performing other tasks that require extensive administrator work.

Set Up Users

If you have several people using your computer, each person should be set up as a separate user. To add users to your computer, or even to change your user characteristics (as well as to perform most other tasks in this chapter), you must be logged on as an administrator, so you first need to accomplish that. Then you may want to change the characteristics of your account and add a Standard User account for yourself. Finally, if you have multiple people using your computer, you may want to set up separate user accounts and have each user sign in to his or her account.

LOG ON AS AN ADMINISTRATOR

The procedure for logging on as an administrator depends on what was done when Windows 7 SP1 was installed on your computer:

- If you installed Windows 7 SP1 on your computer, or if you bought a new computer with it already installed and did nothing special to the default installation regarding administrator privileges, you should be the administrator and know the administrator's password (if you established one).

- If you did not do the installation or you got the computer with Windows 7 SP1 already installed and you are unsure about your administrator status or password, the instructions here will help you log on as an administrator. The first step is to determine the administrator status on your computer.

   Click **Start** and in the Start menu click **Control Panel**. In Category view, click **User Accounts And Family Safety**, and then in any view click **User Accounts**. The User Accounts window opens, as shown in Figure 8-1.

Figure 8-1: **Setting up users provides a way of protecting each user from the others and the computer from unauthorized use.**

If the window shows you are an administrator, you can skip these steps. To make changes to an account, see the next section, "Change Your Account."

–Or–

If you are not an administrator, someone else on your computer must be. Ask that administrator to change your account type or facilitate your signing on as an administrator. Once that is done skip to "Change Your Account."

CHANGE YOUR ACCOUNT

You can change an account name, change the display picture, add or change a password, and possibly change the account type.

1. Click **Start** and click **Control Panel**. In Category view, click **User Accounts And Family Safety**, and then in any view click **User Accounts**.

2. Click **Change Your Account Name**. If you are not already logged on as an administrator, the User Account Control dialog box will appear and ask you to type an administrator's password.

3. Type a new name, and click **Change Name**.

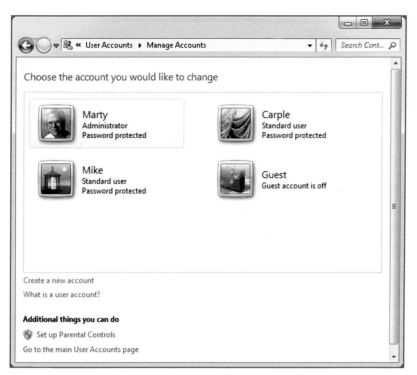

Figure 8-2: *The Manage Accounts window allows you to create and manage user accounts.*

In a similar manner, you can change your display picture. If you are the only administrator, you will not be allowed to change your account type or delete your account. Changing and setting passwords are discussed in the "Use Passwords" section in this chapter.

SET UP ANOTHER USER

To set up another user account, possibly a Standard User account for your use:

1. Click **Start** and click **Control Panel**. In Category view, click **User Accounts And Family Safety**, and then in any view click **User Accounts**. The User Accounts window opens.

2. Click **Manage Another Account**, and, if needed, type a password and click **Yes** to open the Manage Accounts window, shown in Figure 8-2.

3. Click **Create A New Account**. Type a name of up to 20 characters. Note that it cannot contain just periods, spaces, or the @ symbol; it cannot contain " / \ [ ] : ; | = ,+ * ? < >; and leading spaces or periods are dropped.

4. Accept the default account type, **Standard User**, or click **Administrator** as the account type. You can see a summary of the privileges available to each user type.

5. Click **Create Account**. You are returned to the Manage Accounts window. Changing other aspects of the account is described in later sections of this chapter.

Use Passwords

Passwords are the primary keys used to allow some people to use a computer and to keep others away. While there are recent alternatives to passwords (see "Replace Passwords" in this chapter), most computer protection depends on them.

Create a password for Jim's account

Jim
Standard user

You are creating a password for Jim.

If you do this, Jim will lose all EFS-encrypted files, personal certificates and stored passwords for Web sites or network resources.

To avoid losing data in the future, ask Jim to make a password reset floppy disk.

New password

Confirm new password

If the password contains capital letters, they must be typed the same way every time.
How to create a strong password

Type a password hint

The password hint will be visible to everyone who uses this computer.
What is a password hint?

Create password   Cancel

*Figure 8-3: **Creating, changing, or deleting a password will remove all items that are based on passwords, such as encrypted files, certificates, and other passwords.***

CREATE A PASSWORD

After setting up a new user account, you can add a password to it that will then be required to use that account.

1. Click **Start** and click **Control Panel**. In Category view, click **User Accounts And Family Safety**, and then in any view click **User Accounts**. The User Accounts window opens.

2. If it is not your account that you want to add a password to, click **Manage Another Account**. If needed, type a password, click **Yes**, and click the account you want. In your account or in the other account that opens (this cannot be the Guest account because that cannot have a password), click **Create A Password**.

   The Create Password window will open, as shown in Figure 8-3. Note the warning message. This is true only if the user already has a password that has been used to encrypt files, create certificates, and access websites and network resources. If you create a new password for this person, it will replace the old one, and all the places where the old one has been used will no longer be available even with the new password. This is the case every time you create, change, or delete a password.

3. Type the new password, click in the second text box, type the new password again to confirm it, click in the third text box, type a nonobvious hint to help you remember the password, and click **Create Password**.

4. Close the Change An Account window.

CHANGE A PASSWORD

It is a good idea to change your password periodically in case it has been compromised.

1. Click **Start** and click **Control Panel**. In Category view, click **User Accounts And Family Safety**, and then in any view click **User Accounts**. The User Accounts window opens.

2. If it is not your account that you want to change, click **Manage Another Account**. If needed, type a password, click **Yes**, and click the account you want to change. In your account or in the other account that opens, click **Change The Password**.

3. In your account, type the current password, and click in the second text box. In either your or another's account, type a new password, click in the next text box, and type the new password again to confirm it. Click in the final text box, type a nonobvious hint to help you remember the password, and click **Change Password**.

4. Close the Change An Account window.

REMOVE A PASSWORD

If you move a computer to a location that doesn't need a password—for example, if it is not accessible to anyone else, or if you want to remove a password for some other reason—you can do so.

1. Click **Start** and click **Control Panel**. In Category view, click **User Accounts And Family Safety**, and then in any view click **User Accounts**. The User Accounts window opens.

2. If it is not your account in which you want to remove the password, click **Manage Another Account**. If needed, type a password, click **Yes**, and click the account you want. In your account or in the other account that opens, click **Remove The Password**.

3. If it is your account, type the current password, and, in any case, click **Remove Password**.

4. Close the Change An Account window.

Reset a Password

Windows 7 SP1 allows you to reset a password you have forgotten if you have previously created a password reset disk, which can be a USB flash drive, memory card, or CD (I recommend an inexpensive smaller USB flash drive).

CREATE A RESET DISK

1. Insert a USB flash drive or memory card in its socket, or insert a writable CD into its drive. Close the AutoPlay window if it opens.

2. Click **Start** and click **Control Panel**. In Category view, click **User Accounts And Family Safety**, and then in any view click **User Accounts**. The User Accounts window opens.

3. Click **Create A Password Reset Disk** in the list of tasks on the left. If needed, type a password and click **Yes**.

4. The Forgotten Password Wizard starts. Click **Next**. Click the drive down arrow, and select the drive on which you want to create the password key. Click **Next**.

5. Type the current user account password, and again click **Next**. The disk will be created. When this process is done, click **Next**. Then click **Finish**. Remove and label the disk, and store it in a safe place.

6. Close the User Accounts window.

TIP

For a password to be *strong*, it must be eight or more characters long; use both upper- and lowercase letters; and use a mixture of letters, numbers, and symbols, which include ! # $ % ^ & * and spaces. It also should *not* be a recognizable word, name, or date. Instead of a password such as "mymoney," consider using something like this: "my$Money23."

CAUTION

With a password reset disk, anyone can reset a password. Therefore, it is important to store the reset disk in a safe place.

CAUTION

If you or someone else changes your password, all passwords and encrypted files tied to the original password are permanently inaccessible with the new password. If you use a password reset disk to reset your password, you will retain access to all your original information.

NOTE

A CD, memory card, or USB flash drive can hold the password reset for only one user at a time, but it is just a file on the device and can store other information if you want.

USE A RESET DISK

If you have forgotten your password and there isn't another person with administrator permissions on your computer who can reset it, you can use a reset disk you have previously created.

1. Start your computer. When you see the Welcome screen, click your user name. If you have forgotten your password, click the right arrow. You will be told that the user name or password is incorrect.

2. Click **OK** to return to the password entry, and look at your hint.

3. If the hint isn't of any help, click **Reset Password**. The Password Reset Wizard starts.

4. Click **Next**. Insert your reset disk in its socket or drive. Click the drive down arrow, select the drive the reset disk is in, and again click **Next**. Type a new password, confirm it, type a password hint, click **Next**, and click **Finish**. (You do not have to create a new reset disk with your new password; Windows updates the reset disk for you.) Remove the reset disk.

5. Enter your new password, and press **ENTER**.

Replace Passwords

The weakest link in the Windows 7 SP1 security scheme is the use of passwords. Users give their passwords to others or forget them, and passwords are often stolen or just "found." There is nothing to tie a password to an individual, which is handy for sharing, but also a security risk. Two potential means of replacing passwords are smart cards and biometric devices.

USE SMART CARDS

Smart cards are credit card–sized pieces of plastic that have a tamper-resistant electronic circuit embedded in them that permanently stores an ID, a password, and other information. Smart cards require a personal identification number (PIN), so they add a second layer of security (smart card plus PIN in place of a password) to log on to a system. Smart cards can also be used to encrypt something only you (or someone with your smart card and PIN) can open.

NOTE

In case you wondered, the PIN is encrypted and placed on the smart card when it is made. The PIN is not stored on the computer.

QUICKFACTS

CUSTOMIZING A USER ACCOUNT

Each user account can be unique, with a custom Start menu, desktop, color scheme, and screen saver. When programs are installed, you can choose whether they are for just the current user or for all users. When you set up a new user, it is as though you are setting up a new computer. The previous chapters of this book talk about the steps to set up a computer.

As you may have seen earlier in this chapter, a number of elements of the account itself can be changed, including the name, password, display picture, and account type. You can change the name and password in a manner almost identical to what you used to create them, as described in the "Set Up Users" section and the "Use Passwords" section earlier in this chapter.

Windows 7 SP1 detects and supports smart cards, and lets them be used to log on to a computer or network, as well for other authentication needs.

Smart cards require a reader be attached to the computer, either through a Universal Serial Bus (USB) port or a Personal Computer Memory Card International Association (PCMCIA) slot. With a smart card reader, users at the logon screen need to insert their card into the reader, click **Switch User**, and then, when prompted, enter their PIN. With a valid card and PIN, users are authenticated and allowed on the system in the same way as they would be by entering a valid user name and password.

Most smart card readers are compatible with Windows 7 SP1. The drivers for these devices either are included with or are available for Windows 7 SP1, and installing them is not difficult; you need only follow the instructions that come with them.

With a smart card reader installed, set up new accounts (as described in "Set Up Users"), and then, for both new and old accounts, open each user's Create Password window, and click **Smart Card Is Required For Interactive Logon**, which will appear when a smart card reader is present. You do not have to enter a password.

USE BIOMETRIC DEVICES

Smart cards do provide an added degree of security over passwords, but if someone obtains both the card and the PIN, he or she's home-free. The only way to be totally sure that the computer is actually talking to the authorized person is to require some form of physical identification.

This is the purpose of *biometric devices,* which identify people by physical traits, such as voice, handprint, fingerprint, face, or eyes. Often, these devices are used with a smart card to replace the PIN. Biometric devices are becoming more common, and Windows 7 SP1 will work with many of them. Devices are available for under $100, for a fingerprint scanner, to several thousand dollars for a face scanner. Many laptops have fingerprint scanners built in. Depending on your needs, you may want to keep these devices in mind.

1

2

3

4

5

6

7

8

9

10

Switch Among Users

When you have multiple users on a computer, one user can obviously log off and another log on; however, with the Welcome screen, you can use Fast User Switching (which is not available in the Starter Edition of Windows 7 SP1). This allows you to keep programs running and files open when you temporarily switch to another user. To use Fast User Switching:

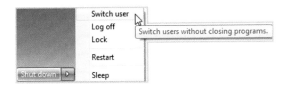

1. Click **Start**, click the **Shut Down** right arrow, and click **Switch User**. The Welcome screen will appear and let the other person click his or her account and log on.

2. When the other person has finished using the computer and has logged off (by clicking **Start**, clicking the **Shut Down** right arrow, and clicking **Log Off**), you can log on normally. When you do, you will see all your programs exactly as you left them.

Control What a User Does

User accounts identify people and allow them to log on to your computer. What they can do after that depends on the permissions they have. Windows 7 SP1 has two features that help you control what other users do on your computer: Parental Controls and the ability to turn Windows features on and off for a given user. In addition, Windows 7 SP1's New Technology File System (NTFS) allows the sharing of folders and drives as well as the assignment of permissions to use a file, a folder, a disk, a printer, and other devices. The permissions are given to individuals and to groups to which individuals can belong. So far, you've seen two groups: Administrators and Standard Users (also called just "Users"), but there are others, and you can create more.

You can limit the sharing of files and folders to the *Public folder* within the Users folder on your computer. To do so, you must create or move the files and folders you want to share into the Public folder. The other option is to share directly the other folders on your computer. This is made easier by the *inheritance* attribute, where subfolders automatically inherit (take on) the permissions of their parent folder. Every object in Windows 7 SP1 NTFS, however, has its own set of *security descriptors* that are attached to it when it is created; with the proper permission, these security descriptors can be individually changed. When permissions

CAUTION

File sharing can be a valuable and useful capability, but it can also open up your computer to significant harm. It is important to think through what your needs are and how you want to do the file sharing to get the value without the harm.

NOTE

A child for whom you want to set up Parental Controls must have a Standard User account. To set up Parental Controls, you must have an Administrator account with a password.

NOTE

For Parental Controls to work, the disk drives on which you want to control the use of games must use the NTFS file system. Parental Controls will not work with the older File Allocation Table (FAT) file system. While you are installing Parental Controls, if a drive with the FAT file system is detected, you will be told this. You can go ahead and install Parental Controls, but content on the FAT drive will not be controlled.

are appropriately set, other users on your computer can access and optionally change your files and folders.

Set Parental Controls

If you have a child or grandchild as one of the users on your computer and you are an administrator with a password, you can control what your child can do on your computer, including hours of usage, programs he or she can run, and access to the Internet. When your child encounters a blocked program, game, or website, a notice is displayed, including a link the child can click to request access. You, as an administrator, can allow one-time access by entering your user ID and password.

1. Click **Start** and click **Control Panel**. In Category view, click **User Accounts And Family Safety**, and then in any view click **Parental Controls**. If needed, type an administrator password, and click **Yes**. You may be asked if you want to sign up for online Family Safety through Windows Live. If you want, enter your Windows Live user name and password, and click **Sign In** to see how it works. Otherwise, click **Cancel**.

2. When you are back in Windows and the Parental Controls window has opened, click the user for whom you want to set Parental Controls to open the individual User Controls window.

3. Click **On** under Parental Controls, as shown in Figure 8-4.

4. Click **Time Limits**, drag the hours to block or allow (you only need to select one or the other, and you can drag across multiple hours and days), and then click **OK**.

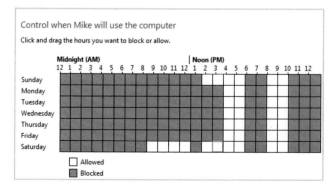

*Figure 8-4: **Parental Controls allows you to determine what a child can do and see on your computer.***

NOTE

In addition to the parental controls that are described here, controls such as web filtering and activity reporting are available for download and use at the bottom of the window that opens when you first open Parental Controls in step 1 of the "Set Parental Controls" section of this chapter.

5. Click **Games** and choose if any games can be played. Click **Set Game Ratings**, choose if games with no rating can be played, click a rating level, choose the type of content you want blocked, and click **OK**. Click **Block Or Allow Specific Games**, click whether to block or allow specific games installed on the computer, and click **OK**. Click **OK** again to leave Game Controls.

6. Click **Allow And Block Specific Programs**, and choose whether to allow the use of all programs or only the ones you choose. If you choose to pick specific programs to allow, a list of all the programs on the computer is presented. Click those for which you want to allow access, and click **OK**.

7. Click **OK** to close the User Controls window.

Control What Parts of Windows Can Be Used

As an administrator, you can control what parts of Windows 7 SP1 each user can access.

1. Log on as the user for whom you want to set Windows feature usage.

2. Click **Start** and click **Control Panel**. In Category view, click **Programs** and then in any view, click **Programs And Features**.

3. Click **Turn Windows Features On Or Off** in the left column. If needed, type a password and click **Yes**. The Windows Features dialog box appears.

4. Click an unselected check box to turn a feature on, or click a selected check box to turn a feature off. Click the plus sign (+) where applicable to open the subfeatures and turn them on or off.

5. When you have selected the features the user will be allowed to use, click **OK**.

6. Close the Programs And Features window.

Set File and Folder Sharing

Files are shared by being in a shared folder or drive. Folders and drives are shared by their creator or owner or by an administrator. To share folders and drives, as well as printers and other devices, both locally and over a network, you must address three components of Windows 7 SP1 that allow you to control access to your computer and its components (see Figure 8-5):

● **The Windows Firewall**, which protects your computer and its contents from network access

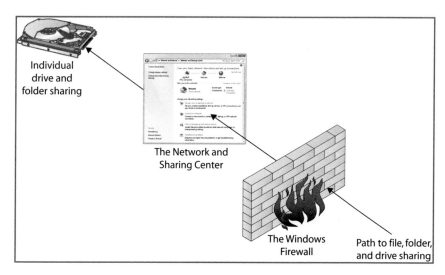

Individual drive and folder sharing

The Network and Sharing Center

The Windows Firewall

Path to file, folder, and drive sharing

Figure 8-5: **Sharing your computer requires that you set up your firewall, the Network And Sharing Center, and the individual drives and folders to accomplish that.**

- **The Network And Sharing Center**, which is the primary means of controlling sharing in Windows 7 SP1

- **Sharing individual drives and folders**, which lets you determine if a drive, folder, or other device is shared; who has permission to access it; and what they can do with the contents

SET UP THE WINDOWS FIREWALL

Windows 7 SP1 includes the Windows Firewall, whose objective is to slow down and hopefully prevent anybody from accessing your computer without your permission, while at the same time allowing those who you want to use your computer to do so. The Windows Firewall is turned on by default. Check to see if it is; if it isn't, turn it on.

1. Click **Start** and click **Control Panel**. In Category view, click **System And Security**, and then in any view, click **Windows Firewall**. The Windows Firewall window opens and shows your firewall status.

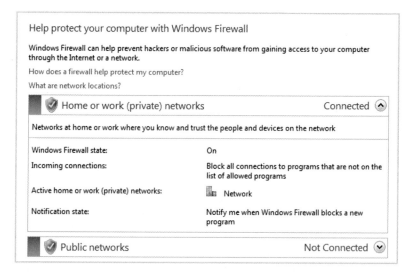

Help protect your computer with Windows Firewall

Windows Firewall can help prevent hackers or malicious software from gaining access to your computer through the Internet or a network.

How does a firewall help protect my computer?

What are network locations?

Home or work (private) networks	Connected ⌃
Networks at home or work where you know and trust the people and devices on the network	
Windows Firewall state:	On
Incoming connections:	Block all connections to programs that are not on the list of allowed programs
Active home or work (private) networks:	Network
Notification state:	Notify me when Windows Firewall blocks a new program

Public networks	Not Connected ⌄

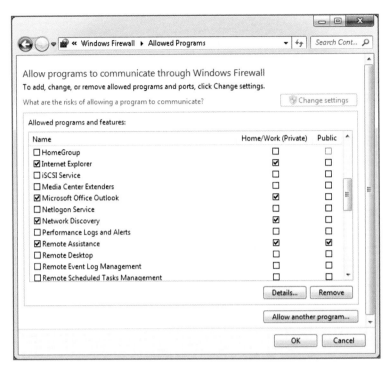

Figure 8-6: *The Windows 7 SP1 Firewall can be configured to allow certain programs and features to come through.*

TIP

In the Windows Firewall Allowed Programs window, you can determine what each option does by highlighting it and clicking **Details** at the bottom of the dialog box.

NOTE

You will probably have other programs selected, such as Internet Explorer and Windows Live Messenger, that can be used on the Internet.

2. If your firewall is not turned on, or if you want to turn it off, click **Turn Windows Firewall On Or Off** in the pane on the left. If needed, type a password and click **Yes**. The Windows Firewall Customize Settings window opens. Click the respective option button to turn on your firewall (highly recommended) or to turn it off (not recommended). You can do this for both your local network and for a public network to which you may be connected. Click **OK**.

3. To change the settings for what the firewall will and won't let through, click **Allow A Program Or Feature Through Windows Firewall** at the top of the left column. The Allowed Programs window opens, shown in Figure 8-6.

4. In the Allowed Programs And Features list, select the services running on your computer that you want to allow people from the Internet to use. To share information across a LAN, click the following items:

- Core Networking
- File And Printer Sharing
- HomeGroup
- Network Discovery
- Windows Collaboration Computer Name Registration Service (optional)
- Windows Peer To Peer Collaboration Foundation (optional)

5. Click to select each program or feature you want to allow through the firewall. Click **OK** to close the Windows Firewall Allowed Programs window, and then click **Close** to close the Windows Firewall Control Panel.

USE THE NETWORK AND SHARING CENTER

The second layer of file-sharing protection in Windows 7 SP1 is controlled with the Network And Sharing Center, shown in Figure 8-7, which allows you to turn on or off the primary components of sharing information among users on a computer and across a network.

The first time Windows 7 SP1 was run, a choice was made between a public and private network. The Network And Sharing Center allows you to change that.

If you are primarily sharing your computer with other computers within an organization or a residence, you should select either Home or Work Network, where network sharing is relatively simple. If you are primarily using public wireless or cable Internet connections and very little sharing of your computer, select Public, which makes it more difficult for someone to get into your computer.

1. Click **Start** and click **Control Panel**. In Category view, click **Network And Internet**, and then in any view, click **Network And Sharing Center**. The Network And Sharing Center window opens, as shown in Figure 8-7.

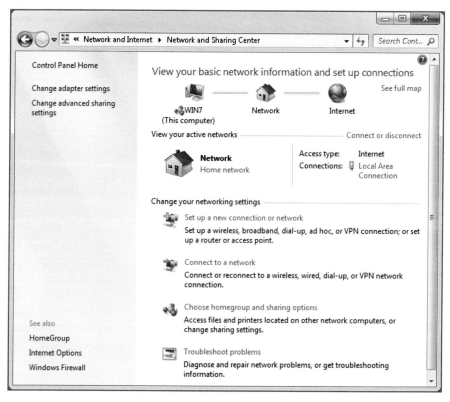

Figure 8-7: **The Network And Sharing Center is the primary means of sharing your computer.**

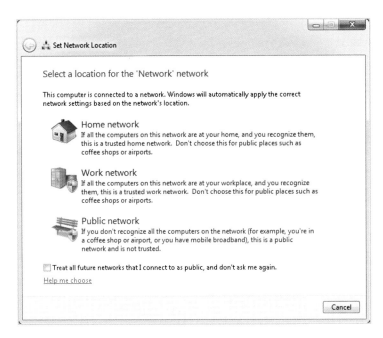

Set Network Location

Select a location for the 'Network' network

This computer is connected to a network. Windows will automatically apply the correct network settings based on the network's location.

Home network
If all the computers on this network are at your home, and you recognize them, this is a trusted home network. Don't choose this for public places such as coffee shops or airports.

Work network
If all the computers on this network are at your workplace, and you recognize them, this is a trusted work network. Don't choose this for public places such as coffee shops or airports.

Public network
If you don't recognize all the computers on the network (for example, you're in a coffee shop or airport, or you have mobile broadband), this is a public network and is not trusted.

☐ Treat all future networks that I connect to as public, and don't ask me again.

Help me choose

Cancel

TIP

If you have a specific program not on the Windows Firewall Allowed Programs And Features list, you can include that program by clicking **Allow Another Program** at the bottom of the Windows Firewall Allowed Programs window. Select the program from the list or browse to its location, and click **Add**.

2. If you want to change the type of network (home, work, or public) you are connected to, click the current type of network to the right of the icon (in Figure 8-7, it is Home Network). The Set Network Location dialog box will appear, as shown to the left.

3. Read the conditions that are expected in each network type, and then click the type that is correct for you. If needed, type a password and click **Yes**. Your choice will be confirmed. Click **Close**.

4. Each type of network has sharing settings that are automatically set. Home Network is the most open, with just about everything shared; Public Network is the other extreme. If you want to review the settings that have been made with your choice and possibly make changes, click **Change Advanced Sharing Settings**. The Advanced Sharing Settings window will open.

5. Review the settings that are shown. In a home or work network, you probably want and will have already set the following:
   - Turn On Network Discovery
   - Turn On File And Printer Sharing
   - Turn On Sharing So Anyone With Network Access Can Read And Write Files In Public Folders
   - Media Streaming Is On
   - Use 128-Bit Encryption
   - Turn Off Password Protection Sharing (With A Home Network)
   - Allow Windows To Manage HomeGroup Connections (With A Home Network)

   For a public network, you probably want the opposite settings.

6. Make any changes that you feel you need, and then, if you made changes, click **Save Changes**. If needed, enter the password and click **Yes**. Otherwise, click **Cancel**.

7. When you have finished with the Network And Sharing Center, click **Close**.

USE HOMEGROUP FOLDER SHARING

The final layer of sharing settings is the determination of the disks and folders you want to share. Windows 7 SP1's HomeGroup makes

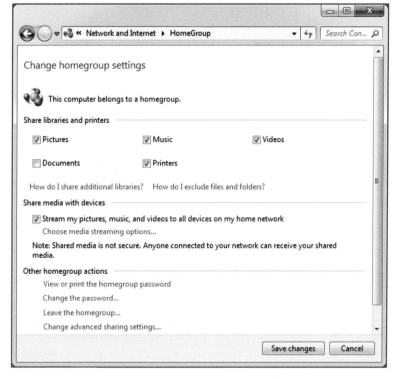

NOTE

A *homegroup* is a group of networking computer users who want to easily share information and resources on their computers. Such a group can be in a residence or in a smaller organization. Only Windows 7 (original Windows 7 or SP1) computers can join a homegroup.

sharing files and folders within the homegroup much easier. When Windows 7 SP1 is first installed or started, you are asked if you want a home, work, or public network. If you choose Home, which may also be a good idea for small businesses, a homegroup is either set up or joined, depending on whether a homegroup already exists. You are then shown a list of your libraries and asked if you want to share them. By default, your pictures, music, printers, and videos are shared for anyone to read, view, or use but not change. Documents are not shared, but you can change this at the time of installation or at a later time. You can make these changes at the library level or at the disk and folder level. To do this at the library level:

1. Click **Start** and click **Control Panel**. In Category view, click **Network And Internet**, and then in any view, click **HomeGroup**. The HomeGroup window opens. If this is the first time you are looking into HomeGroup, you'll be asked if you want to share any libraries. Click **Choose What You Want To Share**. The HomeGroup wizard will appear and walk you through selecting what to share within the network and creating a password to join other Windows 7 computers to HomeGroup. When you are done, and if you have previously reviewed HomeGroup, the Control Panel HomeGroup window will open, as shown in Figure 8-8.

2. Make any changes that you feel you need, and then, if you made changes, click **Save Changes**. If needed, enter the password and click **Yes**. Otherwise, click **Cancel**.

To go beyond the sharing of libraries within the homegroup, and even then only for someone to read, view, or use your libraries, you need to go to the individual drives and folders. You can change the sharing of libraries so that other users can change contents in addition to reading or viewing them. To do that:

1. Click **Start** and click **Computer**. In the folders (left) pane, click **Libraries** so the detail libraries (documents, music, pictures, or videos) are shown in the right pane.

Figure 8-8: The HomeGroup default is to share three of your libraries plus your printer within your homegroup.

2. Right-click the library whose sharing you want to change, and click **Share With**. The context menu and file-sharing submenu will appear.

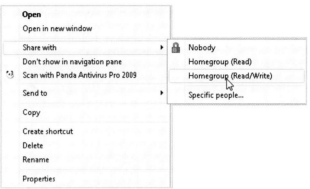

3. By default, the libraries are shared among the homegroup to be read-only. You can allow homegroup members both read and write access to your libraries, or you can select specific people and give them specific permissions. Click the option you want, and when you are finished, close the Windows Explorer window.

SHARE STANDARD FOLDERS WITH SPECIFIC PEOPLE

Standard folders are shared differently than disk drives and the Users folders, but are similar to sharing libraries, where you can share them with specific people. To share standard folders with specific people:

1. Click **Start** and click **Computer**. In the folders (left) pane, open the disk and folders necessary to see in the right pane the folder you want to share.

2. Right-click the folder and click **Share With**. The file-sharing menu will appear, as you saw in the last section.

3. Click **Specific People** to open the File Sharing dialog box. This shows you the current sharing of the folder, as you can see in Figure 8-9.

Figure 8-9: **The sharing of standard folders with specific people takes you to a permissions dialog box.**

NOTE

When you share a folder, all folders and files within it are given the same sharing status due to inheritance. If that is not what you want for a particular folder, you must individually change the sharing status of the folders within it.

NOTE

Your AutoPlay dialog box may look different from the one shown here, depending on the options that have been selected in the past.

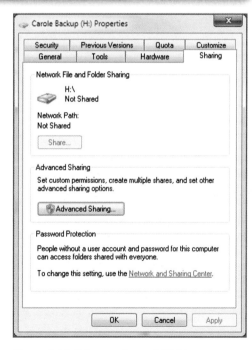

Figure 8-10: *Drives and special folders use a different sharing procedure.*

4. Click the down arrow on the right of the top text box to open a list of users and groups known to your computer. Click the user or group you want to give permission to use this disk or folder, possibly the Everyone group, and click **Add**. The user or group is added to the list in the lower part of the dialog box with the minimal permission level of Read.

5. Click the **Permission Level** down arrow for your new user or group to open the alternative permission levels. Click the level you want for the addition:
   - **Read** allows the user to view the files in the shared folder.
   - **Read/Write** allows the user to view, add, change, and delete any of the files in the shared folder.

6. Click **Share** and, if needed, type a password and click **Yes**. Click **Done** to complete the process.

SHARE DRIVES AND SPECIAL FOLDERS

Disk drives and special folders—like the Users, Program Files, and Windows folders—have a more detailed sharing process.

1. Click **Start** and click **Computer**. Navigate to the drive or folder you want to share.
2. Right-click the drive or folder you want to share, click **Share With**, and click **Advanced Sharing**. The Properties dialog box will appear with the Sharing tab displayed, as shown in Figure 8-10.
3. Click **Advanced Sharing** and, if needed, type a password and click **Yes**.
4. Click **Share This Folder**, change the share name if desired, and click **Permissions**.

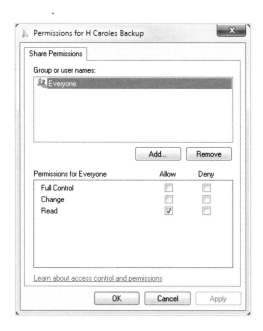

5. Select a listed user or group; or, if the one you want is not listed, click **Add**, click **Advanced**, click **Find Now**, double-click a user or group, and click **OK**.

6. With the user or group selected, click the permission level you want for that entity. The levels of permission are as follows:

- **Read** allows the user or group to read but not change or delete a file or folder.
- **Change** allows the user or group to read and change but not delete a file or folder.
- **Full Control** allows the user or group to read, change, or delete a file or folder.

7. Click **OK** twice and close the Properties dialog box and Windows Explorer.

Use and Add Groups

Groups, or *group accounts*, are collections of user accounts that can have permissions, such as file sharing, granted to them. Most permissions are granted to groups, not individuals, and then individuals are made members of the groups. You need a set of groups that handles both the mix of people and the mix of permissions that you want to establish. A number of standard groups with preassigned permissions are built into Windows 7 SP1, but you can create your own groups, and you can assign users to any of these.

OPEN EXISTING GROUPS

If you have Windows 7 Professional or Ultimate, you can open existing groups and see what permissions they contain.

1. Click **Start** and click **Control Panel**. In Category view, click **System And Security**, and then click **Administrative Tools**.

2. In the right pane, double-click **Computer Management**. If needed, type a password and click **Yes**.

3. In the left pane, click the triangle opposite **System Tools** to open it, click the triangle opposite **Local Users And Groups** to open that (not available in Windows 7 Home Premium), and click **Groups**. The list of built-in groups is displayed, as shown in Figure 8-11.

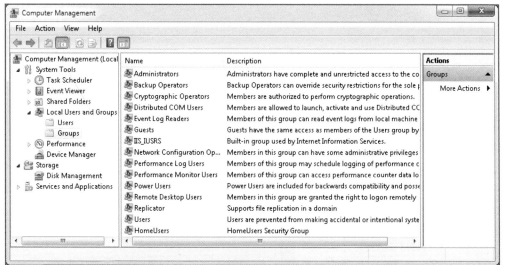

Figure 8-11: **There are a number of built-in groups to which users can be assigned.**

NOTE

"Standard Users" are called just "Users" in the list of groups.

QUICK**FACTS**

UNDERSTANDING PERMISSIONS

Permissions authorize a user or a group to perform some function on an object, such as files, folders, disks, and printers. Objects have sets of permissions associated with them that can be assigned to users and groups. The specific permissions depend on the object, but all objects have at least two permissions: Read and either Modify or Change. Permissions are initially set in one of three ways:

- The application or process that creates an object can set its permissions upon creation.

- If the object allows the inheritance of permissions and they were not set upon creation, a parent object can propagate permissions to the object. For example, a parent folder can propagate its permissions to a subfolder that it contains.

- If neither the creator nor the parent sets the permissions for an object, the Windows 7 SP1 system default settings will do it.

Once an object is created, its permissions can be changed by its owner, an administrator, or anyone else who has been given authority to do this.

4. Double-click a few groups to open the Properties dialog box for each and see the members they contain.

ADD USERS TO GROUPS

1. Right-click a group to which you want to add a user, and click **Add To Group**. Click **Add**. The Select Users dialog box will appear.

2. Either type a name in the text box and click **Check Names**, or click **Advanced** and then click **Find Now**. A list of users on that computer will be displayed. Select the user that you want to add (hold down **CTRL** to select several), and click **OK**.

3. When you are done, click **OK** twice.

ADD A GROUP

1. In the Computer Management window, in the list of groups in the middle (subject) pane, right-click in a white area so that no group is selected, and then click **New Group**. The New Group dialog box appears.

2. Enter a group name of up to 60 characters (Windows 7 SP1 lets you enter more, but if you ever want to use the group in Windows 2000 or NT systems, it will not work). It cannot contain just numbers, periods, or spaces; it can't contain " / \ [ ] : ; | = ,+ * ? < >; and leading spaces or periods are dropped.

3. Enter the description of what the group can uniquely do, and click **Add**. Then follow the instructions in "Add Users to Groups" except for clicking OK the final time in step 3.

4. When your group is the way you want it (see Figure 8-12), click **Create** and then click **Close**. The new group will appear in the list in the middle of the Computer Management window. Close the Computer Management window.

*Figure 8-12: **Creating your own group lets you give it your own set of permissions.***

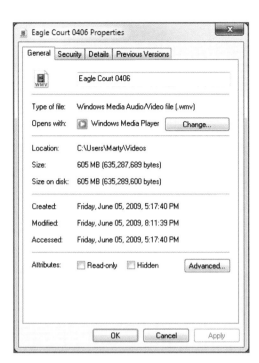

Figure 8-13: *Protecting files and folders is accomplished from the files and folders Properties dialog boxes.*

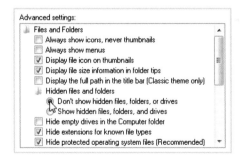

Protect Stored Data

Protecting stored data is another layer of protection. It works to make unusable whatever is found on the computer by someone who managed to break through the other layers of protection.

Protect Files and Folders

You can protect files and folder by hiding them and encrypting them. The easiest way is to hide them. Start by opening the Properties dialog box for the file or folder.

1. Click **Start** and click **Computer**. In the navigation pane, open the disk and folders necessary to locate in the right pane the file or folder you want to protect.

2. Right-click the file or folder you want to protect, and click **Properties**. The Properties dialog box will appear, as shown for a file in Figure 8-13 (there are slight differences among file and folder Properties dialog boxes).

HIDE FILES AND FOLDERS

Hiding files and folders lets you prevent them from being displayed by Windows Explorer. This assumes the person from whom you want to hide them does not know how to display hidden files or how to turn off the hidden attribute. To hide a file or folder, you must both turn on its hidden attribute and turn off the Display Hidden Files feature.

1. In the file or folder Properties dialog box, on the General tab, click **Hidden**, click **OK**, and click **OK** again to confirm the attribute change. If needed, type a password and click **Yes** (the object's icon becomes dimmed or disappears).

2. In the Windows Explorer window, click the **Organize** menu, click **Folder And Search Options**, click the **View** tab, and make sure **Don't Show Hidden Files, Folders, Or Drives** is selected. Click **OK** to close the Folder Options dialog box. Close and reopen the parent folder, and the file or folder you hid will disappear.

3. To restore the file or folder to view, click the **Organize** menu, click **Folder And Search Options**, click the **View** tab, click **Show Hidden Files, Folders, And Drives**, and click **OK**. Then, when you can see the file or folder, open its Properties dialog box, and deselect the **Hidden** attribute.

TIP

Because many applications save temporary and secondary files during normal execution, it is recommended that folders rather than files be the encrypting container. If an application is then told to store all files in that folder, where all files are automatically encrypted upon saving, security is improved.

ENCRYPT FILES AND FOLDERS

File and folder encryption, called the *Encrypting File System (EFS),* is built into Windows 7 SP1 using NTFS (it is not available in the Starter, Home Basic, or Home Premium editions). Once EFS is turned on for a file or a folder, only the person who encrypted the file or folder will be able to read it. However, you can back up the encryption key and use that to access the file or folder. For the person who encrypted the file, accessing it requires no additional steps, and the file is re-encrypted every time it is saved.

To encrypt a file or folder from Windows Explorer, starting with files:

1. From the General tab in the file's Properties dialog box, click **Advanced**. The Advanced Attributes dialog box appears.

2. Click **Encrypt Contents To Secure Data**, and click **OK** twice.

3. If you are encrypting a file, you will see an encryption warning that the file is not in an encrypted folder, which means that when you edit the file, temporary or backup files might be created that are not encrypted. Choose whether to encrypt only the file or to encrypt both the file and its parent folder, and then click **OK**.

4. If you are encrypting a folder, the Confirm Attribute Changes dialog box appears, asking if you want to apply the encryption to this folder only or to both the folder and its contents. If you click **This Folder Only**, *existing* files and folders in the folder will *not* be encrypted, while files and folders later created in or copied to the encrypted folder will be. If you click **This Folder, Subfolders, And Files**, all files and folders will be encrypted. Choose the setting that is correct for you, and click **OK**. If needed, type a password and click **Yes**.

5. Log off as the current user, and log on as another user. Click **Start**, click **Computer**, and open the drive and folders necessary to display in the right pane the file or folder you encrypted. You can see that the file exists, but when you try to open it, edit it, print it, or move it, you will get a message that access is denied.

6. To decrypt a file or folder, log on as yourself (given you're the person who encrypted it), reopen the file or folder Properties dialog box, click **Advanced**, deselect **Encrypt Contents To Secure Data**, and click **OK** twice (three times with folders).

BACK UP YOUR ENCRYPTION KEY

If you use file encryption, it is important to back up your file encryption key so that you do not lose the information you have, and you may be reminded

CAUTION

If you encrypt a shared folder and select This Folder, Subfolders, And Files, any files or subfolders belonging to others will be encrypted with your key and the owners will not be able to use what they created.

of this. It is also important, of course, to keep the media that you back up on safe so that it can't be used. The key is part of a digital certificate, so this section refers to backing up the certificate.

1. Click **Start** and click **Control Panel**. In Category view, click **User Accounts And Family Safety**, and then click **User Accounts**. Your User Account window opens.

2. Click **Manage Your File Encryption Certificates** in the left column. If needed, type a password and click **Yes** to open the Encrypting File System dialog box.

3. Read about what you can do with this wizard, and click **Next**. By default, a certificate was automatically created when Windows was installed—that certificate or a more recent one will appear in the Certificate Details area, as shown in Figure 8-14. Click **Next**.

4. Click **Browse** and navigate to the removable disk and folder you want to hold the certificate (it is not recommended to save the key on the same machine where the encryption is located). Type a filename and click **Save**.

5. Type a password and confirm it, and then click **Next**. Select the folders with encrypted files that you want the new certificate and key applied to, and click **Next**. Your files will be updated with the new key.

6. When you are told the files have been updated and where the key is stored, click **Close** and close the User Accounts window.

7. Store the removable disc or USB flash drive in a safe place.

Use Encrypted Files and Folders

If you are the person who encrypted a file or folder and you log on as yourself, you can use the file or folder exactly as you would if it hadn't been encrypted. The only way you know the files or folders are encrypted is that Windows Explorer shows them in green, as shown in Figure 8-15. If you log on as someone else, or

Figure 8-14: **A security certificate is required to use file encryption.**

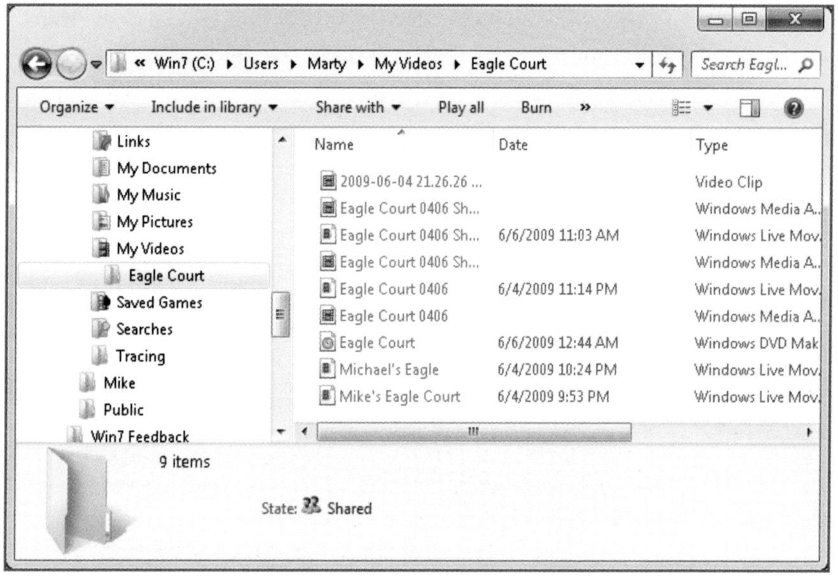

Figure 8-15: *Windows Explorer shows the information for encrypted files in green.*

if someone else logs on as anyone other than you, they will not be able to use the files or folders. Copying and moving encrypted files and folders, however, has a special set of rules:

- If you copy or move a file or folder into an encrypted folder, the item copied or moved will be encrypted.

- If you copy or move a file or folder to an unencrypted folder, the item moved remains as it was prior to being moved. If it was unencrypted, it remains so. If it was encrypted, it is still encrypted after being moved.

- Someone other than the owner who tries to copy or move encrypted files or folders to a different computer sees an error message that access is denied.

- If the owner copies or moves an encrypted file or folder to another file system, such as Windows NT 4 NTFS or Windows 98 FAT32, the encryption is removed, but a warning message is generated before the copy or move is complete.

- Backing up encrypted files or folders with Windows 7 SP1 Backup leaves the items encrypted.

Back Up Your Information

Computers are a great asset, but like any machine, they are prone to failures of many kinds. Once you have started using your computer regularly, it becomes important to make a copy of your information and store it in another location should your hard drive fail or something else happen to your computer.

There are several solutions to copying and saving your information. The term normally used for this is *backup* (or to back up—the verb form). This means storing a copy of your information in a location other than on your computer. You can back up both on your computer and on the Internet.

BACK UP ON YOUR COMPUTER

Within your computer, you can back up your information to a CD or DVD, to another drive that is connected to your computer (including an external hard

TIP

To use a backed-up encryption key, insert the removable media with the key, open the drive in Windows Explorer, and browse to and double-click the file with the key. In the Certificate Import Wizard that opens, click **Next**, confirm that you have the right file, and click **Next**. Type the password used to back up the key, select how you want to use the key, and click **Next**. Select the certificate store you want, click **Next**, and click **Finish**.

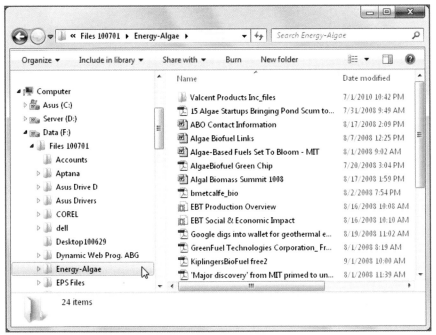

drive and a USB flash or thumb drive), or to a hard drive on another computer. You may want to perform backups to a couple of these items on a periodic basic, and a couple of times a year back up your data to a DVD and put it in your bank safety deposit box.

Windows 7 SP1 has a backup program (see Chapter 3), but without a lot of setup, it backs up things you don't really care about, like programs you already have on CDs or DVDs. A simpler way to do a backup is to copy your files from the hard disk in your computer to an external device, like a CD, DVD, USB flash drive, or external hard drive. Here's how to copy some files to a writable (or "burnable") DVD:

Figure 8-16: **You must first locate the files on your computer that you want to back up.**

1. Click **Start**, click **Computer**, and open (click the triangle on the left) the drive and folders in the left column needed to display the files you want to back up in the right column, as you see in Figure 8-16.

2. Open your DVD drive, insert a blank writable disc, and close the drive. An AutoPlay dialog box will open offering you several options, as shown here.

3. Click **Burn Files To Disc** to open the Burn A Disc dialog box, as shown to the left. Type a title, click **Like A USB Flash Drive**, and click **Next**. You will see a message that the disc is being formatted and then another AutoPlay dialog box will appear.

4. Click **Open Folder To View Files** to open another window with a blank right pane with the message "Drag Files To This Folder To Add Them To The Disc."

5. In your original folder, similar to the one shown in Figure 8-16, select the files you want to back up by clicking the first file, pressing and holding **SHIFT** while clicking the last file (if the files are contiguous), or pressing and holding **CTRL** while individually clicking the other files (if they are not contiguous).

6. When all the necessary files in a folder are selected, drag them (point on the selected files, press and hold the left mouse button, and move the mouse) to the right pane of the new folder for the DVD, as you can see in Figure 8-17, and release the mouse button.

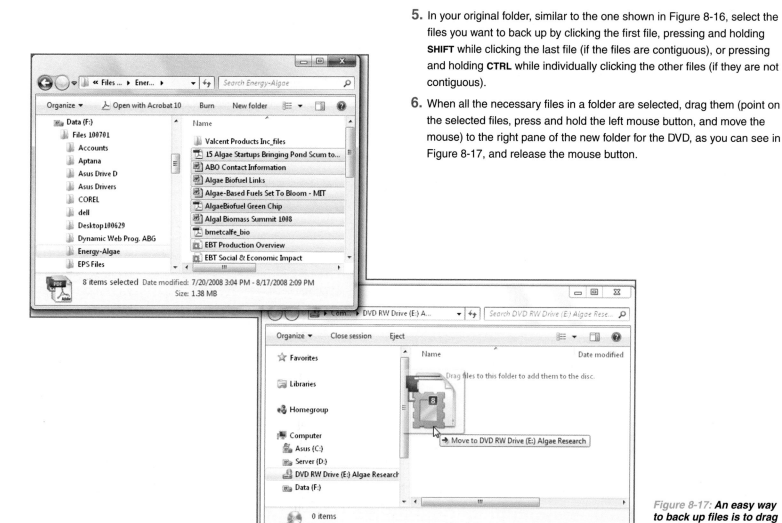

Figure 8-17: **An easy way to back up files is to drag them to a DVD or external drive.**

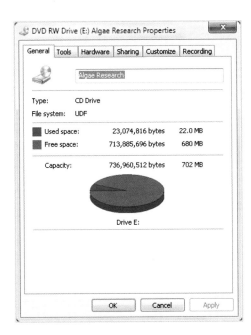

7. You can open other folders and drives and drag other files to the DVD folder. Periodically look at how much space on the DVD has been used by right-clicking the drive in the left pane of its window and clicking **Properties** in the context menu. In the Properties dialog box, look at how much free space you have left, and then click **OK**.

8. When you have all the files you want to back up in the DVD, click **Close Session**. You'll see a message that the disc is being closed. When that is done, you'll get a message that the disc is ready. Click **Eject**, remove the disc, label it with a soft felt-tip pen, and store it with a paper or plastic sleeve in a safe place, preferably away from your computer and in a fireproof container.

BACK UP OVER THE INTERNET

Recently, many people are choosing to save their information to the *cloud*, meaning that they back up the data on their computer to a location (a server) accessed through the Internet. This method makes it easy to access your data from any location, as well as your new computer, should your old computer fail. These services are reasonable in cost or even free and easy to set up.

Some programs, once you have subscribed to them, install a small software program on your computer. These programs work behind the scenes, copying new photos, data files, deposits, or letters to a secure, encrypted location. Should your old computer break down, you can restore your files and data to your new computer.

Some personal financial management programs also offer this service for their data. For example, Quicken's Online Backup service charges a nominal fee per month to protect your financial information.

An example of a currently free cloud service is Microsoft's SkyDrive. Microsoft gives you 25GB of storage. You'll need to set up an account with a user ID and a password.

NOTE

A disc created with the Like A USB Flash Drive option can be put into the DVD disc drive again and have files deleted and added to it, as well as edited and restored to the disc.

1. Click the **Internet Explorer** icon on the taskbar to open it. In the address bar, type skydrive.live.com and press **ENTER**. Windows Live will open, and if you are not already signed up as a Windows Live or Hotmail client, you will be asked to do that. Click **Sign Up**, fill out the form that opens, and click **I Accept**. Your SkyDrive page will open, where you can use existing folders or set up your own, as you can see in Figure 8-18.

Figure 8-18: ***Online, "cloud" Internet storage is a good and safe way to back up important files.***

2. Click a folder you want to use to open it, and then click **Add Files**; or click **New**, click **Folder**, enter a name for the folder, click **Create Folder**, and then click **Add Files**. In either case, a window will open inviting you to drop documents there or select documents from your computer.

3. You can use steps 1, 5, and 6 under "Back Up on Your Computer" and drag the files to the window shown in the previous step; or you can click **Select Documents From Your Computer**, select the files as in step 5, and click **Open**.

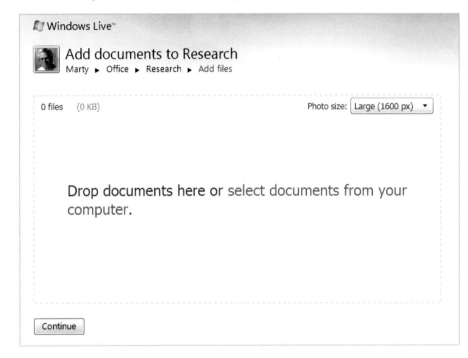

4. You'll see the files being added. When the files have been added, you can remove individual files by clicking the X after the file size of each file. You can add files using either method in step 3.

5. When you have added all the files you want, click **Continue**. A list will appear of the files you have added. You can select a particular file and share, move, copy, rename,

---

Figure 8-19: **You can password-protect your system when you leave it unattended by having the logon screen appear when you return after using the screen saver.**

and delete it. If the file is for Microsoft Word, Excel, or PowerPoint, you can edit it directly in your browser (Internet Explorer) using the Microsoft Office Web Apps.

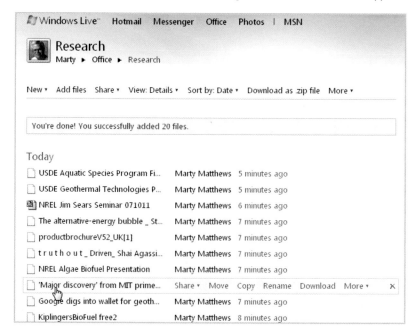

6. When you are done, close the SkyDrive website and if desired, the Internet Explorer.

Other cloud sites work similarly.

Chapter 9
Setting Up Networking

Networking is the ability to connect two or more computers and allow them to share information and resources, whether at home, in an organization, or around the world. The Internet, as was discussed in Chapter 4, is a form of networking. This chapter discusses a *local area network,* or *LAN,* which is generally confined to a single residence or building, or perhaps just a section of a building. (The Internet is a *wide area network,* or *WAN.*) You'll see what comprises a LAN, how to set it up, and how to use it.

Plan a Network

Windows 7 SP1 is a *network operating system.* This allows the interconnection of multiple computers for many purposes:

- **Exchanging information**, such as sending a file from one computer to another
- **Communicating**, for example, sending email among network users

- **Sharing information** by having common files accessed by network users
- **Sharing network resources**, such as printers and Internet connections

Networking is a system that includes the connection between computers that facilitates the transfer of information, as well as the scheme for controlling that transfer. The scheme makes sure that the information is transferred correctly and accurately. This is the function of the networking hardware and software in your computer and the protocols, or standards, they use.

Select a Network Architecture

Your network *architecture* is the combination of hardware, software, and standards that are used to perform networking. Today, the majority of LANs use the *Ethernet* standard, which determines the type of network hardware and software needed by the network, and *TCP/IP* (Transmission Control Protocol/Internet Protocol), which determines how information is exchanged over the network. With this foundation, you can then choose between using a peer-to-peer LAN or a client-server LAN.

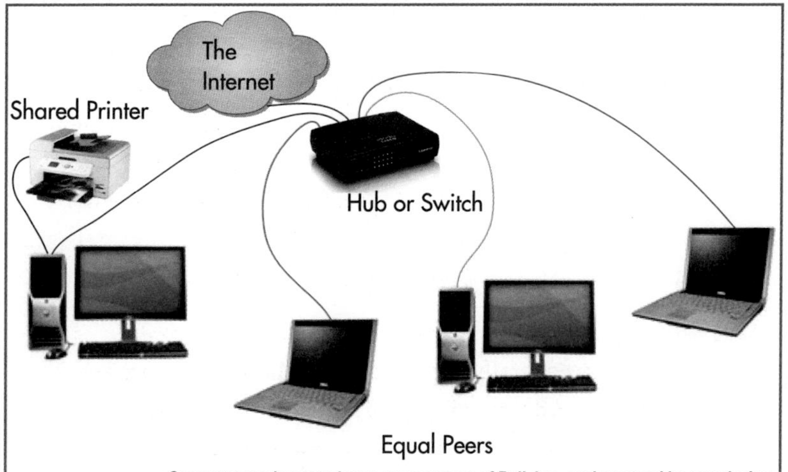

PEER-TO-PEER LANS

All computers in a *peer-to-peer LAN* are both servers and clients and, therefore, share in both providing and using resources. Any computer in the network may store information and provide resources, such as a printer, for the use of any other computer in the network. Peer-to-peer networking is an easy first step to networking, accomplished simply by joining computers together, as shown in Figure 9-1. It does not require the purchase of new computers or significant changes to the way an organization is using computers, yet resources can be shared (as is the printer in Figure 9-1), files and communications can be transferred, and common information can be accessed by all.

Computer equipment photos are courtesy of Dell, Inc., and are used by permission.
Network equipment photos are courtesy of LinkSys by Cisco and are used by permission.

Figure 9-1: **In a peer-to-peer LAN, all computers are both servers and clients.**

Peer-to-peer LANs tend to be used in smaller organizations that do not need to share a large central resource, such as a database, or to have a high degree of security or central control. Each computer in a peer-to-peer LAN is autonomous and often networked with other computers simply to transfer files and share expensive equipment. Putting together a peer-to-peer LAN with existing computers is easy, and can be inexpensive (less than $40 per station).

CLIENT-SERVER LANS

The computers in a *client-server LAN* perform one of two functions: they are either servers or clients. *Servers* manage the network, centrally store information to be shared on the network, and provide the shared resources to the network. *Clients,* or *workstations,* are the users of the network and are standard desktop or laptop computers. To create a network, the clients and server(s) are connected together, with the possible addition of stand-alone network resources, such as printers, as shown in Figure 9-2.

The management functions provided by the server include network security, managing the permissions needed to implement security, communications among network users, and management of shared files on the network. Servers generally are more capable than clients are in terms of having more memory, faster (and possibly more) processors, larger (and maybe more) disks, and more special peripherals, such as large, high-speed tape drives. In general, servers are dedicated to their function and are infrequently used for normal computer tasks, such as word processing.

Clients generally are less capable than servers are and, infrequently, may not even have a disk. Clients usually are standard desktop and laptop computers that perform the normal functions of those types of machines in addition to being part of a network. Clients can also be "mini-servers" by sharing some or all of their disk drives or other resources.

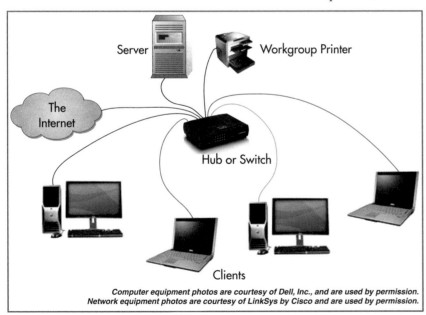

Computer equipment photos are courtesy of Dell, Inc., and are used by permission.
Network equipment photos are courtesy of LinkSys by Cisco and are used by permission.

Figure 9-2: **In a client-server LAN, one or more computers are servers and the rest are clients.**

So the principal difference between peer-to-peer networks and client-server networks is the presence of a dedicated server.

Windows 7 SP1 and Windows Server 2008 R2 work together to form a client-server network operating environment, with Windows Server performing its function and Windows 7 SP1 acting as the client. Several Windows 7 SP1 computers (as well as computers using other versions of Windows, or even other operating systems) can operate in a peer-to-peer network.

There are simple client-server networks, and there are client-server networks where one or more servers are set up as *domain controllers* and the entire network is considered a *domain.* In a large organization, a domain provides many benefits—most importantly, a central registry for all users so that one registration provides access to all the computers and resources in the domain. Domains, however, are complex and require significant expertise to set up and manage. This book, therefore, focuses on setting up and using a peer-to-peer network and on connecting to a client-server network.

Select a Network Standard

Windows 7 SP1 supports the two predominant networking standards: wired Ethernet and wireless. These, in turn, determine the type of hardware you need.

USE WIRED ETHERNET

The wired Ethernet standard comes in several forms based on speed and cable type. The most common, called 10/100/1000BaseT, provides a network that operates at the regular Ethernet speed of 10 Mbps, at the Fast Ethernet speed of 100 Mbps, or at the Gigabit Ethernet speed of 1000 Mbps.

A wired Ethernet 10/100/1000BaseT system, shown in Figure 9-3, has three major components:

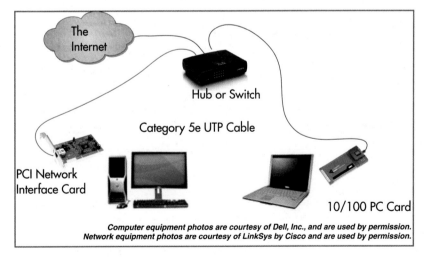

Computer equipment photos are courtesy of Dell, Inc., and are used by permission.
Network equipment photos are courtesy of LinkSys by Cisco and are used by permission.

Figure 9-3: **A wired Ethernet network consists of a card in your computer, a hub or switch into which other computers are connected, and a cable connecting the two.**

● The **network interface card (NIC)** plugs into your computer or is built into it and connects it to the network.

- A **hub**, **switch**, or **router** joins several computers together to form the network:

  - A **hub**, the simplest and oldest device, is where all computers are on the equivalent of a telephone party line (everybody can hear everybody else).

  - A **switch** is a newer device, about the same price as a hub and has virtually made them obsolete, where all computers are on the equivalent of a private telephone line.

  - A **router** joins two different networks, for example, the Internet to a local area network. Often, a router is combined with a hub or a switch, either in one device or in two devices, to join the Internet to several computers.

- An **unshielded twisted-pair (UTP)** telephone-like cable with a simple RJ-45 connector (similar to that for a telephone but larger) joins the NIC to the hub, switch, or router. This cable is called Category 5, enhanced Category 5, or Category 6 ("Cat 5," "Cat 5e," or "Cat 6," respectively).

Ethernet networks are easy to set up (see "Set Up a Network" later in this chapter), have become pervasive throughout organizations, and have an average cost for all components of less than $40 per computer on the network.

USE A WIRELESS LAN

Wireless LANs (WLANs) replace the cable used in a wired network with small radio transceivers (transmitter and receiver) at the computer and at the switch and/or router. There are several wireless standards, but the most common are 802.11b, 802.11g, and 802.11n. All three are Wi-Fi–compliant (Wi-Fi is a trademark for a set of wireless fidelity standards) and are compatible with one another:

- **802.11b** is the oldest and provides data transfer of *up to* 11 Mbps using a secure transmission scheme.

- **802.11g** came next, is currently the dominant standard, is *up to* five times faster than 802.11b (54 Mbps) but generally operates at 22 to 24 Mbps, and is built into many computers.

- **802.11n** is between three and seven times faster than 802.11g, operating between 70 and 140 Mbps under normal conditions, and it can be as much as 10 times faster (300 Mbps) under perfect conditions, which are difficult to achieve. 802.11n will operate proportionally faster at a longer distance than 802.11g will, but all three standards are range-sensitive (the greater the distance between the computer and the wireless access point, the slower the speed).

Most public Wi-Fi locations will handle 802.11b or g, while "n" is usually only available in private businesses and homes.

A WLAN has two components (see Figure 9-4):

- An **access point** is connected to the wired Ethernet network by being plugged into a hub, a switch, or a router. It uses a transceiver to communicate wirelessly with cards that are added to computers using the WLAN.

- An **adapter** plugs into or is built into your computer, and has a transceiver built in to communicate wirelessly with an access point within its range. There are various adapters for use in both notebook and desktop computers.

If the access point is plugged into a hub or switch on a wired network, the wireless computers within the range of the access point operate on the network in exactly the same way as they would with a cable connection, except they are slower. A WLAN has some significant benefits over a normal wired LAN:

- You do not have the expense of cabling and the even higher expense of installing and maintaining cabling.

- Adding and removing users from the network is extremely easy.

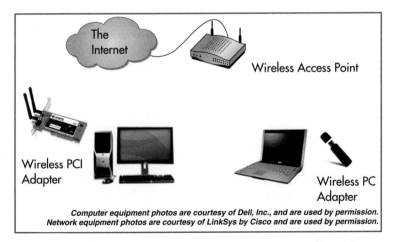

Computer equipment photos are courtesy of Dell, Inc., and are used by permission. Network equipment photos are courtesy of LinkSys by Cisco and are used by permission.

*Figure 9-4: **A wireless network consists of an adapter that plugs into or is built into your computer and an access point that is connected to a wired network, the Internet, or both.***

QUICKSTEPS

SELECTING WIRED ETHERNET HARDWARE

Selecting networking hardware for wired Ethernet means selecting a NIC, a hub or switch, and cabling. For all hardware, a brand-name product giving you a company that stands behind what you are buying can be beneficial. Respected brands of networking gear include 3Com, Cisco and its subsidiary Linksys, D-Link, Netgear, and RealTek.

SELECT A NETWORK INTERFACE CARD

Most new computers come with a built-in 10/100 Ethernet NIC, and some now include 1000 (Gigabit), so you may not need to add this. You already have a NIC if your computer has two telephone-style jacks, one slightly larger than the other. The larger one is the connection to the NIC. The other jack is for the modem.

If you don't have a NIC, you can generally add one to your computer. For a desktop computer, you want a 10/100 or 10/100/1000 NIC for either the PCI (Peripheral Component Interconnect) bus or the USB (Universal Serial Bus). If you use a NIC that plugs into the PCI bus,

Continued . . .

QUICKSTEPS

SELECTING WIRED ETHERNET HARDWARE *(Continued)*

you will need to open the computer case and plug it in. If you are uncomfortable doing that, most computer stores will do it for little more than the cost of the card ($25 to $50). You need to carry in only the computer itself, not the monitor, keyboard, or mouse. If you choose to use a USB NIC, it will cost slightly more, but it plugs into a socket on the outside of the case.[1]

For a laptop computer, the NIC plugs in from the outside, so it is easy to add. It uses one of three connections (in all cases, you want a 10/100/1000 NIC):

- **PC Card,** short for PCMCIA (Personal Computer Memory Card International Association), which goes into a slot on the side of laptops

- **Express card**, which also goes into a slot on the side of newer laptops

- **USB connector**, which plugs into a USB port on the computer, either in laptops or desktops

SELECT CONNECTING DEVICES

As discussed in "Use Wired Ethernet," there are two common connecting devices: hubs, which are like a party-line telephone system where everybody hears all

[1] Network equipment photos are courtesy of LinkSys by Cisco and are used by permission.

Continued . . .

- Users can move easily from office to office.
- Users can roam within an area, say, carrying their laptops to a meeting.
- Visitors can easily get on the network.

The downsides are (potentially) cost, speed, and security, but all of these are manageable. The cost per computer of a wired network, as was said previously, is less than $40 per computer. The cost per computer of a wireless network may be the same or less, considering that a wireless adapter is built into most laptops. The speed difference is more significant, not just because of the difference between a 54-Mbps or higher access point and a 100-Mbps network, but because of the net rate of dividing the 11- or 54-Mbps access point by the number of people trying to use it. Despite these drawbacks, there is a large movement to WLANs, and a number of systems are being sold for both offices and homes.

Set Up a Network

When you installed Windows 7 SP1, a basic set of networking services was installed and configured using system defaults. This setup may, but doesn't always, provide an operable networking system. Look at these three areas to set up *basic networking*, which means that your computer can communicate with other computers in the network:

- Be sure the NIC is properly set up.
- Install the networking functions that you want to perform.
- Review your network security settings.

Set Up Network Interface Cards

If the computer you are setting up has a NIC that is both certified for Windows 7 and fully Plug and Play–compatible, then your NIC was installed by Windows Setup without incident and you don't need to read this section. Otherwise, this section examines how the NIC was installed and what you need to do to make it operational.

QUICKSTEPS

SELECTING WIRED ETHERNET HARDWARE *(Continued)*

the traffic; and switches, which are like a private-line telephone system. Switches once cost a lot more, so hubs were used. Today, switches and hubs are virtually the same price. A simple switch runs from under $20, for a 10/100 four-port one, to under $50 for an eight-port Gigabit switch. You need a port for each user on the system, plus one for your broadband (DSL or cable) Internet connection. The largest switches have 48 ports, but you can stack switches by plugging them into one another. You want at least an Ethernet 10/100 switch and possibly a Gigabit one with the number of ports that meet your needs.

SELECT CABLING

For 10/100 Ethernet networking, you need either Category 5 or Category 5e cabling with RJ-45 male connectors on each end. Such cables come in various colors and lengths, up to 100 feet with the ends molded on, or in lengths up to 1,000 feet without the ends, where you need a crimping tool to add the ends (*not* a simple task!). Cat 5e cable, which provides better transmission capability, is almost the same price as Cat 5, so I recommend it, and if you are going to use Gigabit Ethernet, you need Cat5e or even Cat 6.

Assuming that a NIC *is* properly plugged into the computer, any of these things could be causing it to not operate:

● The NIC driver is not recognized by Windows 7 SP1; it is either missing or not properly installed.

● The NIC is not functioning properly.

Look at each of these possibilities in turn.

CHECK THE NIC AND ITS DRIVER

Check the status of your NIC and whether you have a driver installed. If you don't, you can install one.

1. Click **Start** and click **Control Panel**. In Category view, click **Network And Internet**, and then click **Network And Sharing Center**. The Network And Sharing Center window opens.

2. In the Network And Sharing Center, the top of which is shown in Figure 9-5, you can see if you are connected to a network by looking for the double line between your computer and the network icon in the center. See if you are connected to the Internet by looking for the double line between the network icon and the Internet icon on the right. In the middle-right area of the Network And Sharing Center, you can see if you have a local area connection (wired) and/or a wireless connection. If your Network And Sharing Center looks like Figure 9-5, you have all these connections (you don't need both a local area connection and a wireless connection) and you can be assured your NIC is working, and you can skip to the next chapter.

3. If you do not see the connections shown in Figure 9-5, you need to start the process of figuring out why and getting it fixed. Click **Change Adapter Settings** in the left pane. The Network Connections window opens. If you have an icon in the window labeled "Local Area Connection" and/or "Wireless Network Connection," as shown here, you have the NIC driver properly installed and you can go on to the section "Enable Windows 7 SP1's Networking Functions."

4. If you do not have a Local Area Connection icon, you must first install a Windows 7 driver for the NIC. Since a driver was not automatically installed by Windows 7 SP1, you will need to get one before proceeding. If a driver did not come with the NIC (most likely on a CD), you need to use another computer attached to the Internet to locate and download it.

NOTE

Lessened security is also a potential downside with wireless if it isn't set up properly. For example, if you don't turn on encryption and the use of passwords, your neighbor (or hacker cruising your neighborhood) might be able to get on your network or look at your network traffic.

TIP

If you want to network only two computers, you can do so without a hub or a switch, but you need a special *crossover* cable where the connections are reversed on each end. Most computer stores carry such a cable.

QUICKSTEPS

SELECTING WIRELESS HARDWARE

Selecting networking hardware for a wireless network means selecting a wireless adapter and a wireless access point. The same manufacturers as were listed for wired Ethernet hardware are recommended.

SELECT A WIRELESS SPEED

If you are installing a new wireless network, the up-to-54-Mbps 802.11g standard is the minimum, and you probably want to consider the up-to-300-Mbps 802.11n, although "n" is new and may be more expensive.

SELECT A WIRELESS ADAPTER

Most laptops come with a built-in wireless adapter, so you may not need to buy one. For a desktop computer, you will need a PCI or USB wireless adapter for the speed you have chosen, and, with PCI, you will need to open up the computer to plug it in or have a store do it. For a laptop computer without the built-in capability, you

Continued . . .

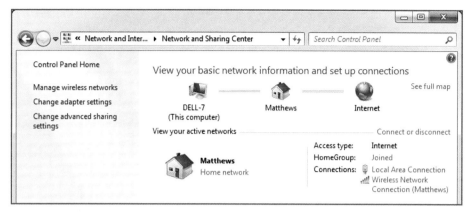

*Figure 9-5: **The Network And Sharing Center will tell you if you are connected to a local area network or a wireless network and to the Internet.***

5. On the other computer, bring up the manufacturer's website, locate and download the Windows 7 driver (you need to know the make and model of the NIC), copy it onto a disc or a USB flash drive, and then go back to the original computer.

6. Click **Start** and click **Control Panel**. In Category view, click **Hardware And Sound**, and then, under Devices And Printers, click **Device Manager**. The Device Manager window opens.

7. Double-click **Network Adapters** to display the network adapter in your computer. If you see your NIC and it doesn't have a problem icon (an exclamation point), Windows thinks that the NIC is installed and running properly. If you double-click the device, you should see the device status, "This device is working properly." If so, you may need to only install a new driver. Skip to step 14.

8. If you see your NIC with a problem icon, double-click the NIC. You will most likely see a device status message telling you that a driver was not installed. Skip to step 14.

9. If you don't see your NIC in the Device Manager window, click the **Action** menu, and click **Add Legacy Hardware**. The Add Hardware Wizard will open. Click **Next**. Click

QUICKSTEPS

SELECTING WIRELESS HARDWARE

(Continued)

need a PC Card, Express Card, or USB wireless adapter of the appropriate speed, which you can easily plug in (you need to check whether your laptop uses a PC Card or Express Card adapter by looking at the information that came with your computer).

SELECT A WIRELESS ACCESS POINT

Wireless access points come in simple versions that plug into a wired Ethernet network, as well as more sophisticated versions, called "wireless broadband routers," that terminate a DSL, FiOS (fiber optic), or cable Internet connection. You have that choice and a choice of speeds when you choose a wireless access point.

Install The Hardware That I Manually Select From A List—you don't want Windows to search for new hardware; if it was *going* to find it, it would have—and click **Next**.

10. Double-click **Network Adapters** in the Common Hardware Types list. A list of network adapters appears. If your NIC had been on the list, Windows Setup would have found it, so you need to insert and use either the disk that you made prior to step 3 or the disk that came with the NIC.

11. Click **Have Disk**. Click **Browse**, locate the appropriate drive, and click **OK**. When the drive is displayed, select the driver for your adapter, and click **Next**. When told that the device will be installed, click **Next** again.

12. You may see a message stating that the driver you are about to install does not have a Microsoft digital signature. Click **Yes** to go ahead and install it anyway. The driver and its necessary supporting software will be installed.

13. Click **Finish**. The Network Connections window should now show the Local Area Connection icon. If you see this icon, go to the section "Enable Windows 7 SP1's Networking Functions."

14. If you saw your NIC in the Device Manager window, with or without a problem icon, you can install or reinstall a driver from there. Place the disk with the driver software in the drive. Right-click your NIC and click **Update Driver Software**, as shown in Figure 9-6.

15. Click **Browse My Computer For Driver Software**, click **Browse**, locate the drive and folder with the driver, and click **Next**. You will be told when the driver is installed. Click **Close** to close the Update Driver Software dialog box.

If you still do not have a Local Area Connection icon, or if some other problem occurred in the preceding process that does not point to an obvious solution, continue through the next section to see if a solution is presented.

DETERMINE IF A NIC IS FUNCTIONING

If installing a NIC driver did not cause the Local Area Connection icon to appear, it is likely that the NIC itself is not functioning properly. The easiest way to test that is to replace the NIC with a known good one, ideally one that is both Windows 7–certified and Plug and Play–compatible. It is wise to have a spare NIC; they are not expensive (as low as $20), and replacing a suspected bad one can quickly solve many problems.

NOTE

In many of the steps in the following sections of this chapter, you will be interrupted and asked by User Account Control (UAC) for permission to make changes to the computer. So long as it is something you started, click **Yes** and, if needed, enter an administrator's password. To keep the steps as simple as possible, we have left out the UAC instructions. Chapter 8 discusses UAC in more detail.

TIP

You can change the name, "Local Area Connection," that appears in the Network Connections window. For example, if you install two NIC cards, you can give each of them a descriptive name by right-clicking the icon and clicking **Rename**.

TIP

I went through the process of downloading a driver and found it painless. The hard part is figuring out what type of card you have, because often it is not written on the card. You may be able to see it in step 6 of "Check the NIC and Its Driver." If not, you need to locate purchase records or documentation—if you know which records go with the card.

TIP

If you suspect that your NIC is not working and it is built into the computer, you can still add another NIC and use it. Almost all systems allow you to have two or more NICs installed.

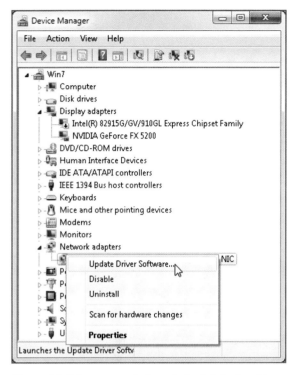

Figure 9-6: *It is common to have to install device driver software for older hardware.*

Enable Windows 7 SP1's Networking Functions

Windows 7 SP1's networking functions provide the software for a computer to access other computers and, separately, for other computers to access the computer you are working on. In other words, the two primary functions allow the computer to be a client (it accesses other computers) and to be a server (other computers access it). Make sure that these two services are enabled by following these steps (the steps are the same for both a wired and a wireless network—only the option and title names are different; the figures show a wired network).

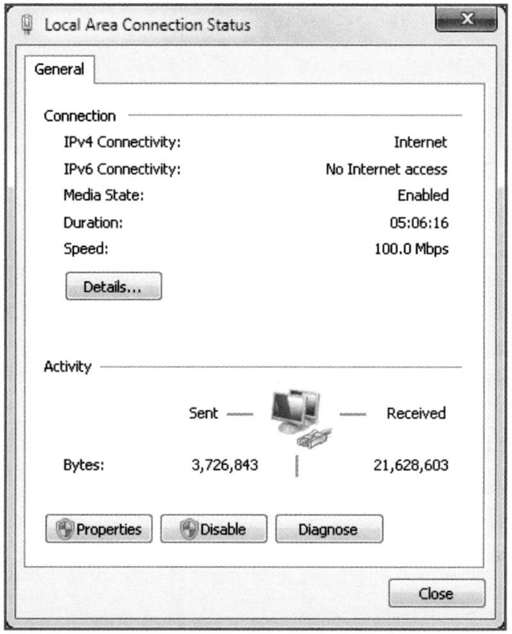

1. Click **Start** and click **Control Panel**. In Category view, click **Network And Internet**, and then click **Network And Sharing Center**. The Network And Sharing Center window opens.

2. Click **Local Area Connection** (or **Wireless Network Connection** in the middle-right area). The Local Area Connection Status dialog box appears, as shown in Figure 9-7. In the particular case shown here, the computer indicates it is connected to the network and that it is sending and receiving information, which indicates it is correctly set up.

3. Click **Properties**. The Local Area Connection Properties dialog box, shown in Figure 9-8, appears and displays the services and protocols that have been installed automatically.

   The minimum services needed for networking are Client For Microsoft Networks and File And Printer Sharing For Microsoft Networks, plus one protocol, Transmission Control Protocol/Internet Protocol Version 4 (TCP/IPv4). By default, Windows 7 SP1 installs an additional service and three additional protocols.

4. Click **Install**. The Select Network Feature Type dialog box appears, in which you can add clients, services, and protocols.

Figure 9-7: If your NIC is working correctly, you should see a lot of information being sent and received.

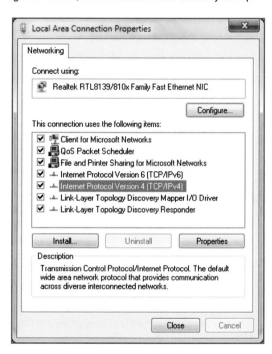

Figure 9-8: Windows 7 SP1 automatically installs the networking services and protocols shown here.

NOTE

In "Enable Windows 7 SP1's Networking Functions" and "Configure a Networking Protocol" you can use the Have Disk button to install unique, non-Windows services for special purposes.

INSTALL A CLIENT

1. Double-click **Client**. If you already have Client For Microsoft Networks installed, you will not have any services to install.

2. If Client For Microsoft Networks is not installed, select it and, in any case, click **OK**.

INSTALL A SERVICE

Windows 7 SP1 provides two services, both of which are automatically installed:

- **File And Printer Sharing For Microsoft Networks** handles the sharing of resources on your computer.

- **QoS (Quality of Service) Packet Scheduler** helps balance a network and alleviate bottlenecks when one part of the network is fast and another part is slow.

1. In the Select Network Feature Type dialog box, double-click **Service**. If you already have File And Printer Sharing For Microsoft Networks and QoS Packet Scheduler installed, you will not have any services to install.

2. If File And Printer Sharing For Microsoft Networks and QoS Packet Scheduler are not installed, select them and, in any case, click **OK**.

Configure a Networking Protocol

Networking protocols are a set of standards used to package and transmit information over a network. The protocol determines how the information is divided into packets, how it is addressed, and what is done to assure it is reliably transferred. The protocol is, therefore, very important to the success of networking, and its choice is a major one. Windows 7 SP1 offers three Internet protocols and two network-mapping protocols:

- **Internet Protocol Version 4 (TCP/IPv4)**, for use with the Internet and most LANs

- **Internet Protocol Version 6 (TCP/IPv6)**, the newest system for use with the widest variety of networks (some Internet service providers and the routers they provide for DSL and cable Internet service do not handle IPv6, but that will change very quickly, because the world is about to run out of the over four billion IPv4 addresses in 2011)

- **Reliable Multicast Protocol**, which is a special one-to-many protocol used in conferencing

- **Link-Layer Topology Discovery Mapper I/O Driver** that goes out and finds devices on the network

- **Link-Layer Topology Discovery Responder** that responds when it is queried by a Discovery Mapper

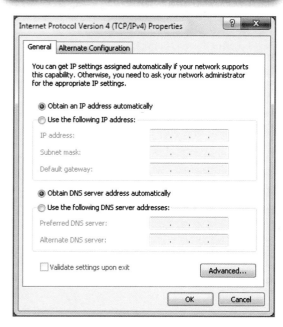

Figure 9-9: If you use dynamic IP addresses that are automatically assigned, you don't have to worry about having two devices or computers with the same IP address.

All of these protocols, except Reliable Multicast Protocol, are installed by default. If the computer you are working on is or will be connected to the Internet, it will require TCP/IPv4.

CHECK AND CHANGE PROTOCOLS

Check (and change if necessary) the protocols that have been installed and the settings that are being used.

1. In the Select Network Feature Type dialog box, double-click **Protocol**. The Select Network Protocol dialog box appears listing the available protocols.

2. If you see any protocol you want installed, double-click it. If you want to install another protocol, double-click it too. Otherwise, click **Cancel** twice to close the Select Network Protocol and Select Network Feature Type dialog boxes.

3. Select the **Internet Protocol Version 4 (TCP/IPv4)** protocol in the Local Area Connection Properties dialog box, and click **Properties**. The Internet Protocol (TCP/IP) Properties dialog box appears, shown in Figure 9-9. Here you can choose either to use a dynamic IP (Internet Protocol) address automatically assigned by a server or DSL router or to enter a static IP address.

   If you have a server or a DSL router that automatically assigns IP addresses, you need to leave the Obtain An IP Address Automatically option selected (it is selected by default).

ENTER YOUR OWN IP ADDRESS

1. If you are working on a computer that you know must have a static IP address, click **Use The Following IP Address** and enter an IP address. The IP address that you use should be from the block of IP addresses that an ISP or other authority has assigned to your organization.

2. If you entered a static IP address, you must also enter a subnet mask. This mask tells the IP which part of an IP address to consider a network address and which part to consider a computer, or *host,* address. If your organization was assigned a block of IP addresses, it was also given a subnet mask. If you used the APIPA range of addresses, use 255.255.0.0 as the subnet mask.

OBTAIN AN IP ADDRESS AUTOMATICALLY

1. If you don't have a specific reason to use a static IP address, click **Obtain An IP Address Automatically**, and use the addresses from either a server or DSL router on the network or APIPA.

TIP

If the server is down or nonexistent, Automatic Private IP Addressing (APIPA) assigns an IP address. APIPA is limited insofar as a computer using it can talk only to other computers in the same range of numbers. If all computers in a small network are using Windows 98/Me, Windows 2000/XP, or Windows Vista/7/7SP1 and have Obtain An IP Address Automatically selected, without a DHCP server, they will all automatically use the 169.254.0.0 through 169.254.255.255 range of IP addresses.

TIP

If your organization doesn't plan to directly access an outside network like the Internet or you have a router between your network and the Internet, the static IP address can be from the block of APIPA numbers or from several other blocks of private IP addresses. (See the "Getting a Block of IP Addresses" QuickSteps.)

2. Click **OK** to close the Internet Protocol Version 4 (TCP/IPv4) Properties dialog box, click **Close** to close the Local Area Connection Properties dialog box, click **Close** to close the Local Area Connection Status dialog box, and close all open dialog boxes and windows.

3. Click **Start**, click the **Shut Down** right arrow, and click **Restart**. This is required to utilize your network settings.

VERIFY YOUR CONNECTION

1. When the computer restarts, reopen the Local Area Connection Status dialog box (click **Start** and click **Control Panel**; in Category view, click **Network And Internet**, and then click **Network And Sharing Center**). Click **Local Area Connection** in the middle-right area to open the Local Area Connection Status dialog box. You should see activity on both the Sent and Received sides.

2. If you do not see both sending and receiving activity, click **Start**, click in the **Search Programs And Files** text box, enter a computer name in your same subnet in the form *computername*\, and press **ENTER**. Windows Explorer will open and you should see the drives on the computer you entered, as shown in Figure 9-10. If you see this,

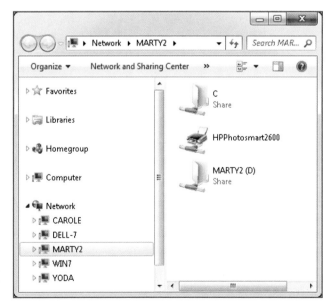

Figure 9-10: **When networking is functioning properly, you'll be able to see shared resources on other computers in your network.**

GETTING A BLOCK OF IP ADDRESSES

The block of IP addresses you use with the Internet Protocol depends on whether the computers to be assigned the addresses will be private or public.

GET PRIVATE IP ADDRESSES

If the computers will be operating only on an internal network, where they are separated from the public network by a router or bridge, they are *private* and need only organizational uniqueness. Four blocks of IP addresses have been set aside and can be used by any organization for its private, internal needs without any coordination with any other organization, but these blocks should not be used for directly connecting to the Internet. These private-use blocks of IP addresses are:

- 10.0.0.0 through 10.255.255.255
- 169.254.0.0 through 169.254.255.255 (the APIPA range)
- 172.16.0.0 through 172.31.255.255
- 192.168.0.0 through 192.168.255.255

GET PUBLIC IP ADDRESSES

If your computer(s) will be interfacing directly with the Internet, they are *public* and thus need a globally unique IP number. If you want a block of public IP addresses, you must request it from one of several organizations, depending on the size of the block that you want. At the local level, for a moderate-sized block of IP addresses, your local ISP can assign it to you. For a larger block, a regional ISP may be able to handle the request. If not, you have to go to one of three regional Internet registries:

- American Registry for Internet Numbers (ARIN), at arin.net, which covers North and South America, the Caribbean, and sub-Saharan Africa

Continued . . .

the computer is networked. If this doesn't work, you need to double-check all the possible settings previously described:

- If you are using APIPA, make sure that the computer you are trying to contact is also using that range of numbers, either as a static assigned address or with automatic assignment.
- If all the settings are correct, check the cabling by making a simple connection of just several computers.
- If you do a direct connection between two computers, remember that you need a special crossover cable with the transmitting and receiving wires reversed.
- If all else fails, replace the NIC.
- It could also be that network security is getting in your way of seeing the drives and resources on the other computer. See "Review Network Security" later in this chapter.

With a good NIC, good cabling, the correct settings, and network security properly handled, you'll be able to network.

Test a Network Setup and Connection

You can use several command-line utilities to test a TCP/IP installation. The more useful of these commands are the following:

- **Ipconfig** is used to determine if a network configuration has been initialized and if an IP address is assigned. If an IP address and valid subnet mask are returned, the configuration is initialized and there are no duplicates for the IP address. If a subnet mask of 0.0.0.0 is returned, the IP address is a duplicate.
- **Hostname** is used to determine the computer name of the local computer.
- **Ping** is used to query either the local computer or another computer on the network to see whether it responds. If the local computer responds, you know that TCP/IP is bound to the local NIC and that both are operating correctly. If the other computer responds, you know that TCP/IP and the NICs in both computers are operating correctly and that the connection between the computers is operable. Figure 9-11 shows the testing results on my system.

1. Click **Start**, click **All Programs**, click **Accessories**, and click **Command Prompt**. The Command Prompt window opens.

QUICKSTEPS

GETTING A BLOCK OF IP ADDRESSES (Continued)

- Réseaux IP Européens (RIPE), at ripe.net, which covers Europe, the Middle East, and northern Africa

- Asia Pacific Network Information Centre (APNIC), at apnic.net, which covers Asia and the Pacific

CAUTION

Remember that private ranges work only with other computers in their own subnets and with IP addresses from the same range. You can tell what the subnet is from the subnet mask. For example, with a subnet mask of 255.255.255.0, all computers in the network must have IP addresses with the same first three groups of numbers and vary only in the last group. Thus, computers with the numbers 192.168.104.001 and 192.168.104.002 are in the same subnet.

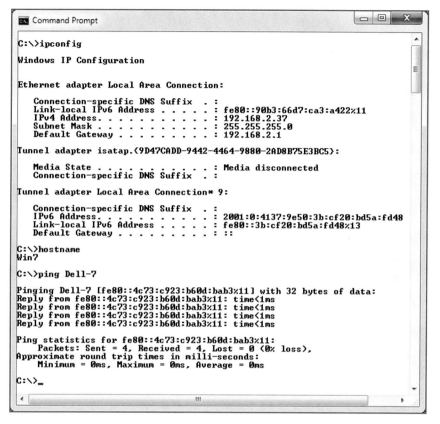

Figure 9-11: *You can test a network with TCP/IP utilities such as Ipconfig, Hostname, and Ping.*

2. Type ipconfig and press **ENTER**. The IP address and subnet mask of the current computer should be returned. If this did not happen, there is a problem with the current configuration.

3. Type hostname and press **ENTER**. The computer name of the local computer should be returned.

4. Type ping, type a space, type the name of another computer on your network, and press **ENTER**. You should get four replies from the other computer.

NOTE

The 127.0.0.1 IP address is a special address set aside to refer to the computer on which it is entered.

5. If Ping did not work with a remote computer, try it on the current computer by typing ping 127.0.0.1 and pressing **ENTER**. Again, you should get four replies, this time from the current computer. If you didn't get a reply here, you have a problem with either the network setup or the NIC. If you did get a reply here but not in step 4, there is a problem either in the other computer or in the cable and devices connecting them.

6. Type exit and press **ENTER** to close the Command Prompt window.

If you do find a problem here, go on to the next section on network security, and then review earlier sections on setting up network hardware, functions, and protocols to isolate and fix the problem.

Review Network Security

Chapter 8 discusses network security in depth. This section provides a brief synopsis of the specific steps you need to take to share your computer across a LAN so that other computers similarly set up can see your computer and access the drives, folders, and printers. You will be able to see and access other computers that do the same thing. The steps to take in the appropriate order are described next. The specific steps to open the required windows and dialog boxes, as well as the specific settings to use, are provided in Chapter 8.

1. When you complete the installation of Windows 7 SP1, or the first time you turn on a new computer with Windows 7 SP1 already installed, you are asked if the network you want to be a part of will be at home, at work, or in some public location, as shown in Figure 9-12. Both Home and Work are considered private locations where you want your computer to be seen and shared. You can change this later on (see step 2).

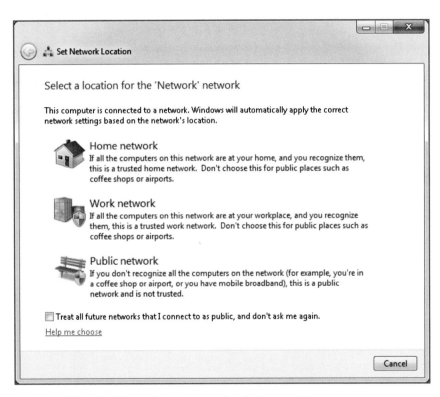

Figure 9-12: **Decide if the network you use is private or public.**

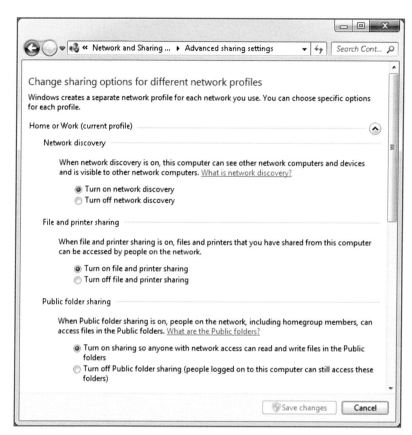

Figure 9-13: **Turn on the sharing of your computer.**

2. If you want to share your computer's resources, such as files, folders, disk drives, and printers, you need to turn on that capability (it is turned off by default in a Work and Public network, but partially turned on in a homegroup Home network). This is done in the Advanced Sharing Settings window, shown in Figure 9-13, for both the private and public aspects of this computer.

3. To share individual drives, folders, and printers, you must turn on that capability for the most senior drive or folder you want to share (also known as the parent). Subsidiary folders and the files within those folders will inherit the sharing aspect of the parent unless you individually change that sharing. Only in a homegroup can you share the full C: (or system) drive. Sharing a drive, folder, or printer is done through the object's Properties dialog box, shown in Figure 9-14.

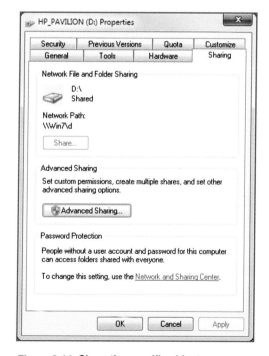

Figure 9-14: **Share the specific objects you want others to be able to use.**

4. Finally, you must set up Windows Firewall to allow the network and its sharing aspects to come through even though you have Windows Firewall turned on (which is highly recommended). Setting up the firewall to allow networking is done in the Windows Firewall Allowed Programs window, shown in Figure 9-15.

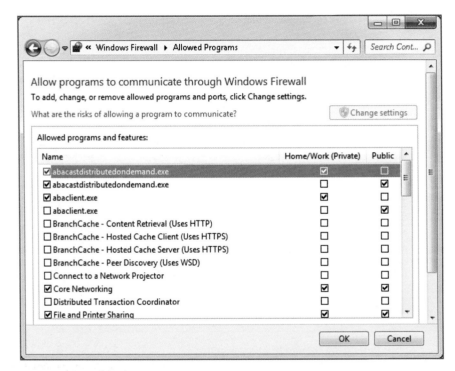

Figure 9-15: *Make sure Windows Firewall allows networking.*

Chapter 10
Using Networking

Networking brings a vastly enlarged world of computing to you, giving you access to all the computers, printers, and other devices to which you are connected and have permission to access. Using a network and its resources is no more difficult than accessing the hard disk or printer that is directly connected to your computer. Your network connection can be either wired or wireless, and you'll notice no difference, except for the hardware and the possibility that wireless is slower.

In this chapter you'll see how to access other computers and printers over a local area network (LAN), how to let others access your computer and resources, and how to access your computer remotely—across a LAN, through a telephone connection, or over the Internet.

Access Network Resources

Begin by looking at the network available to you through your computer. Then access a disk and retrieve files and folders from another computer, use a network printer, and access the Internet over the network.

Explore a Network

Whether you have just installed a small home network or have just plugged into a large company network, the first thing you'll probably want to do is explore it—see what you can see. You can do that from Windows Explorer.

1. Click **Start**, click **Computer**, scroll down the navigation pane, and click **Network** to open it. The network resources will be displayed, as you see in Figure 10-1.

2. Double-click one of the shared computers on your network. It will open and display the drives, printers, and other resources (such as memory cards, USB flash drives, and removable disks) on that computer.

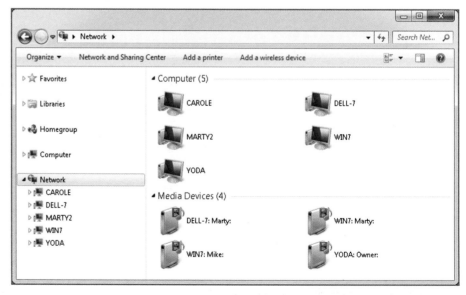

Figure 10-1: *Opening your network displays the computers and media that are being shared.*

TIP

The shared folders, disks, and other resources that appear when you open your network are the result of your computer having searched your workgroup or domain for shared resources. When you first set up networking, you won't see anything until resources have been shared by other computers and your computer has had time to find them.

3. In the navigation pane, click the triangle next to one of the drives to open it, and then click one or more of the folders to see the files available to you (see Figure 10-2).

4. Click **Back** one or more times, and then open other computers, drives, and folders to more fully explore your network.

5. Click **Close** to close Windows Explorer.

Permanently Connect to a Network Resource

If you use a specific network drive or folder a lot, you may want to connect to it permanently so that you can use it as if it were a drive on your computer. This permanent connection is called a "mapped network drive." Note that it is only "permanent" until you decide to disconnect from the drive. See "Disconnect a Mapped Drive" later in this chapter.

CONNECT TO A MAPPED NETWORK DRIVE

To set up a mapped network drive:

1. Click **Start**, click **Computer**, scroll down the navigation pane, and click **Network** to open it. The network resources will be displayed, as you saw in Figure 10-1.

   In the navigation pane, click the triangle opposite **Network**, and click the computer that contains the drive you want to connect to permanently. You should see the drive in the subject pane.

2. Right-click the drive in the subject pane, and click **Map Network Drive** (see Figure 10-3). The Map Network Drive dialog box will appear.

3. Select the drive letter you want to use for the mapped drive or the specific folder, if that is applicable; choose whether you want to reconnect to the drive every time you log on to your computer; and choose whether you need to use different credentials—whether you want to log on to that resource using a different user name and password.

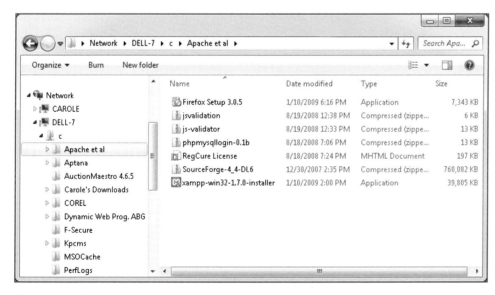

Figure 10-2: If the computers on your network have been shared, you should be able to see the folders, files, and other resources that are available to you.

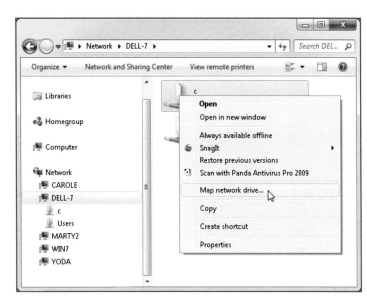

Figure 10-3: Mapping a network drive gives you a permanent connection to that device.

4. Click **Finish**. The drive will open in a separate window. Close that window.

5. In the navigation pane of the original Windows Explorer window, click the triangle to the left of **Network** to close it. Then, if it isn't already displayed, click **Computer** to open that view. Both in the navigation pane and in the subject pane, you should see the new network drive, as shown in the Network Location area of Figure 10-4.

6. Close Windows Explorer.

DISCONNECT A MAPPED DRIVE

1. Click **Start**, click **Computer**, and, if needed, scroll down the navigation pane so you can see your mapped drive(s).

2. In the navigation pane, right-click the mapped network drive, and click **Disconnect**. The drive will disappear from the navigation and subject panes.

If you see an error message saying you have files open on the mapped drive and that you may lose data if you don't close the files before disconnecting, check if you do have files open, and if so, close them. Then once you are sure nothing is open, click **Yes** to disconnect.

In order to connect to a network, one has to first be created. If that hasn't been done, return to Chapter 8 and follow the instructions there.

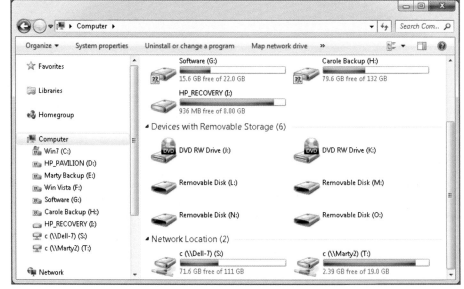

Figure 10-4: You have the same access to a mapped network drive across a network as you do to any drive on your computer.

Connect Outside Your Workgroup or Domain

If you want to connect to another computer or network resource outside of your workgroup or domain, you will not see that computer or resource when you open Network view. You must use a different procedure to connect to it.

1. Click **Start** and click **Computer**. Scroll down and click **Network**. The Network window opens, as you saw in Figure 10-1.

2. Click **Network And Sharing Center** on the toolbar. The Network And Sharing Center window will open.

3. Click **Connect To A Network**. A list of the networks you can connect to is displayed. Click the network you want, and click **Connect**.

4. If requested, enter a user name and a password, and click **OK**. Given the appropriate permissions, you'll see and be able to open the computers in the other network.

5. Close the Network And Sharing Center and Windows Explorer.

Copy Network Files and Information

Once you have opened a network resource, it is easy to copy information from the resource to your local hard disk.

1. Click **Start** and click **Computer**. If needed, scroll through the navigation pane, and click the triangle opposite **Network** to open it. Then open the computer, drive, and folder(s) in order to see the files that you want to copy in the subject pane.

2. In the navigation pane on your local computer, click the triangle opposite the drive and, if needed, open the folder to display the folder you want to hold the information from the network.

3. In the subject pane, click the first file or folder you want to copy, and then hold down **CTRL**, clicking the remaining files and/or folders you want. When all are selected, drag them to the folder in the navigation pane in which you want them, as you can see in Figure 10-5.

4. Close Windows Explorer.

QUICKSTEPS

FINDING OR ADDING A NETWORK PRINTER

There are two ways to find a network printer: by using Find Printer in the Print dialog boxes of some programs and by using Add A Printer in the Printers And Faxes dialog box.

USE FIND PRINTER

Recent versions of Microsoft Office products and other applications have included a Find Printer button to search for and locate network printers. This is the same as the printer search capability, which uses the Windows domain's Active Directory service. To use this, you must be in a domain and not in a workgroup.

1. In an Office 2010 application, click the **File** tab, click the **Printer** down arrow, and click **Add Printer**. If your network is not part of an Active Directory domain, you will get a message to that effect. Otherwise, the Find Printers dialog box will appear and begin a search for a printer.

2. A list of printers will be displayed. When you have located the printer you want, right-click that printer and click **Connect**.

3. Close the Search Results window.

USE ADD A PRINTER

Add A Printer is the most common way to locate a network printer, and is available to both workgroup and domain users.

1. Click **Start** and click **Devices And Printers**. The Devices And Printers window opens.

2. Click **Add A Printer**. Click **Add A Network, Wireless, Or Bluetooth Printer**. A list of printers will be presented to you (see Figure 10-6). Select one and click **Next**.

Continued . . .

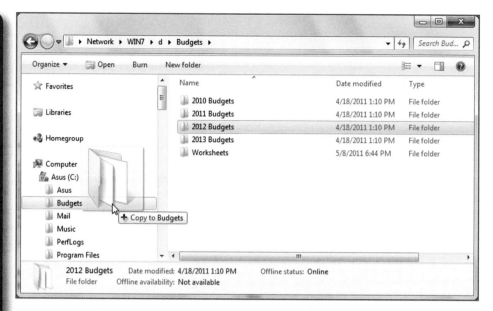

Figure 10-5: *You can locate and copy files and folders across the network.*

Print on Network Printers

Like using other network resources, using a network printer is not much different from using a local printer. To locate a network printer, see the "Finding or Adding a Network Printer" QuickSteps.

To use a network printer that has been previously found, either automatically or manually—from Microsoft Word 2010, for example:

1. Click the **File** tab, and click **Print** to open the Print dialog box.

2. Under Printer, click the down arrow, and choose the network printer you want to use.

3. Make any needed adjustments to the printer settings, and click **Print** to complete the printing.

QUICKSTEPS

FINDING OR ADDING A NETWORK PRINTER (Continued)

3. If you don't see a list of printers, click **The Printer That I Want Isn't Listed**. Click **Select A Shared Printer By Name**, click **Browse**, double-click the computer that has the printer you want, and then double-click the printer. You should see the printer you want in the Add Printer dialog box, as shown in Figure 10-7.

4. Click **Next**. A permanent connection will be made to the printer. Click **Install Driver** if you are asked to do so. Click **Next**.

5. If desired, click the **Set As The Default Printer** check box. Click **Print A Test Page**. When a test page prints, click **Close** and then click **Finish**. If a test page does not print, click **Get Help With Printing**, and follow the suggestions.

6. Close Control Panel.

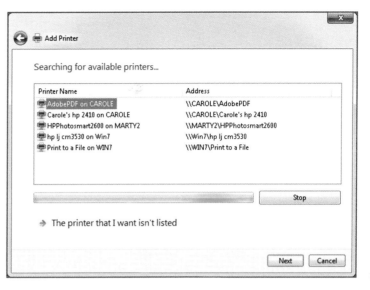

Figure 10-6: The automatic search for a printer may not find the printer you are looking for if you are not on an Active Directory domain.

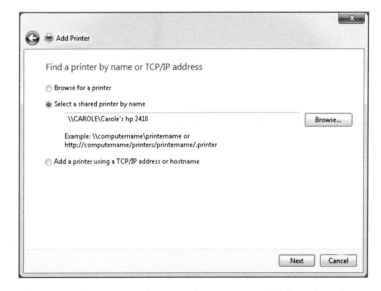

Figure 10-7: If you know of a network computer to which a printer has been attached and it has been shared, you can connect to it easily.

Access a Network Internet Connection

If the network you are on has an Internet connection, you are automatically connected to it and can use it directly, unless it requires a user name and password. In most instances, you simply have to open your browser (click the **Internet Explorer** icon on the taskbar) or your email program (click **Start**, click **All Programs**, and click **Windows Live Mail**), and you are using the Internet. See Chapter 4 for more information.

Let Others Access Your Resources

The other side of the networking equation is sharing the resources on your computer to allow others to use them. This includes sharing your files, folders, and disks, as well as sharing your printers. The mechanics of setting up your computer to share its resources is discussed in depth in Chapters 8 and 9 (in particular, see Chapter 8). Here we'll look at how that is used once it is turned on.

Share Files and Folders

You can share files and folders by putting them into a shared folder. By default, your computer has a series of folders within Libraries that can be shared; however, the folders aren't shared by default unless you are in a homegroup. You can also create more shared folders (see Chapters 8 and 9).

1. Click **Start**, click **Computer**, and open the disk and folder(s) needed to locate and display the files and/or folders you want to share in the subject pane.

2. In the navigation pane, click the triangle opposite Libraries and Documents to display the Public Documents folder. Click its triangle, if shown, to open any currently shared subfolders.

3. Drag the files and/or folders you want to share from the subject pane to one of the Libraries folders in the navigation pane, as shown in Figure 10-8.

4. Close Windows Explorer.

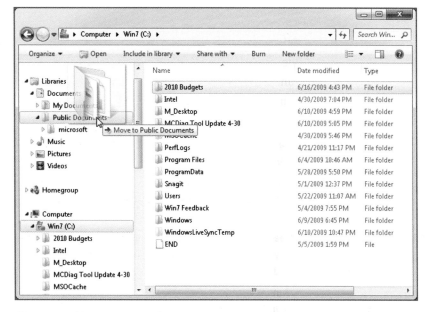

Figure 10-8: You can share a file by putting it into one of the Libraries folders.

Work Remotely

Windows 7 SP1 allows you to work remotely from another computer—for example, from a remote computer (like your laptop) to a computer or server in your office—using Windows 7 SP1's Remote Desktop Connection. The objective is to transfer information and utilize resources from a distance using a LAN connection. Using Remote Desktop Connection requires both a Remote Desktop host and a Remote Desktop client.

Set Up a Remote Desktop Connection

Remote Desktop Connection enables you to literally take control of another computer and do everything on it as if you were sitting in front of that computer. Remote Desktop Connection is run over a LAN, where the computer you are sitting at is the *client* and the computer you are accessing is the *host*. To set up the host, you must first establish user accounts and then enable a LAN-based host.

SET UP REMOTE DESKTOP ACCOUNTS

To use Remote Desktop Connection, the host must have user accounts established for that purpose and the user accounts must have a password. Therefore, the first step in setting up the account is to set up one or more such accounts on the host.

1. Click **Start** and click **Control Panel**. In Category view, click **User Accounts And Family Safety**, and then click **User Accounts**.

2. Click **Manage Another Account**, click **Create A New Account**, enter the name for the account (this example uses "Remote"), select the type of account you want, and click **Create Account**.

3. Click the new account, click **Create A Password**, enter the password, press TAB, type the password again, press TAB twice, enter a hint if you wish (anyone can see the hint), and click **Create Password**. Close the Change An Account window.

4. Click **Start** and click **Control Panel**. In Category view, click **System And Security**, scroll to the bottom, and click **Administrative Tools**.

NOTE

Only Windows 7 or Windows 7 SP1 Professional, Enterprise, and Ultimate editions can be a Remote Desktop host. All versions of Windows 7 SP1 can be a Remote Desktop client, as can Windows Vista, Windows XP, and older versions of Windows with Windows XP Client installed.

Figure 10-9: *User accounts must be members of the Remote Desktop Users group in order to use Remote Desktop Connection.*

Figure 10-10: *Remote Desktop Connection is not turned on by default.*

5. In the subject pane, double-click **Computer Management**. In the Computer Management window that opens, in the left column, if it isn't already open, click the triangle opposite **System Tools** to open it, click the triangle opposite **Local Users And Groups** to open it, and click **Users**. In the list of users in the subject pane, shown in Figure 10-9, double-click the new user you just created.

6. In the user's Properties dialog box that appears, click the **Member Of** tab, and click **Add**. In the Select Groups dialog box, click **Advanced** and then click **Find Now** to search for groups. Click **Remote Desktop Users**; click **OK** three times; and close the Computer Management, Administrative Tools, and Control Panel windows.

SET UP A LAN-BASED HOST

Set up the host for using Remote Desktop Connection within a LAN.

1. Click **Start** and click **Control Panel**. In Category view, click **System And Security**, and then click **System**. Click **Remote Settings** on the left. The System Properties dialog box will appear with the Remote tab displayed.

2. In the bottom Remote Desktop panel, click **Allow Connections From Computers Running Any Version Of Remote Desktop**, as shown in Figure 10-10.

3. Click **Select Users**. Users that you added to the Remote Desktop Users group are displayed.

4. If you want to add more users, click **Add**, click **Advanced**, and click **Find Now**. Select the users you want to include by holding down **CTRL** while clicking them, and then click **OK** four times to close all open dialog boxes. Close Control Panel.

10

SET UP A REMOTE DESKTOP CLIENT

The Remote Desktop Connection client is probably
already installed on the computer you will be
using for the client, since it is part of the default
Windows 7 SP1 installation. Verify this, and, if it is
not installed, do so.

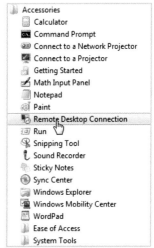

Click **Start**, click **All Programs**, click **Accessories**,
and click **Remote Desktop Connection**.

If you see the Remote Desktop Connection dialog
box, you need to do nothing further here.

If you do not see Remote Desktop Connection, you'll
need to reinstall Windows 7 SP1.

Connect to a Remote Desktop over a LAN

When you are sitting at the client computer connected to a LAN to which the
host is also connected, you can connect to the Remote Desktop host.

1. Click **Start**, click **All Programs**, click **Accessories**, and click **Remote Desktop
   Connection**. The Remote Desktop Connection dialog box appears.

2. Enter the name or IP address of the computer to which you want to connect in the
   form *computer name*.

3. After you have entered the computer name, click **Connect**. The Windows Security
   dialog box appears. If asked, enter the user name and password for the Remote
   Desktop host computer (this was the "Remote" user you created earlier), and click **OK**.
   If you see a message that someone is currently logged on to the remote host, decide
   if you can disconnect them, and click the appropriate choice. (See "Use a Remote
   Desktop Connection.")
   If you see a message that the remote computer does not have a security certificate
   from a trusted certifying authority, click **Yes** to go ahead and connect. (You may have
   created your own certificate in Chapter 8.)

The Remote Desktop toolbar appears in the top center of the screen with the
name of the computer that is hosting you.

10

Use a Remote Desktop Connection

Once you are connected to the host computer, you can perform almost any action that you could if you were sitting in front of that computer—you can run programs, access data, and more. In addition, the Remote Desktop toolbar, called the Connection Bar, allows you to close the Remote Desktop window without logging out so that your programs will keep running, to minimize the window so that you can see the computer you are sitting at (see Figure 10-11), and to maximize the window. In addition, there is a pushpin icon that determines whether the Connection Bar is always on the desktop or if it is only there when you move the mouse to the upper-center portion of the screen.

Remote Desktop Connection also gives you the ability to transfer information between the host computer and the client computer you are using. This means that you can:

- Print to a local printer connected to the client (this is enabled by default)
- Work with files on both the remote host and the client computers in the same window (this is not enabled by default)
- Cut and paste between both computers and documents on either one (this is enabled by default)

The local client resources that are available in a Remote Desktop session are controlled by the Remote Desktop Connection dialog box options.

1. From the Remote Desktop, click **Start**, click **All Programs**, click **Accessories**, and click **Remote Desktop Connection**. The Remote Desktop Connection dialog box appears. Click **Options**, and the box expands to give you a number of controls for Remote Desktop.

2. Click the **Display** tab. The default for a LAN is to use Full Screen mode and up to the maximum color level your computer can use, as well as to display the Connection Bar.

3. Click the **Local Resources** tab. As you can see in Figure 10-12, you can determine your audio settings, which include bringing sound to the client, and if you want the ability to use shortcut keys. Also:

   - If you want to print on the printer attached to the local client, keep the default Printers selection.

TIP

If your LAN has particularly heavy traffic and is slow, you might want to lower the screen size and colors.

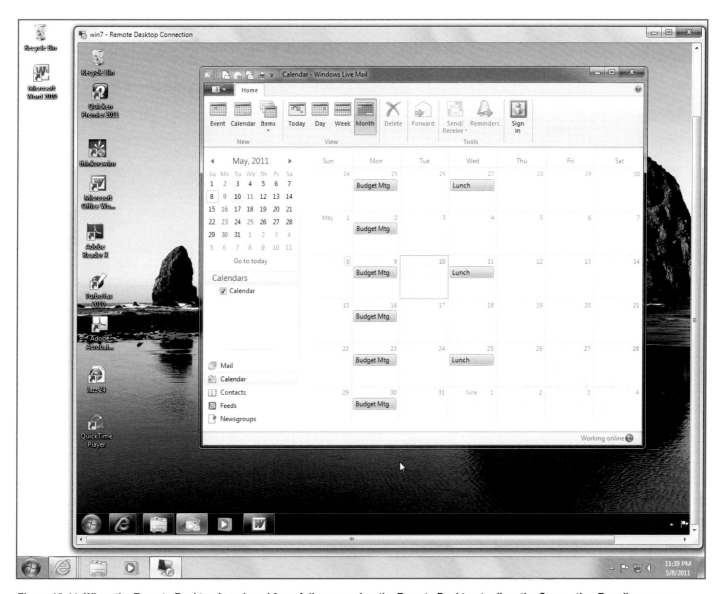

Figure 10-11: When the Remote Desktop is reduced from full-screen size, the Remote Desktop toolbar, the Connection Bar, disappears.

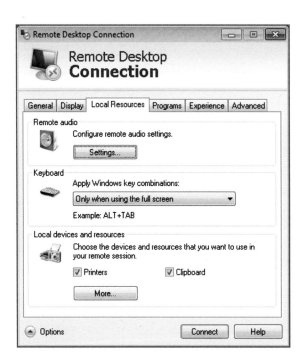

Figure 10-12: You can control what client devices are available with Remote Desktop.

- If you want to transfer information using the Cut and Paste commands between the two computers, the Clipboard should be selected.

- If you want to transfer information by dragging between disk drives, click **More** and click **Drives** to select them all; or click the plus sign (+) next to **Drives**, and select individual drives.

- If you intend to use a Plug And Play device on the local client, click that option.

4. If you want to start a program when you open the Remote Desktop Connection, click the **Programs** tab, click the relevant check box, and enter the path and filename of the program and the starting folder to use.

5. Click the **Experience** tab, and select the connection speed you are using. This will determine which of the items below the drop-down list box are selected. You can change the individual items if you want.

6. Click the **Advanced** tab. Look at the choices for authentication, and select the one that is correct for you. If you have to go through a Remote Desktop (RD) Gateway (generally in larger organizations), click **Settings**, select the option that is correct for you, type any needed information, and click **OK**.

7. Click the **General** tab. If you will use several settings, save the ones you just made by clicking **Save As**, entering a name, and clicking **Save**.

8. If you are not already connected, enter your password and click **Connect**. Otherwise, close the Remote Desktop Connection dialog box.

9. When you are done using Remote Desktop, you may leave it in any of three ways:

- Click **Close** on the Connection Bar. This leaves you logged on, and any programs you have will remain running. If you restart Remote Desktop Connection with the host computer and no one else has logged on locally, you will return to the same session you left.

- Click **Start** and click **Log Off**. This terminates your Remote Desktop session and all programs are stopped. If you restart Remote Desktop Connection with the host computer and no one else has logged on locally, you will begin a new session.

- Click **Start**, click the **Shut Down** right arrow, and click **Disconnect**. This is the same as clicking the Close button on the Connection Bar.

NOTE

The effective range of a wireless access point is highly dependent on which protocol (802.11b, 802.11g, or 802.11n) you are using ("n" is better than "b" or "g"), the types of walls you have to go through (wood and plaster are better than concrete or metal), and your device—see reviews.cnet.com and search on "wireless access points."

Set Up and Use a Wireless Network

Wireless networks have become a popular way to create small networks in homes and small businesses for the simple reason that you don't have to run cables everywhere. With a wireless access point connected to the Internet, any wireless-enabled computer within approximately 150 feet (46 m) of the access point indoors can connect to the Internet and communicate with any other network-connected or wireless-enabled computer. If the access point is also connected to a wired network, all the members of the wired network are available to the wireless computers. Chapter 9 talked about the hardware requirements needed to do this. Here we will talk about what is needed to set up and use a wireless network in Windows 7 SP1 and make it secure.

Set Up a Wireless Connection

The first task is to make a connection with a wireless access point and then set it up so its use is secure. If you have a recent computer with wireless capability that is turned on (there may be a small switch on your computer to do that) and is near a wireless access point, your computer may automatically connect. If you click the network connection in the notification area, you will see a message that you are connected. In any case, continue from here to set up and secure the connection.

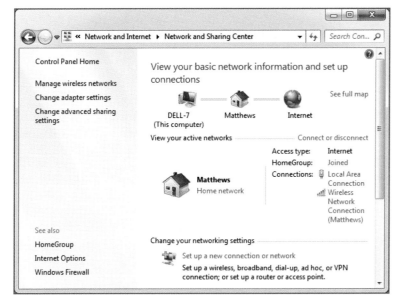

Figure 10-13: *You want the connection between your computer and a wireless access point to be secure so that someone within range of your access point cannot use it.*

1. Click **Start** and click **Control Panel**. In Category view, click **Network And Internet**, and then click **Network And Sharing Center**. If you are already connected, you will see your connection both graphically and textually, as shown in Figure 10-13. Skip to step 6.

2. If you don't see a wireless connection already established, click **Set Up A New Connection Or Network**. Click **Set Up A New Network**, and click **Next**. Your system will search for a wireless adapter in your computer and then for a wireless access point.

3. When a wireless network is found, you are asked to name your network. Type a name and click **Next**. Type a "passphrase" or password of at least eight characters, and click **Next**.

4. Choose the file and printer sharing option you want, or keep your current settings, and click **Next**.

5. Insert a USB flash drive on which you can save your settings, and click **Next**. This drive can be used to transfer these settings to other computers and wireless devices. Click **Close**.

6. In the Network And Sharing Center window (shown in Figure 10-13), look at the type of wireless network you have—Private or Public—and determine the type your situation requires. If you need to change the type, click **Customize**, click the type you want, change the icon if desired, click **Next**, and click **Close**.

Manage Wireless Network Sharing

When you use a wireless connection, you most likely do not want other network users to access your computer. That is the default setting, but check and make sure that is the way your connection is set up.

1. From the Network And Sharing Center, click **Change Adapter Settings** in the Tasks list. The Network Connections window opens, displaying the connections available on the computer.

2. Double-click **Wireless Network Connection** to open the Wireless Network Connection Status dialog box, shown in Figure 10-14.

Figure 10-14: A wireless network is particularly susceptible to intrusion and needs to be protected.

UICKSTEPS

IMPLEMENTING WINDOWS DEFENDER

Windows Defender guards your computer against spyware and other unwanted programs. It watches what is happening on your computer and looks for programs that are trying to install themselves or change important Windows settings, both without your approval. Windows Defender does this on a real-time basis, as well as letting you manually start a scan of your computer. It uses a Microsoft database called the SpyNet Community that tracks, with the user's approval, what programs people think might be dangerous.

REVIEW WINDOWS DEFENDER SETTINGS

By default, Windows Defender is running on your computer and you must take some action to turn it off, if that is what you want, although this is not recommended. To open, review, and possibly change the Windows Defender setting:

1. Click **Start**, click **Control Panel**, click the **Category** down arrow, click **Large Icons**, scroll to the bottom, and click **Windows Defender**. Windows Defender appears.

2. Click **Tools** on the toolbar, and click **Options** to display the many settings you can change to have Defender run the way you want, as shown in Figure 10-15.

3. Click each of the options on the left, and for each, scroll through the settings and make any changes that meet your needs.

4. When you have finished, click **Save** to return to the Tools And Settings window and check out the other options there.

Continued . . .

3. Click **Properties**, click the **Sharing** tab, and look at your connection-sharing settings. In most circumstances where you are using a public Wi-Fi hotspot, you do *not* want these check boxes selected, which is the default in a public network. In a home network, the setup shown next is the default. The primary instance in which you would want this enabled would be in a secure organizational setting.

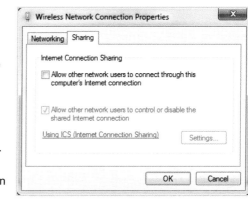

4. When you have assured yourself that the settings are the way you want them, click **OK**, click **Close** in the Status dialog box, and close the Network Connections window.

Figure 10-15: Windows Defender provides some protection against spyware and unwanted programs.

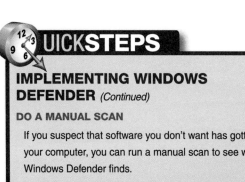

UICKSTEPS

IMPLEMENTING WINDOWS DEFENDER *(Continued)*

DO A MANUAL SCAN

If you suspect that software you don't want has gotten on your computer, you can run a manual scan to see what Windows Defender finds.

1. While in Windows Defender, click **Scan** on the toolbar. The scanning will immediately start. When it completes, you will be told what was found and given the scan statistics, as shown in Figure 10-16.

2. When you have finished, click **Close** and close the Control Panel.

Figure 10-16: *Windows Defender can do a quick manual scan anytime you want it.*

CAUTION

Windows Defender is not designed or recommended as a replacement for antivirus software. It is meant solely to get rid of spyware and unwanted programs. You should also have an antivirus program, most of which also get rid of spyware.

Use a Wireless Network

Once you have a wireless network up and running the way you want, you can use it in the same way you use a wired network.

1. Click the **Internet Explorer** icon on the taskbar to open this browser, and explore the Web in the same way you would with a wired network, as shown in Figure 10-17.

2. Close Internet Explorer and open your email program, which you can use in the same way as with a wired network connection.

3. Close your mail program, and try any other networking program you use.

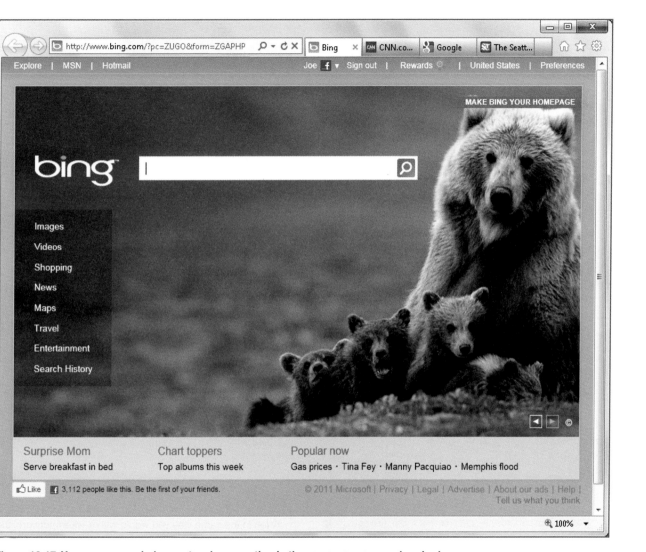

Figure 10-17: You can use a wireless network connection in the same way you used a wired one.

Index

Numbers

127.0.0.1 IP address, explained, 236
802.11b wireless standard, 223
802.11g wireless standard, 223
802.11n wireless standard, 223

A

access points. *See* wireless access points
accessory programs. *See also* programs
    Calculator, 118
    Character Map, 118–119
    Notepad, 119
    Paint, 119
accounts, changing, 191–192
Action Center
    accessing, 6
    using, 121
address bar
    described, 10
    function, 46
    identifying, 9, 46
    navigating with, 53–54
administrative privileges, requirement of, 191
administrator, logging on as, 190–191
advanced system information, getting, 125
Aero Peek
    features, 13, 15
    using, 35
Aero Shake, features, 13, 15–16
Aero Snaps, features, 14, 16–17
All Programs menu, starting programs from, 8
ALT key. *See* keyboard shortcuts
APIPA (Automatic Private IP Addressing), 233
application icons, jump lists for, 17
applications. *See* programs; software
audio. *See also* sounds; volume
    playing CDs, 164–166
    volume control, 167
audio files, playing from Internet, 85

automatic programs, controlling, 116. *See also* programs
Automatic Updates, turning on, 119–120
AutoPlay dialog box, opening, 143

B

Back button
    function, 46
    identifying, 46
backing up
    on computers, 212–215
    files and folders, 63–64
    on Internet, 215–218
Backup And Restore window, displaying, 65
backups of files, flagging, 62
Bing search engine, using, 79
biometric devices, using, 196
broadband connections, setting up, 74
browser, starting, 77
browser navigation
    Back and Forward buttons, 78
    Pages recently entered button, 78
Burn Files to Disc option, using, 64
burning music CDs, 173–176

C

C: disk, 51
cable service Internet connection, 71–72
Calculator program, running, 118
calendar, displaying, 37
Calendar in Windows Live Mail
    adding email messages to, 98
    adding events to, 98
    closing, 97
    expanding, 97
    opening, 97
    returning to Windows Live Mail, 98
camcorder, importing video from, 179–180

camera images, importing, 142–144
cameras, installing, 139–141
CDs
    backing up on, 212–215
    copyrighted material on, 173
    playing, 164–166
    ripping to computers, 172
    writing files to, 64–67
    writing folders to, 64–67
Certificate Import Wizard, using, 212
Character Map program, running, 118–119
check box
    described, 13
    identifying, 12
classic menus, turning on, 11
ClearType, adjusting, 28
client-server LANs, features of, 221–222
clock, displaying, 37
Close button
    described, 10, 13
    identifying, 9, 12
    using with programs, 113
cloud service, SkyDrive, 215–218
color scheme, choosing for windows, 26–27
Command button
    described, 13
    identifying, 13
Command Prompt window
    entering DOS commands in, 115
    opening, 116
communications
    broadband connections, 74
    defined, 71
    dial-up connections, 72–73
    installing modems, 71–72
compressed format, using, 62
compressing files and folders, 63–64
Computer folder, 7
computer information, getting, 124
computers, locking, 217–218

DVDs
backing up on, 212–215
copyrighted material on, 173
playing, 178
saving movies to, 187–188
writing files to, 64–67
writing folders to, 64–67
dxdiag option, choosing, 178

E

ease-of-access settings
changing, 38–40
reading tools, 39
turning on, 39
typing tools, 39
EFS (Encrypting File System), 210
email. *See also* Web mail; Windows Live Mail
adding to Calendar, 98
attaching files to, 96–97
copying text to, 84
creating, 91–92
receiving, 92
responding to, 93
sending, 91–92
email address, adding to Contacts list, 95
encrypted files, using, 211–212. *See also* files
encrypted folders, using, 211–212. *See also* folders
Encrypting File System (EFS), 210
encrypting files and folders, 61–62, 210
encryption, removing, 62
encryption key
backing up, 210–211
using, 212
Error Checking feature, using, 66–67
Ethernet. *See* wired Ethernet
Ethernet, using, 222–223
events, adding to Windows Live Mail Calendar, 98
Exit command, using with programs, 113
Explorer. *See* Windows Explorer

F

Favorites
adding sites to, 79
creating folders, 82
opening, 79
putting in folders, 82–83
Favorites bar, adding sites to, 83
Favorites list
deleting sites from, 83
rearranging, 82
fiber optic Internet connection, 71
file and folder sharing, 197, 199–200, 246. *See also* folders; sharing
HomeGroup folder sharing, 203–204
Network and Sharing Center, 201–203
setting up Windows Firewall, 200–201
file attributes, changing, 62–63
files. *See also* encrypted files; network files
backing up, 63–64
copying, 58–59
creating, 60
deleting, 55–56
encrypting, 61–62, 210
hiding, 209
moving, 58–59
protecting, 209–211
renaming, 55
searching for, 58–60
selecting, 55
undeleting, 55–56
writing to CDs or DVDs, 64–67
zipping, 63–64
Filter Keys typing tool, 39
firewall
configuring, 238
setting up, 200–201
Flash Drive option, choosing, 64–65, 215
folder attributes, changing, 62–63
folder trees, opening, 53

folders. *See also* encrypted folders; file and folder sharing
backing up, 63–64
copying, 58–59
creating, 54
deleting, 55–56
encrypting, 61–62, 210
hiding, 209
hierarchy of, 51
moving, 58–59
navigating, 52–54
opening, 52
pinning to Windows Explorer, 35
protecting, 209–211
renaming, 55
searching for, 58–60
selecting, 52, 55
sharing, 205–207
subfolders in, 51
system-related, 6–8
undeleting, 55–56
user-related, 6–7
writing to CDs or DVDs, 64–67
zipping, 63
fonts
adding, 162
deleting, 162
selecting, 162
using, 162
Forward button
function, 46
identifying, 46
FreeCell, playing, 21–22

G

gadgets, managing, 44
Gmail, using, 96
Google Search, using, 77–78

speakers, configuring for sounds, 42
Speakers icon, identifying, 6
spinner
    described, 13
    identifying, 12
spyware, guarding against, 255–256
Start button
    described, 4
    identifying, 3, 5
    in taskbar, 32
    using, 5
Start menu
    adding programs to, 32
    changing pictures in, 33
    customizing, 31–32
    opening, 6
    removing programs from, 32
    session-end choices, 6
    system-related folders, 6–8
    user-related folders, 6–7
startup screen, 3
Sticky Keys typing tool, 39
Sticky Notes, using, 148
storage devices, identifying, 51
strong password, requirements, 194
subfolders, contents of, 51
subject pane
    described, 10
    function, 46
    identifying, 9, 46
switch, using with wired Ethernet, 223
Switch User feature, explained, 19, 197
Sysprint.sep file, explained, 159
Sysprtj.sep file, explained, 159
System Configuration dialog box, 116
system features, opening, 5
system icons, displaying, 36. *See also* icons
system information, getting, 124–125
system messages, icon, 6
System Recovery, running, 123
System Restore
    requirements, 122

running from Start menu, 124
running from System Recovery,
    123–124
running from Windows, 123
setting up, 122
system-related folders
    Computer, 7
    Control Panel, 8
    Default Programs, 8
    Devices and Printers, 8
    Help And Support, 8

T

tab row, tabs in, 80
Tablet PC Input Panel, opening, 33
tabs
    closing, 81
    opening pages in, 80
    switching among, 81
task list, accessing, 32
Task Manager
    Applications tab, 112
    Performance tab, 114
    Processes tab, 114
    Run command, 114
    Services tab, 114
Task Scheduler
    using with email messages, 111
    using with programs, 110
taskbar
    changing properties of, 34–35
    described, 4
    hiding, 34
    identifying, 3
    moving and sizing, 33–34
    notification area, 32
    pinning icons to, 34–35
    programs pinned to, 5
    rearranging icons in, 35
    removing icons pinned to, 35

Show Desktop button, 32
Start button, 32
task list, 32
ungrouping tasks in, 112
unlocking, 34
using, 5
using small icons, 34
taskbar buttons, customizing, 34–35
taskbar previews
    described, 14
    features, 18
taskbar properties
    closing, 35–36
    opening, 34
    using Aero Peek, 35
tasks
    repeating, 110
    working with, 111
TCP/IPv4 protocol, 231–232
TCP/IPv6 protocol, 231–232
text box
    described, 13
    identifying, 12
text file printer, creating, 155. *See also* printers
text size, changing, 25–26
themes, changing, 25
thumbnails, opening, 18
time and date
    impact of settings, 43
    setting, 5, 36–38
time formats, specifying, 43
time zone, changing, 37
title bar
    described, 10, 13
    identifying, 9, 12
Toggle Keys typing tool, 39
toolbar
    described, 10
    function, 46
    identifying, 9, 46
TV, using Media Center with, 187–188
typing tools, availability of, 39

U

UAC (User Account Control), 189, 191
UAC dialog box, appearance of, 24, 74, 108
UNC (Uniform Naming Convention), 243
Undo option, using, 55
updates, applying, 120
USB Flash Drive option, choosing, 64–65, 215
user accounts
    changing, 191–192
    customizing, 196
user-related folders, 6–7
users
    adding to groups, 208
    logging on as administrator, 190–191
    setting up, 191–192
    switching among, 197
utilities, accessing, 6
UTP (unshielded twisted-pair) cable, 223

V

video
    importing from camcorder, 179–180
    playing DVDs, 178
video clips, trimming, 181–182
video files, playing from Internet, 85
visualizations, displaying in Media Player, 176
volume, controlling, 6, 167. *See also* audio; sounds

W

Web History feature
    deleting and setting, 82–83
    using, 81–82
Web mail, using, 96. *See also* email; Windows Live Mail
webpages. *See also* recent pages
    copying from Internet, 84
    opening in tabs, 80
    printing, 155–156

websites. *See also* site navigation
    adding to Favorites bar, 83
    categorizing, 84–85
Wi-Fi standard, function of, 223
window border
    described, 10
    identifying, 9
window color, changing, 26–27
window elements
    address bar, 9
    Close button, 9
    details pane, 9
    library pane, 9
    Maximize/Restore button, 9
    Minimize button, 9
    navigation pane, 9
    next button, 9, 11
    preview pane, 9
    previous button, 9, 11
    scroll arrow, 9
    scroll bar, 9–11
    scroll button, 9
    sizing handle, 9
    subject pane, 9
    title bar, 9
    toolbar, 9
    window border, 9
windows
    controlling access to, 199
    versus dialog boxes, 12–13
    hiding, 15
    left-aligning, 16
    maximizing, 16
    minimizing, 15–16
    opening from thumbnails, 18
    restoring, 16–17
    right-aligning, 17
    snapping to screen areas, 16–17
    unhiding, 15
Windows
    logging onto, 2
    starting, 2

Windows 7 SP1
    changing appearance of, 24–28
    installing manually, 2
    as network operating system, 219–220
    restoring, 121–124
    updating, 118–120
Windows Defender, implementing, 255–256
Windows desktop. *See* desktop
Windows Explorer
    address bar, 46–47
    Back button, 46–47
    closing, 49
    customizing, 48–49
    details pane, 46–48
    Edit menu, 50
    file information, 50
    File menu, 50
    folder options, 50
    Forward button, 46–47
    layout options, 48
    library pane, 46–47
    menus, 49–51
    Name option, 49
    navigation pane, 46–47
    opening, 47–48
    Organize menu, 49
    Pictures options, 48–49
    pinning folders to, 35
    preview pane, 46–48
    rearranging objects, 49
    Refresh button, 46–47
    search box, 46–47
    starting, 7
    subject pane, 46–47
    toolbar options, 46–49
    Tools menu, 50
    turning off panes, 11
    turning on classic menus, 11
    turning on panes, 11
    View menu, 50
    View tab, 50